SIBLINGS

The EFPP Book Series

Editor-in-Chief: Anne-Marie Schloesser

SIBLINGS

Envy and Rivalry, Coexistence and Concern

Edited by

Katarzyna Skrzypek,
Beata Maciejewska-Sobczak,
and
Zuzanna Stadnicka-Dmitriew

KARNAC

First published in 2014 by
Karnac Books Ltd
118 Finchley Road, London NW3 5HT

British Library Cataloguing in Publication Data

A C.I.P. for this book is available from the British Library

ISBN 978 1 78049 181 3

Edited, designed and produced by The Studio Publishing Services Ltd
www.publishingservicesuk.co.uk
e-mail: studio@publishingservicesuk.co.uk

Printed in Great Britain

www.karnacbooks.com

CONTENTS

ACKNOWLEDGEMENTS

We would like to thank Ken Robinson from the British Psychoanalytic Association for his encouragement, careful advice, and extensive help with the Introduction.

Our thanks are also due to Anne-Marie Schloesser, Editor-in-Chief of the EFPP book series, for choosing "Siblings" as the theme for the Cracow EFPP Conference 2011: it proved to be such an inspiring area of interest for many contributors.

We are grateful to all the authors who presented their papers at the Conference—it was impossible to include every contribution in this volume, but those who could be present and listen did benefit enormously from their papers.

We would like to thank Katarzyna Lipiec, our proof-reader, for her dedication to the work on the book, her skilfulness in solving problems, and her knowledge of the English language. Without her commitment this book would have never appeared.

Thanks, too, to Maurice O'Brien for his extensive help with the translation of Mrs Daune's paper.

Finally, we thank our families for their patient assistance and tolerance for the time and work that editing the book demanded.

Our teamwork was part of the experience of editing the book. It was meaningful for all of us to be part of this "lateral" group, with each of us contributing in their own special way.

*   *   *

Prophecy Coles' chapter, "The transgenerational pattern of trauma transmission", uses some material from her book, *The Uninvited Guest from the Unremembered Past*, published in 2011 by Karnac, London.

The paper "Sibling rivalry: psychoanalytic aspects and institutional implications", by Franz Wellendorf, is a revised and updated version of the paper published by the *Bulletin of the British Psychoanalytic Society*, 45(3) November 2009, and is reprinted with permission of the Bulletin Editorial Board.

ABOUT THE EDITORS AND CONTRIBUTORS

Ewa Bąk is a psychologist, group analyst, and graduate of postgraduate studies on philosophy of the twentieth century and sociology. She is a founding member of the Institute for the Study of Attachment and Social Relations Klinika, a full member of the Institute of Group Analysis Rasztów. She works in private practice with adults, couples, adolescents, and children.

Francesco Bisagni, MD, NCPsyA, is a member of the Society of Analytical Psychology (SAP), British Psychoanalytic Council (BPC), Affiliate Member and Training Analyst in the Association of Child Psychotherapists (ACP), and President of the Centre for Studies in Contemporary Psychoanalysis (CSPC).

Rachel Blass is a psychoanalyst in private practice in London, visiting professor at University College London, Convener of the Psychology of Religion Programme at Heythrop College, University of London, and is on the board of the *International Journal of Psychoanalysis*, where she is editor of the "Controversies" section. She has published and lectured widely on the conceptual, epistemological and ethical foundations of psychoanalysis.

Deborah Blessing is a clinical social worker and psychoanalyst and a member of the Washington Center for Psychoanalysis and the Washington School of Psychiatry in Washington, DC. She is a founding faculty member of the Infant and Young Child Observation Training Program at the Washington School of Psychiatry and sits on the faculties of the Close Attention and Psychoanalytic Couple and Family Therapy training programs at the Washington Center for Psychoanalysis.

Daniela Cantone is a psychoanalytical psychotherapist and a member of the Italian Association for Psychoanalytic Psychotherapy of Childhood, Adolescence and Family (AIPPI), Naples. (AIPPI is a member of the EFPP.) She works with children, adolescents, and young people. She is Assistant Professor at the Faculty of Psychology, Second University of Naples.

Prophecy Coles trained as a psychoanalytic psychotherapist at the Lincoln Clinic and is a member of the London Centre for Psychotherapy. She has written numerous articles and her book, *The Importance of Sibling Relationships in Psychoanalysis*, was published by Karnac in 2003.

Rossella Coveri accomplished her training at the CSMH (Martha Harris Study Centre) in Florence, which is a Tavistock model school of psychoanalytic psychotherapy for children, adolescents, and their families. She works in private practice as a psychoanalytic psychotherapist for children, adolescents, and their families and at the Under Five service of the Municipality of Sesto Fiorentino (Melograno Family Centre). She is a member of the Martha Harris Childhood and Adolescence Psychoanalytical Psychotherapy Association (AMHHPPIA).

Françoise Daune is a psychoanalytical psychotherapist, ex-President of FFBPP (Belgian Francophone Federation for Psychoanalytic Psychotherapy), a member of ARPP (Association for the Research on Psychoanalytic Psychotherapy), and a trainer at IFSAM Institut Jules Bordet, Université Libre de Bruxelles.

Evalotta Enekvist is an authorised psychotherapist and psychoanalyst in the Swedish Psychoanalytical Association (IPA). She accomplished her training in psychoanalysis at the Swedish Psychoanalytic Institute and works in the Erica Foundation in Stockholm and in private practice.

Anna Faber is a sociologist, psychoanalytic psychotherapist, and full-time member of the Polish Society for Psychoanalytic Psychotherapy. She works in private practice in Sopot, and co-operates with the public sector and NGOs. Together with her colleagues, she has established a successful psychoanalytic mother–infant programme in a hospital setting.

Carmela Guerriera is a psychoanalytical psychotherapist, member of the Italian Association for Psychoanalytic Child Psychotherapy (AIPPI), Naples, and a member of the EFPP. She works with children, adolescents, and young people. She is an associated professor at the Faculty of Psychology, Second University of Naples, Italy.

Michael D. Kahn, PhD, ABPP (American Board of Professional Psychology) is a clinical associate professor of psychiatry at the University of Connecticut School of Medicine and Professor Emeritus of Clinical Psychology at the University of Hartford. He is a graduate analyst of the Massachusetts Institute of Psychoanalysis, co-author of *The Sibling Bond* (1982, 1997), and co-editor of *Siblings in Therapy* (1988). He practises in Hartford, Connecticut.

Lech Kalita is a psychologist, psychoanalytic psychotherapist, full-time member of the Polish Society for Psychoanalytic Psychotherapy, works in private practice in Gdynia, and co-operates with NGOs and the public sector. He is chief editor of the magazine, *Psychoanaliza i Sztuka* ("Psychoanalysis and Art").

Alison Knight-Evans was Deputy Head of Psychotherapy at Springfield Eating Disorders Unit, St George's Hospital in Tooting, London. She has retired from the NHS after twenty years, but continues to practise privately. She is a psychoanalytic member of the British Association of Psychotherapists.

Beata Maciejewska-Sobczak is a training psychoanalytic psychotherapist and supervisor of the Polish Society for Psychoanalytic

Psychotherapy, which is a member of the EFPP. She is a Polish Psycho-analytic Association candidate, and works in Warsaw in private practice.

Jeanne Magagna was Head of Psychotherapy Services at Great Ormond Street Hospital for Children for twenty-four years. She currently works as a consultant psychotherapist in the Ellern Mede Centre for Eating Disorders in London. She formally completed three separate trainings at the Tavistock Clinic to become a child and adolescent psychotherapist (PhD level), family therapist, and adult psychotherapist. She is Vice-President and joint co-ordinator of train-ing for the CSMH (Martha Harris Study Centre) Tavistock model trainings in Florence, Rome, Venice, Bologna, and Naples.

Sarah Mandow is a consultant psychotherapist at The Cassel Hospital in South West London. She provides a consultancy service to non-NHS institutions and also works in private practice. She is a psychoanalytic member of the British Association of Psychotherapists.

Miriam Monticelli is a child, adolescent, and family psychotherapist, and teaches the postgraduate Masters programme in "Psychoanalytic Observational Studies" at the CSMH in Florence and in Lunigiana. She is the secretary of the AMHPPIA (Martha Harris Childhood and Adol-escence Psychoanalytical Psychotherapy Association). She works in the "Under Five" Service of the Municipality of Sesto Fiorentino at the Melograno Family Centre and in the Raggio Verde Parents' Space of the SdS of Florence N/W over the Library of the Municipality of Scandicci.

Maria Papagounou is Scientific Director of the Hellenic Centre for the Mental Health of the Child and his Family, To Perivolaki—a day centre for children with pervasive developmental disorders. She is an exter-nal supervisor in the Child Psychiatric Department at General Children's Hospital "Agia Sofia" in Athens. She is a delegate of Greece to the Child and Adolescent Section in the EFPP, and a Board Member of the Hellenic Institute of Psychoanalytic Psychotherapy of the Child and Adolescent.

Joanna Skowrońska is Head of the Training Committee of the Institute of Group Analysis Rasztów, Warsaw, and a member of the Manage-ment Committee of the Group Analytic Society, London.

Katarzyna Skrzypek is a psychologist, training psychoanalytic psychotherapist, and supervisor of the Polish Society for Psychoanalytic Psychotherapy, and a delegate of the Polish Society to the Adult Psychotherapy Section of the EFPP.

Zuzanna Stadnicka-Dmitriew is a psychologist, psychoanalytic psychotherapist, and member of the Polish Society for Psychoanalytic Psychotherapy, which is a member of the EFPP. She is a Polish Psychoanalytical Association candidate (IPA).

Nancy Taloumi is a child and adolescent psychotherapist, clinical psychologist, and member of the Hellenic Association of Child and Adolescent Psychotherapy. She is a training therapist at the Day Centre for Autistic and Psychotic Children—To Perivolaki in Athens, and works in private practice with children and adolescents.

Agnieszka Topolewska is a psychologist and a psychoanalytic psychotherapist. She lives in Gdansk and works in private practice. For several years, she worked in the public sector psychotherapy centres with adolescent and adult patients addicted to alcohol. She is a member of the Polish Society for Psychoanalytic Psychotherapy.

Sabine Trenk-Hinterberger is a member of the German Psychoanalytic Association (DPV) and works in private practice as a psychoanalyst in Marburg. As a training and control analyst and lecturer, she belongs to the DPV Institute Giessen.

Franz Wellendorf is a member and training analyst of the German Psychoanalytic Society (DPG) and the IPA, affiliated member of the German Psychoanalytic Association (DPV), and guest member of the British Psychoanalytic Society. He was Supervisor and Counsellor of Psychiatric Clinics, Psychological Information Centres and Schools, and President of the DPG. He is a member of the IPA Board, and the author of several publications on psychoanalytic theory, supervision, counselling, and psychoanalytic interpretation of literature.

Marie-Ange Widdershoven is a psychologist and psychotherapist, member of the Hellenic Institute of Psychoanalytic Psychotherapy, Child and Adolescent Section, and a Delegate for Greece to the EFPP.

She is Head of the Psychotherapeutic Department in the Diagnostic and Therapeutic Unit, Spiros Doxiadis in Athens, and an external supervisor in the Child Psychiatric Department at Children's Hospital "Agia Sofia" in Athens.

Chava Yanai-Malach is a clinical social worker and a candidate at the Tel Aviv Institute for Contemporary Psychoanalysis. She works in a private clinic in Tel Aviv. She is a supervisor of The Homeless Unit in Tel Aviv. She teaches in the Psychoanalytic Psychotherapy Programme in the Barzilay Medical Centre in Ashkelon.

Anne-Marie Schloesser

This book is about a topic that has been mostly neglected by psycho-analytic thinking, for reasons yet to be examined more profoundly. This fact is even more surprising as the horizontal relation between sisters and brothers is, in contrast to the vertical child–parent relation, a lifelong one, accompanying us from early childhood until the last phase of life.

The contributions in this book try to fill this gap. They examine the psychodynamic meaning of the sibling relationship, the role of the sibling in the outer and the inner world, and its contribution to the formation of the self.

Powerful affects, such as love, hate, and envy, occur between siblings; we find rivalry, but also coexistence and concern for each other. What does it mean when there is a brother or a sister close in age whom one can never reach or overcome since he/she will always be older and bigger? How can a child cope with the existence of a disabled sibling, where rivalry and testing one's own forces might be experienced as dangerous? Are siblings necessary ingredients for the development of a healthy personality?

These and other questions are raised and discussed in this book, which is a selection of papers that were presented at the EFPP conference in Cracow in 2011.

FOREWORD

Rachel Blass

In contrast to the killing of the father in *Totem and Taboo*, in biblical tradition it is the killing of the preferred brother that is noted as the first and most significant murderous act. In fact, Cain's slaying of Abel is the first story to be recounted at all after man is expelled from the Garden of Eden, a story perhaps best remembered for Cain's failed attempt to deny his deed (and, one might suggest, his guilt) with the words, "Am I my brother's keeper?" Indeed, from one psychoanalytic vantage point, both father and brother (or sister) may be regarded similarly as interchangeable "thirds". As such, they are hated oedipal rivals standing in the way of the phantasised complete possession of the beloved object and, at the same time, they are beloved objects in their own right, who also serve as a source of support and protection from the horror of the phantasised total dyadic relation. Yet, psychoanalysis also has always described the role of the father and of siblings in our lives and in our phantasies as significantly different. Most notably, the father is recognised as a rightful part of the parental couple and is associated with all the phantasies of that special relation, whereas siblings are recognised as products of that couple—competing children, but also companions to the shared fate of exclusion from the couple. Parents are regarded as primary internal objects in ways that siblings are not (e.g., as inherent components of the superego in Freud's description of its development or as primary good and bad objects in Klein's thinking). Consequently, transference and counter-transference tend to be considered in terms of parent–child object relationships and the role of the sibling finds its secondary place within that context.

Further reflection on the role of the sibling in our inner world and how it manifests itself in analytic treatment is of great importance and interest. This includes the study of the ways in which the sibling is an internal object, the processes of identification that take place in relation to siblings, the psychodynamic meaning of the family in the light of sibling relationships, and how these interact with child–parent object relations and the implications of such inner processes and meanings for the analytic relation. The present volume, compiled of selected papers from the European Federation of Psychoanalytic Psychotherapy's (EFPP) 2011 conference held in Cracow, brings together a wide range of psychotherapeutic and analytic perspectives to the understanding of these issues. It addresses them in the light of specific questions of psychopathology and treatment and under varying environmental circumstances, and also invites us to consider how early sibling relationships affect our present-day interactions, including how they affect the dynamics within psychoanalytic institutes. The book is a valuable contribution to contemporary reflection and study in the area of sibling relationships.

Given the great breadth of its scope, I find the book's relatively large number of chapters dealing with the topic of death to be striking. While this might be explained by accidental factors, perhaps the fact that, in comparison to our relation to our parents, we feel in relation to our siblings physically strong and independent, makes the internal danger of killing them off (or being killed by them) more profound and real. In a sense, we do know that we are, indeed, "our brother's keeper".

The EFPP is to be commended for the significant work it has done in making the fruits of its conference on this topic available to a broad audience of readers.

Introduction

Katarzyna Skrzypek, Beata Maciejewska-Sobczak,
and Zuzanna Stadnicka-Dmitriew

There seems to be a rising interest in sibling dynamics and their place in the formation of the self. Prophecy Coles and Juliet Mitchell both explore the question of why this area has been neglected in psychoanalytic theory, and if there are reasons for the subject to be emerging at this time. The development of the theory shifted from focusing on the relation with the father and the Oedipus complex to the centrality of the mother–child relation. Is the sibling relation going to receive such interest?

This book consists of selected texts presented at the EFPP Conference in Cracow, Poland, in October 2011. It is an attempt at finding the place of sibling relationships in psychoanalytic theory and practice. Like the Conference, it is in dialogue with the emerging interest in the role of siblings in the formation of the self.

The texts show not only the theory, but also the practice, of dealing with sibling-related problems and their impact on psychoanalytic institutions. Practitioners share their experience of working with siblings of disabled children, dealing with cancer in the family, coping with the loss of a sibling, helping families to adapt to a new baby, dealing with phantasy and reality of murderousness towards siblings, and transgenerational transmission of trauma. Another field of interest is the specificity of transference–countertransference issues related to siblinghood. The findings of a preliminary research programme on the impact of having "brothers and sisters in analysis" are cited. We also have an opportunity to draw from the knowledge of group analysts about sibling issues. The nature of the sibling relation is shown from different perspectives.

Mitchell has introduced two axes to organise thinking about the issues concerning siblinghood (2003). The vertical one concerns what happens in the relation with parents, and the horizontal one depicts siblings and their later substitutes—peers. She postulates that the lateral relationships that we have with our siblings provide structure to our mind just as the vertical oedipal dimension does. In Freudian thinking, the appearance of a sibling was felt as traumatic because it was evidence of the parents' intercourse confirming the fact of being excluded from the parental couple, or siblings served as a recipient for displaced oedipal feelings. In the Kleinian approach, the babies in the mother's womb are felt to be part of the mother's richness that evokes envy in the child. Siblings were seen as part of the vertical dynamics.

Mitchell gives siblings a meaning and structuring power of their own. In "Sibling trauma: a theoretical consideration" (2006), she shows how sibling trauma can be theorised in parallel to the castration complex, and how it provides a structure to the unconscious. In all her writings on siblings, Mitchell describes how discovering that one has siblings—or could have siblings, in the case of the only child—is an experience of being annihilated. The "Unique Baby of the Parents", "His Majesty the Baby"—the baby's identity up to that point—is felt to be dead, replaced by the next child. This stands as an experience of death in the unconscious, a notion contradictory to Freud's that man is not capable of imagining his death because he does not have such an experience. As a consequence, the child has murderous impulses towards the other one. The impulse to kill is mitigated by a powerful prohibition—the "Law of the Mother": "thou shall not kill your brother/sister, as he/she shall not kill you". Theoretically, it is analogous to the "Law of the Father", from the Freudian theory, which forbids taking the place of the father and possessing the mother. The "Law of the Mother" ensures rights for every coming child, in the seriality of their appearance, with a prohibition against killing, incest, and determining that the mother is the person who can have babies, not the child. Mitchell states that before "they are equal in their sameness to each other for their father, children must be equal in their difference from each other for their mother. This will be the crucial first vertical relation for siblings" (Mitchell, 2003, p. 11). Analogously to the forbidden wishes of the oedipal complex, the wish to kill becomes repressed under the demand of the Law. Mitchell argues that the hate evoked by the experience of being annihilated is much more powerful and intense than the envious feelings experienced in the oedipal–vertical relation due to the loss and annihilation, which is incomparably stronger with siblings. When the prohibition on killing is withdrawn, as it is in war, the "repression . . . fails and violence against siblings or their substitutes is acted out" (Mitchell, 2003, p. 36).

Franz Wellendorf points to an important difference between the oedipal, or vertical, struggles and those concerning the sibling level. In trying to trespass the oedipal boundaries, the child is psychologically in a safer position—there is an obvious difference between itself and the parents, a difference of a generation because of which it feels too small and weak to really threaten them; besides, it knows that fundamentally it needs the parent. The father–mother–child triangle forms an entity. This is different from the sibling dimension, which is a sequence, an open-ended one: there can be next ones, where the sibling is not indispensable—"one can do without a sibling, one's existence does not depend on the sibling, siblings are not necessary". This brings forth a basic fear, that Mitchell also points to, as a basic, formative, although threatening discovery: since one can think that the sibling is unnecessary, one also has to confront the idea that it concerns the subject as well—"the sequence can also do without me, it might not matter whether I do exist or not". The "Law of the Mother" can attenuate such fears.

In order to overcome the trauma of being replaced by a sibling, the infantile, unique self, as Trenk-Hinterberger names it in her chapter from this book, the "paradise lost" must be mourned. Mitchell widely describes the consequences of the failure to acknowledge this loss: they transpire as hysteria, psychopathy, and paranoia. The individual lives entrenched in narcissism and grandiosity.

If the process of mourning the death of oneself as "His Majesty the Baby" (a Freudian expression) being in an ideal unity with the mother can take place, we discover "the huge relief of that dreaded fact that we are ordinary" (Mitchell, 2003, p. 29). Self-esteem, an internalised notion of one's subjecthood, emerges as a result of this process of the loss of the unique, pre-sibling self (Mitchell, 2003). It is a process that, just like the Oedipus complex, needs reworking during one's lifetime. The hateful feelings—effects of trauma—are channelled into aggressiveness and rivalry. Some of the hate is reversed into its opposite—love. There is also another dynamic that mitigates the murderousness, and that is narcissistic love of oneself in the other baby. The other is expected to be "more of oneself". Part of this expectation is destroyed when the child sees that the other is different and has taken one's place, but some of the narcissistic love stays. The sibling is "adored", as Mitchell puts it, in a narcissistic way. The simultaneity of love and hate directed at the same object, compared with the oedipal triangle, where love can be felt toward one of the parents and hate to the other, make the matter a very intense and difficult one.

Mitchell's statement that the feelings evoked by the sibling are much more intense than the ones experienced in the oedipal triangle is in accordance with Sharpe and Rosenblatt (1994). They depict the influence of the sibling relation as a triangle constellation parallel to the child–parents triangle, where the brother or sister is either the prized love object, or the rival, while the other sibling or a parent stand for The Third. Sibling relationships, as they describe them, "exert definitive effects on the individual's identifications, adult object choices, and patterns of relating" (Sharpe & Rosenblatt, 1994). They disagree, like Mitchell and most authors exploring sibling dynamics, with the common psychoanalytical approach that depicts siblings as replacements for one of the parents in the child–parent oedipal strivings. They outline the development of the sibling relation as parallel to the pre-oedipal and oedipal child–parent development. Like Mitchell, they point to the importance of other children to an infant: "in the normal symbiotic phase (about six weeks to five months of age), infants watch other children with particular interest and will often choose a child to observe, rather than an adult" (Sharpe & Rosenblatt, 1994), thus confirming the narcissistic "adoration" of a human who is not like the mother. The later developmental phases show the vicissitudes of the rivalrous and idealising affects. Identification, guilt feelings, and crushing narcissistic injuries between siblings are described with their influence on the self, spouse choice, and character formation. The sibling relation is depicted as loaded with strong passions. Sharpe and Rosenblatt do not picture the birth of a sibling as a trauma suicide, or eating disorders. Those individuals establish inner enclaves, in which the deceased object is resurrected and kept as if in a crypt. As Coles insightfully discusses, this kind of haunting presence of the dead is linked with a great feeling of guilt of the one who survived, and can be passed on from generation to generation. The majority of chapters stresses the significance of the omnipotent fantasies about causing the death of the siblings. Following Mitchell, the authors discuss the significance of murderous fantasies towards siblings and their connection with the real or symbolic death of brothers and sisters. The main source of this kind of fantasies is the trauma of being replaced by a newborn sibling. Re-enactment of this trauma, along with the accompanying fear of annihilation, the feelings of harm, and murderous rage often becomes the dominating internal reality. If this state is reinforced by the actual loss of a sibling, there is a risk that the self will be overtaken by a psychotic state of mourning.

Part IV, "Transference and countertransference related to sibling-hood", puts together chapters in which the issue is distinct. The influence of the repression of early negative feelings in the sibling relation and their later forms is explored: it might affect not only patients, but therapists as well, and, as a consequence, working through some defences is impossible and some important issues, such as deep psychic devastation wrought by sibling hatred, are left unaddressed. The importance for the analyst/psychotherapist of being able to discern when the transference develops along the vertical and when along the horizontal axes transpires through the chapters of this section.

The special issues of the transference–countertransference with twin patients are extensively examined in the clinical material of Topolewska and Bisagni. In Bisagni's paper, we see a careful analyst working through the twinning transferential relation. The twinning relation is a kind of psychic retreat protecting from agonising fear of total abandonment and separateness that stems from experiencing the care-taker object as unreliable. The analyst needs to differentiate between what would be colluding with the patient's wish to form a twinning relation and his developmental need to experience having a containing mothering object.

Topolewska's chapter on twin relationships explores their enmeshed and extremely rivalrous character. Her clinical material shows the process of the therapist liberating herself from a collusion with the patient that obliterated the strong hateful sibling transference, which now could be dealt with (lateral transference), and how the opening up of a space for the twin brother in the therapist's mind (a developmental need stemming from the vertical transference) resulted in the patient's progress in therapy.

Part V contains chapters by authors who agree on the interdependence of the vertical and horizontal axes, "there are no such things as siblings, there are only siblings and parents".[1] Constellations in which parents unconsciously transfer a relation with a sibling to one of their children are examined in Magagna's chapter. The impact of unconscious identifications with a particular child that affect the way the parent relates to the other child, enacting feelings from the past relation with a sibling, are also explored in Coveri, Monticelli, and Bertocii's contribution. Magagna depicts how unprocessed issues with siblings can affect the parents' containing function towards the sibling issues of their children. The notion of the "special time"—where the firstborn has an opportunity to work through some of his/her issues with the coming baby before its birth—is presented.

The impact of children's and parents' unconscious phantasies about the child damaging the sibling in the mother's womb, and working on their resolution, is shown in Guerrriera and Cantone's chapter.

Enkevist presents how excessively focusing on the relation with siblings at the cost of the importance of the vertical dimension in an attempt to avoid the necessary generation clash and working through the oedipal conflict has inhibited the developmental process of her adolescent patients.

Note

1.   We would like to thank Ken Robinson for this transposition of Winnicott.

References

Arlow, J. A. (1972). The only child. *The Psychoanalytic Quarterly*, 41: 507–536.

Mitchell, J. (2003). *Siblings: Sex and Violence*. Cambridge: Polity Press.

Mitchell, J. (2006). Sibling trauma: a theoretical consideration. In: P. Coles (Ed.), *Sibling Relationships* (pp. 155–174). London: Karnac.

Morley, E. (2006). The influence of sibling relationships on couple choice and development. In: P. Coles (Ed.), *Sibling Relationships* (pp. 197–224). London: Karnac.

Parsons, M. (2007). From biting teeth to biting wit: the normative development of aggression. In: S. Ruszczyński, & D. Morgan, (Eds.), *Clinical Lectures in Delinquency, Perversion and Violence* (pp. 117–136). London: Karnac.

Sharpe, S. A., & Rosenblatt, A. D. (1994). Oedipal sibling triangles. *Journal of the American Psychoanalytic Association, 42*: 491–523.

Vivona, J. M. (2007). Sibling differentiation, identity, development and the lateral dimension of psychic life. *Journal of the American Psychoanalytic Association, 55*: 1191–1215.

Winnicott, D. W. (1945). Primitive emotional development. *International Journal of Psychoanalysis, 26*: 137–143.

horizontal level of the sibling relation to the vertical dimension of the father–son relation. As Jones writes,

> I had known that Rank had suffered much in childhood from a strongly repressed hostility to his brother, and that this usually covered a similar attitude toward a father. This was now being unloaded onto me, and my dominant concern was how to protect Freud from the consequences. . . . For three years I lived with the fear lest Rank's 'brother-hostility' regress to the deeper 'father-hostility' and I hoped against hope that this would not happen in Freud's lifetime. (Jones, 1957, p. 49)

Jones' hypocritical formulation leads one to understand his assertion—that hate for the father lies behind Rank's hostility—as a powerful strategic argument in the battle between the psychoanalytic brothers. A brother's insinuation of his sibling rival's hatred of the common father can serve as a weapon, invoking the father and his power as an ally in the conflict. This is, however, not to deny the central significance of the ambivalence toward Freud as an overpowering father figure.

The personal relationships between the members of the *Brüderhorde* interfered with their analytic relationships, lending additional, confusing complexity to the rivalries among the psychoanalysts. Freud, Ferenczi, and Jung mutually analysed each other's dreams during their trip to America in 1909. Ferenczi was in analysis with Freud, Jones with Ferenczi. Freud was also the analyst of Jones' girlfriend, Loe. I believe that the conflict was significantly heightened by this mixing of the psychoanalytic parent–child relation and the psychoanalytic sibling relation, for a blurring of these lines is a source of disquieting identity and relation disturbances. Right up to the present, psychoanalytic institutes have been a hotbed of such confusion of the parent–child dimension with that of the sibling relation. We frequently observe that the rivalry is fought out using a tactic of damning suspicion, which takes the form of "wild interpretations" of one's opponent. Even left unarticulated, these "wild interpretations" carry the power of symbolic and sometimes also material destruction—all the more when they come cloaked in psychoanalytic terminology as expert judgements.

With regard to the mortal danger that National Socialism posed to psychoanalysis and many psychoanalysts (Brecht, Friedrich,

Hermanns, Kammer, & Jülich, 1985, p. 64), I would like to remind you that the Jewish members of the German Psychoanalytic Society were pressured to leave the society in the illusory hope that it could thus be saved. The institution took the place of sibling and collegial solidarity. I wonder whether this extreme situation did not bring to light a concealed truth about psychoanalytic institutions, which is that the preservation of the institution rests on a hidden fratricide and sorori-cide. The internal and external adaptation necessary for the institution to persist and hold its members together is inseparable from the tacit acceptance of the elimination of disturbing individuals. In the face of the extreme threat to personal safety and to the individual's sense of self, posed by the terror of National Socialism, the firm walls of the institution appear as indispensable protection.

This brief look at the history of the psychoanalytic movement makes visible the discrepancy between, on the one hand, the neglect of the sibling relation in theory and clinical practice and, on the other, the frequency and intensity of sibling rivalry among psychoanalysts. I would like to add here that this rivalry is by no means an exclusively male domain. To grasp the dynamic of the sibling relation in all its complexity, it would be necessary also to examine the rivalry between sisters. The conflicts in the British Psychoanalytical Society around Anna Freud and Melanie Klein might serve as an example here— conflicts that also hugely contributed to the fertilisation of theoretical and clinical psychoanalysis.

The dynamic of the sibling relation

What is specifically threatening about the sibling relation as opposed to the oedipal threat? Whereas a parent–child relation is a relation between members of different generations, with a sibling relation we are dealing with members of one and the same generation. A child's every contact with his parents also means a confrontation across the generational boundary. The Oedipus complex encompasses the child's experiences in attempting, in his desires and his aggressive impulses, to defy and cover up the generational divide. With the formation of the superego at the end of the Oedipus phase, this boundary becomes an element of the psychic structure. The child's contact with his or her siblings, on the other hand, does not cross such a boundary; there are differences of age between them, but not of generation. Age differences can be of great significance in the relation of the child to his parents, for example, when they lead to preferential or discriminatory treatment, but they remain a matter of degree. In contrast, the difference in generations is fundamental and structural.

This difference has considerable consequences for the vicissitudes of instincts and the structuring of unconscious phantasies that have as their object the parents or siblings. The desiring of the mother and the murderous impulses towards the father, which underlie the oedipal conflicts, are a powerful source of anxiety and guilt. None the less, murdering the great and powerful father is so far from the young child's reality that, on the generational divide, its oedipal desires can only be articulated and differentiated as wishes and phantasies. The child is completely dependent on its parents for material and psychic survival; oedipal love and oedipal hate exist entirely against the background of existential dependence. While Oedipus's position is charged with conflict, his place in the constellation is also very clear. Father–mother–child: no point in the triad is conceivable without the other two. The triad is closed. It cannot exist without any one of its poles. Every person needs a father and mother.

Siblings, on the other hand, belong to the same generation. They are not as dependent on one another for their material and psychic survival as they are—each in their own right—on their parents. The principle of the sibling relation is the sequence. In contrast to the triad, the sequence is open. Siblings are not necessary. Without them, I would still exist. Conversely, this also means that the sequence can do without me. The sibling relation breeds the elemental fear that it might not matter whether or not I exist.

Closeness in the sibling relation offers special opportunities for personal development. Siblings can mutually support each other in coping with developmental challenges and crises. This includes what we can call—differentiating it from the oedipal triad—secondary triangulation. It opens a psychosocial space beyond the oedipal triad. In this space, siblings can find an access to love and hate that is less conditioned by existential dependence and, thus, allows a significant expansion of their ego. The sibling relation opens up a space in which the individual can learn to deal with rivalry productively. Living out, and deriving creative power from, rivalry is part of what it means to be an adult.

However, the existence of siblings also poses disturbing and painful questions. Behind feelings of rivalry, envy, and jealousy, an elemental narcissistic threat looms. The birth and existence of siblings is the visible evidence that my parents have other needs and wishes beyond me: not only in the sense that they devote attention and love to another child, my brother or sister, but also in that father and mother have a sexual relation with one another which is not accessible to me and which bears fruit that has a life independent of my own. Siblings are living proof of the primal scene.

In this way, siblings can be living evidence of an ever-present threat to the self. Seen from this angle, rivalry between siblings is closely connected to unconscious death wishes towards the sibling. After all, there could be no clearer difference than that I live, whereas the other is dead. The oedipal drama is marked by the threat of castration. The drama of sibling rivalry, however, is characterised by the threat of annihilation — annihilation at the hands of the other, who lays claim to the place that I occupy (see also Freud, 1917b).

The price of neglecting the sibling relation

I am convinced that neglecting the sibling relation and the inherent rivalry limits psychoanalytic understanding in both theory and practice. Here, I will look at just two areas: (1) possible consequences for analytical work with patients, and (2) the consequences for psychoanalytic institutions.

1. Although experiences with siblings come to life again in the analytic relation, many patients hardly mention their siblings and their rivalry with them in their associations, or do so only in a stereotyped way. This seems especially to be the case when they have developed a fused relation with a brother or sister, such that the ego boundaries between the siblings have remained blurred. In this case, the psychic structure with regard to the sibling relation is comparatively undifferentiated, but even when siblings do not come up in free association, they remain present in the process of transference–countertransference. If the conflicts and rivalries that characterise the horizontal level of the sibling relation are not thoroughly worked through and, furthermore, if

there is no clarifying theoretical reflexion, the transference and the analyst's countertransference reactions will not be understood and remain inaccessible. Unable to be worked with, they will constitute a hindrance to the analysis. The transference–countertransference process can then be infused with destructive sibling rivalry without this being recognised.

A lack of empathy can be an expression of a lacking openness on the part of the patient to the feelings of a sibling whom the analyst "greeted . . . with adverse wishes and genuine childhood jealousy" (Freud's letter to Fliess, 3 October, 1897, in Masson, 1985, p. 268). It is important that transference and countertransference phenomena of this kind are understood as a repetition of the patient's experiences with siblings. This is not easy, when the patient produces only scant thoughts about his siblings and when, in addition, the analyst has no conceptual frame of reference with which to understand the particular dynamic of the sibling relation. Patients can feel not understood in their phantasies, desires, and fears, stemming from internalised sibling relationships, and condemned for their rivalrous impulses, if their analyst fails to recognise the relative autonomy of this issue or, due to countertransference processes, cannot acknowledge it. This is the case, for example, when he understands a sibling transference only as a new manifestation or continuation of the oedipal theme. A double misunderstanding arises, as neither the parent nor the sibling transference can be appropriately understood or interpreted. To respond to a sibling transference with an interpretation aimed at the patient's relation to his parents is to systematically misunderstand him. It means the failure of a necessary process of differentiation and can lead to tenacious resistances in analysis.

2.   In my comments on the history of psychoanalysis, I indicated that I see a connection between the conflicts of psychoanalysis in the institutional context and the dynamic of sibling relationships and rivalry. In my view, we must simultaneously analyse the horizontal level of sibling and collegial relationships and the vertical dimension of oedipal authority relationships (and their interconnection) in order to understand institutional processes and structures. This applies particularly to psychoanalytic institutions. Without an analysis of the dynamic of sibling rivalry, we

are hardly in a position to understand the institutional conflicts in psychoanalytic institutes—neither those from the history of psychoanalysis nor those which plague us in our psychoanalytic institutes today. More than thirty years ago, Limentani stressed that sibling rivalries heavily burden training analyses (Limentani, 1974); I would maintain, not only these, but the entire institutional life of the system of psychoanalytic education and training. When we avoid an unflinching analysis of hidden wishes for love and murder between psychoanalytic siblings, we run the risk of interpreting conflicts and rivalries in analytic education prematurely and one-sidedly as an expression of problems with authority and with dependence on parent figures. As we could see with Jones, psychoanalysis has a tradition of just such displacements.

If we do not analyse independently problems that occur specifically in the horizontal dimension, there can be no psychoanalytic concept of a mature solidarity in which rivalry is not seen as a destructive force, but as a potential for development and creativity. In a vertically organised professional society, we risk losing sight of the sibling relation—and the development of solidarity generally—as a dimension in its own right. For this reason, the central focus of psychoanalytic attention on the vertical, parent–child, dimension also reflects society. Solidarity depends on reconciliation with internalised objects—parents and siblings. This requires adhering to the specific dynamics of, as well as to the interconnection between, these two dimensions, the vertical and the horizontal. Our reconciliation with parental figures remains incomplete if the autonomous reality of our sibling relationships is ignored, just as sibling reconciliation is doomed to fail if the oedipal dimension is denied.

References

Brecht, K., Friedrich, V., Hermanns, L. M., Kammer, I. J., & Jülich, D. H. (Eds.) (1985). Hier geht das Leben auf eine sehr merkwürdige Weise weiter [Here life goes on in a most peculiar way]. In: *Zur Geschichte der Psychoanalyse in Deutschland*. Hamburg: Kellner.

Ferenczi, S. (1911). On the organization of the psycho-analytic movement. In: *Final Contributions to the Problems & Methods of Psycho-Analysis* (pp. 299–307). London: Hogarth, 1955.

Freud, S. (1914d). On the history of the psychoanalytic movement. *S.E., 14*: 6–66. London: Hogarth.

Freud, S. (1917b). A childhood recollection from "Dichtung und Wahrheit". *S.E., 17*: 145–156. London: Hogarth.

Fromm, E. (1963). Psychoanalysis: science or party line. In: E. Fromm (Ed.), *The Dogma of Christ and other Essays on Religion, Psychology and Culture* (pp. 266–269). New York: Holt, Rinehart & Winston, 1963.

Jones, E. (1957). *Sigmund Freud: Life and Work*. Vol. 3: *The Last Phase 1919–1939*. London: Hogarth.

Limentani, A. (1974). The training analyst and the difficulties in the training psychoanalytic situation. *International Journal of Psychoanalysis, 55*: 71–77.

Masson, J. M. (Ed.) (1985). *The Complete Letters from Freud to Fliess 1887–1904*. Cambridge, MA: Harvard University Press.

CHAPTER TWO

Siblings in psychotherapy: a report from a preliminary psychoanalytic research project

Lech Kalita and Anna Faber

Introduction

T his chapter is a report from a preliminary research project focused on situations where an individual who undergoes psychotherapy knows other patients of her/his therapist. We have decided to use the term "therapeutic siblings" to describe this situation, both for the sake of clarity and for being based on theoretic considerations. The nature of our preliminary research is an exploratory one; our goal was to start the process of systematic organisation of observations in the area of "therapeutic siblings".

Theoretic considerations

Why should we study "therapeutic siblings"?

Transference is one of the absolutely fundamental concepts in psychoanalysis (Joseph, 1985). Inequity of patient's and therapist's roles in analysis and psychoanalytic psychotherapy (Frosh, 2006) makes transferential configurations concerning parental figures the ones that are most commonly encountered and described; one important dimension of those configurations is the fact that the parental figure belongs to a generation older than the patient. Nevertheless, we all have a great number of very early experiences, constituting the foundations of our internal world, that can be seen not only in a vertical dimension (relations with figures belonging to an older generation), but also in a horizontal dimension (relations with figures belonging to one's own generation—siblings and peers) (Joyce, 2011). According to norms in our culture, the infant and the young child usually enters the wider world of her or his peers in a more advanced phase of his childhood, while his earliest years are spent with his family: parents or their substitute (grandparents, nannies, etc.). It is in those earliest years that, alongside relations with care-takers, relations with siblings develop (in reality or in phantasy—see Joyce, 2011). Assuming that experiences connected with siblings are activated in course of psychoanalytic psychotherapy, we shall—as we always do—search for their expression in transference (Joseph, 1985). If we refer to the wide definition of transferential work, in which we consider not only those feelings that are orientated directly towards the therapist, but also all those experiences that stem from the fact of being immersed in a psychotherapeutic process, we can identify an area very vulnerable to transference experiences connected with siblings. This area would be all that is experienced due to the awareness of one's therapist's other patients (Larmo, 2007). The horizontal nature of such relations—as no patient is (or, no patient should be) more privileged than the others—is in obvious contrast with asymmetrical therapeutic relation, where one participant (therapist) is given much more power than the other (patient). Another issue that could make the "patient–therapist–other patients" constellation more similar to sibling experiences is the focus on the horizontal sibling rivalry dimension of oedipal strivings (Joyce, 2011). Thus, we understand that experiences concerning one's therapist's other patients can become a valuable source of information about one's transferential experiences and can be included in a therapeutic process to one's benefit.

A special position of "therapeutic siblings" in psychotherapeutic institutions

Our preliminary research was conducted on a group of psychotherapists that was undergoing (or had undergone in the past) psychotherapy and had experiences of "therapeutic siblings". Such choice of subjects was dictated by two main considerations. First, we considered ethical issues: recruiting subjects who were not therapists would require passing the information about our project to them, which would in turn require them to voluntarily breach confidentiality (inform the researchers about the fact of undergoing therapy) (Pope & Vasquez, 2010). As far as psychoanalytically orientated psychotherapists were concerned, it was obvious that they were undergoing, or had undergone, their own psychotherapy, so the request to participate in this project in itself would not break their confidentiality. The other important consideration that led us to choose this group of subjects for our preliminary research was the ubiquity of studied phenomenon in the population of psychotherapists. While, in the case of other patients, most often we can observe their fantasies about the therapist's other patients, in a group of therapists it is common to know one's own therapist's other patients in person. It seems to us that those situations (especially if they are not analysed in a transferential context during one's therapy) can shape further relations on the institutional level (Wellendorf, 2001). The degree and nature of such shaping remains unclear and its study surely stretches far beyond our preliminary research project. Nevertheless, it seems to be a valuable venture to undertake.

Stage one: the creation of a method

The creation of a method that would be best suited for the goal sketched out in the introduction to this chapter (i.e., to start the process of systematic organisation of observations in the area of "therapeutic siblings") raised a number of issues right from the beginning. In our attempt to organise our observations in a systematic way, should we relinquish some of the meanings that psychoanalytic perspective can supply and focus our attention on quantitative data? Are we able to come up with a method that would constitute a compromise between the rigorous demands of scientific research and a wish to capture some of the truth about subjects' subjective experiences? It occurred to us that if we aim at capturing subjective experiences, we should base our research on interviews rather than questionnaires, but how should we construct such interviews? We found the procedure described by Frosh (2006) quite helpful in coping with those problems; we decided to consistently stand our psychoanalytic ground and enquire into our own motivation to conduct this study. The personal interest of both researchers into the subject and the decision to undertake this project stemmed from the fact that we shared the experience of being "therapeutic siblings" (we had our own therapies with the same therapist). We decided not to exclude this fact from the procedure of constructing our method, but, rather, to utilise it: we had an unstructured talk about our experiences of having a "therapeutic sibling". The material that emerged in this talk helped us in constructing the interview. We came to a conclusion that the most important part of this structure would be the open-ended question; we realised that free-floating associations on the topic gave us the most valuable material. In addition, we agreed on some supplementary questions that referred in a more specific way to issues that we both identified as meaningful aspects of experiencing "therapeutic sibling". The sequence of questions was also important; we started the interview with the open-ended question, without any further suggestions, in the hope of receiving material unburdened by researchers' expectations; additional questions were biased by our ideas (and our expectations), so we asked interviewees to answer those only after the open-ended question had been answered. The structure of interview was as described in the following sections.

Open-ended question

I would like you to tell me, as fully as possible, if your awareness that other particular persons are undergoing or had undergone psychotherapy with your therapists affects you, and in what way?

Additional questions

Questions concerning: (a) the dominant feelings towards "therapeutic siblings"; (b) the interplay between actual sibling experience and "therapeutic siblings"; role of (c) sex and (d) sequence of "therapeutic siblings" and role of (e) sequence and (f) phantasies concerning actual siblings. The last question concerned (g) the experience of interview itself.

Stage two: commencing the interviews

After having the structure of the interview prepared, we started to recruit subjects. A group of subjects was recruited from a population of psychoanalytic psychotherapists; we briefly presented the idea of a research and asked them to participate in the interview. Thus, we cannot claim that our group was randomised in any way—participation was voluntary and no subjects were rejected. We are aware of the need to eliminate this methodological weakness in further studies. The preliminary project was commenced on a group of ten persons. We provided intimate, confidential external conditions; the interview was recorded. The gathered material was processed in a way partly based on a method of multi-step hermeneutic analysis and interpretation of empiric material, described by Kruchowska (2010). The recordings were transcribed into text documents, which in turn were analysed by the judges. In this preliminary version of the research, researchers themselves took on roles of judges; the exploratory nature of this study eliminated the risk of biasing the judgement of the material by any hypotheses. After this judgement, material underwent quantitative and qualitative analyses at the level of single text, and then the same procedure at the level of the complete set of texts. Data acquired from meta-analysis of the complete set of texts were further analysed statistically. These proceedings led us to formulate some conclusions.

Stage three: qualitative and quantitative analysis: the level of a single text

The judges' task was to define threads, sub-threads and categories in the transcript of the answers to the open-ended question from each interview. The thread was a description of general characteristics of the whole answer; the sub-thread was a more precise description of a particular portion of a thread; the categories were the basic elements of the sub-threads. We can illustrate this procedure by defining the thread, sub-thread, and categories in a short excerpt from an answer to the open-ended question:

> "I was glad to see him [subject's 'therapeutic sibling'], we travelled together [to attend sessions in a distant city] and it was pleasant in a way. I had been travelling by myself for years . . ."

Thread: Meaning of subject's experience of "therapeutic sibling".

Sub-thread: Actual relation with a "therapeutic sibling"

Categories: External intensity of an actual relation with a "therapeutic sibling"; feelings stemming from an actual relation with a "therapeutic sibling".

Defining threads, sub-threads, and categories in each text resulted in the creation of thread–sub-thread–category tables. An example, describing the whole answer to the open-ended question, is given in Table 2.1.

At this point, we were able to formulate internal and external interpretations of each text. Internal interpretations were formulated at the level of the text itself—it was an attempt to read the text consistently without venturing beyond it. External interpretations were

Table 2.1. An example of an answer to the open-ended question examined through the thread, sub-thread, and categories.

Thread	Sub-thread	Categories
Meaning of subject's experience of "therapeutic sibling"	Actual relation with a "therapeutic sibling"	External intensity of an actual relation with a "therapeutic sibling"
		Feelings stemming from an actual relation with a "therapeutic sibling"
	Similarities between "therapeutic siblings" and actual siblings	Similarities between "therapeutic siblings" and actual siblings
A history of subject's psychotherapy	Difficulties in subject's psychotherapy	Particular disturbances in subject's psychotherapy
		Specific feelings stemming from disturbances in subject's psychotherapy
	Issues connected with setting of subject's therapy	Differences in therapeutic setting between subject and her "therapeutic sibling"
		Analogies in therapeutic setting between subject and her "therapeutic sibling"

based on a theory that was external to the text: in our case, it was a psychoanalytic theory. We can demonstrate fragments of those interpretations.

Internal interpretation (excerpt)

The subject's focus on a scarce amount of encounters with her "therapeutic sibling" goes hand in hand with her emphasis on inner meanings and experiences: the intensity of feelings stemming from her relation with "therapeutic siblings". In spite of declaring that her contact with "therapeutic siblings" was scarce, it seems that it was very important to her (twenty-four statements of sixty-one statements in total).

External interpretation (excerpt)

The subject tended to speak about her feelings in a one-dimensional, positive way; we could infer that she avoided her feelings of aggressiveness and rivalry, as some material suggests them: "I didn't like those dogs in the [therapist's] courtyard, they were . . . not really aggressive, but they scared me and I wasn't sure about their intentions, they always kept barking when I came by".

After the qualitative analyses of threads, sub-threads, and categories, we analysed their quantitative characteristics. We counted the number of statements that qualified into each category and then we ordered those categories. This kind of qualitative–quantitative process resulted in the creation of tables of categories, exemplified in Table 2.2.

We started the same procedure for the additional questions; we came to think that the directed nature of those questions imposes a thread, so we limited ourselves to defining sub-threads and categories. In our preliminary study, we focused mainly on an open-ended question; what follows is material concerning those open-ended questions.

At this point, we had already created ten external and internal interpretations and ten tables of categories (one for each interview) ordered by frequency of category. In those ten texts—treated separately—we managed to identify thirty-four categories. Thus, we gained a systematic picture of each of the interviews alone. However, what we focused on was the systematic picture of the whole phenomenon.

Table 2.2. An example of a table of categories.

Categories total: 66	
External intensity of an actual relation with a "therapeutic sibling"	24 = 36.3%
Particular disturbances in subject's psychotherapy:	22 = 33.3%
Feelings stemming from an actual relation with a "therapeutic sibling"	20 = 30.3%
Specific feelings stemming from disturbances in subject's psychotherapy	16 = 24.2%
Differences in therapeutic setting between subject and her "therapeutic sibling"	13 = 19.6%
Analogies in therapeutic setting between subject and her "therapeutic sibling"	11 = 16.6%
Similarities between "therapeutic siblings" and actual siblings	2 = 3%

So, we needed to commence a qualitative meta-analysis—group categories defined in each text into common meta-categories. We proceeded to the next stage of our research.

Stage four: qualitative and quantitative meta-analysis: the level of the complete set of texts

The categories defined on the basis of each text were grouped by the judges into eight meta-categories, which included all thirty-four categories from separate texts. We shall present the list of meta-categories and an example of categories included in one of these meta-categories.

The list of meta-categories

1. External intensity of an actual relation with "therapeutic siblings".
2. Ambivalence towards "therapeutic siblings".
3. Relation with subject's therapist.
4. Fantasies about "therapeutic siblings".
5. Feelings towards "therapeutic siblings".

6. Early feelings in a triangular relation (subject–therapist–"thera-peutic sibling").
7. The triangular relation (subject–therapist–"therapeutic sibling").
8. Relations with actual (biological) siblings.

Categories included in meta-category No. 3—"relation with subject's therapist":

- relation with subject's therapist;
- relation with subject's therapist (second category same as the first);
- length of subject's therapy;
- particular disturbances in subject's psychotherapy;
- recognising subject's own place in her therapy;
- change in sessions' timetable;
- fantasies about therapist's comfort;
- difficulties in therapeutic process;
- specific feelings stemming from disturbances in subject's psychotherapy.

We used this set of meta-categories to process the complete set of texts once again. Each interview received a new table; this time, they described the quantity of statements that fell into each meta-category (in contrast to earlier tables based on categories derived from this text treated separately). In the next step, we created a table that was a quantitative description of the total set of text based on meta-categories. Thus, we ended up with a picture of the total set of data, ordered by meta-categories. It can be shown on a graph.

Stage five: interpretations

The data acquired in the previous stage allowed us to formulate some conclusive interpretations: an external qualitative meta-interpretation, an internal qualitative meta-interpretation, and an interpretation based on a statistical analysis.

As far as the internal qualitative meta-interpretation is concerned, we formulated an interpretation that was based solely on the set of texts themselves. We observed that a large number of statements referred to subjects' relation with their therapists, even though we did not suggest this in the open-ended question. The three most frequently recurring meta-categories might suggest that experiences in a triangular relation (subject–therapist–"therapeutic sibling") could be the most important issue for subjects, but it turned out that the meta-category directly addressing this issue was represented only marginally. Only one interview seemed to be a mature description of working through those issues in psychotherapy. The third observation concerned the focus of the subjects' statements, which was on direct, actual relations (external relation and feelings stemming from it) rather than childhood relationships or indirect relations (i.e., relations in phantasy). All those observations made us think that—on the level of texts themselves, without reference to external theories—subjects seemed more focused on direct, actual relationships with their therapist and with their "therapeutic siblings" than on thinking about those relationships in the light of their very intense triangular dimensions, in reference to the past or to phantasies.

The external meta-interpretation was based on meta-categories in the set of texts, but it referred to a theory which was external to those texts (in our case, a psychoanalytic theory). A large number of statements that fell under the "relation with therapist" category could—as we see it—suggest an important role of primary (parental) objects in structuring the psychic contents. The open-ended question encouraged subjects to formulate free associations connected with experiences of having "therapeutic siblings"; the fact that subjects devoted so much space to their dyadic relations with their therapist (in this context representing their parent/primary object) seems to confirm the concept of an organising role of a relation with a primary object in a triangular configuration (Rusbridger, 2004). The dominance of statements concerning actual experiences in the relation between subjects, their therapist, and their "therapeutic siblings" (three most frequently occurring meta-categories) over statements concerning the possibility of observing the triangular dimension of those relationships (meta-category, "the triangular relation") suggests that the oedipal contents saturate the conscious material, but are much less prone to conscious processing. A very limited number of statements focusing on biological siblings (although these seemed to be quite emotional during interviews) led us to think that, while experiences with actual siblings might influence further transferential feelings, they remain mostly unconscious (beyond the main flow of consciousness). The dominance of the three meta-categories focused on actual and/or direct feelings over the other five meta-categories connected with indirect observations, phantasies, and the past could be seen as evidence of subjects being immersed in the here-and-now experience, even if it was rooted in the past.

Statistical analysis of data was based on testing correlations between meta-categories. Correlations that proved significant are presented in Table 2.3

It occurs to us that this result allows the formulation of three interpretations. The strongest correlation was observed in the pair "external intensity of actual relation with a 'therapeutic sibling'"/"feelings towards 'therapeutic sibling'". It could be said that this proves that actual relations with "therapeutic siblings" are almost always connected with intense feelings, but we need to note that those meta-categories could have been inadequately differentiated, so areas they aim to describe might overlap. Very strong correlation in the pair "the triangular relation"/"external intensity . . ." seems to emphasise the idea that while the actual relation with "therapeutic siblings" activates strong oedipal feelings, what we observe (as we pointed out in the external meta-interpretation) are their derivatives, since oedipal issues themselves operate mainly outside conscious associations. Correlations in pairs "the triangular relation"/"feelings towards 'therapeutic siblings'" and "the triangular relation"/"relation with therapist" are seen by us as an expression of inextricable connection between being in a relation with one object in a triangular constellation and activating oedipal feelings.

Table 2.3. Significant correlations based on testing between meta-categories.

Pairs of meta-categories	N	Correlation	Significance
External intensity . . ./Feelings . . .	10	0.896	0.000
External intensity. . ./Triangular relation	10	0.773	0.009
Feelings . . ./Triangular relation	10	0.797	0.006
Relations with therapist/Triangular relation	10	0.774	0.009

Conclusions

Our study must be treated as preliminary research, constituting only the first tentative step into further attempts at clarifying the phenomenon of "therapeutic siblings". Having a very small group of subjects casts a shadow of doubt over our conclusions, although they might be used as guiding points in further research. The main conclusion that we arrived at concerned the intensity and vividness of feelings which stem from the existence of therapeutic siblings, as well as from being placed in a triangular relation—between the subject, the therapist, and the "therapeutic sibling"—while, at the same time, having limited insight into the triangular (oedipal) nature of this relation and its roots in the past. We feel that this conclusion remains consistent with above-mentioned theoretic considerations about studying siblings. In the light of our work as therapists, we feel it is vital to pay more attention to our patients' feelings towards their (actual and phantasised—see Joyce, 2011) "therapeutic siblings", as those feelings can become extremely intense while simultaneously remaining outside the material due to the lack of patients' insight into the triangular nature of such situations (with the therapist constituting one vertex of this triangle). In an institutional context, we feel that it is worth noting that unavoidable "therapeutic siblings" relationships (even more inescapable in relatively small societies, such as our Polish Society for Psychoanalytic Psychotherapy) probably result in many intense feelings in members of psychotherapeutic institutions, but those feelings might receive little working through on a conscious level. This can lead to abundant development of oedipal rivalry, jealousy, and hatred in present and future relationships with "therapeutic siblings" in institutions.

Conclusions derived from multi-step analysis of answers to the open-ended question could be supported by a few observations from our initial qualitative analysis of answers to additional questions; those have not yet been adequately processed qualitatively, but some regularities are already emerging.

Feelings most frequently identified by subjects were anger and jealousy. In the case of having older "therapeutic siblings" (i.e., when the subject knows the people who had started therapy with the subject's future therapist before the subject did), subjects talked about anxiety and/or a wish to have closer relations with their older "siblings".

As far as the question regarding the sex of "therapeutic siblings" is concerned, answers that stressed its relevance prevailed—subjects added that the opposite sex of the "sibling" made this relation easier. Interpretations of each interview let us observe that the opposite sex of the subjects' therapist seems to be the factor that facilitates development of oedipal issues in psychotherapy. Where differences of sex occurred, interviews were saturated with oedipal issues and subjects were able to talk about them more directly during the interview (even though they might not have been so directly conspicuous during therapy). An example from one of those interviews

"Actually it [the theme of 'therapeutic sibling'] opened up the whole trauma, all the angry, furious, hateful feelings and the anxiety: What comes next? What about me? I'm older, I wouldn't receive any more care and understanding! I remember this moment as a very traumatic one, as it—in a way—threatened my therapy due to difficult feelings in this complicated situation".

Another example:

"There was a moment when we [the subject and her 'therapeutic sibling'] broke apart, we had a kind of conflict, each started to ascribe something to one another. M was angry that I started to meet with her friends without her presence. But I did this anyway, though I knew it enrages her. Then our ways parted; I terminated this therapy, and after some time she terminated hers. Then we refreshed this friendship and we're friends up to this day. But back then—it was really strange."

We had an impression that subjects undergoing therapy with a therapist of the same sex cope with oedipal contents by taking a position of someone who is excluded from an oedipal situation, as if they unconsciously thought that their "therapeutic siblings" of a different sex are in a somewhat closer relation with their therapist. Interviews with those people were characterised by an increased level of anxiety. The following example can illustrate this:

"Another thing that stimulated my anxiety was arriving on time and leaving right after the session had ended—not to confront reality."

Some interesting observations were made concerning the sequence of birth and the sequence of starting therapy with one's therapist. In every interview, we identified a sense of longing for being the first or only child, which resulted either from losing that position or from not having such experience. First-born subjects were, in a way, convinced of their special, dominant, and "adequate" role, which they experienced as being somehow unique, sometimes also being better or smarter. Big differences of age seem to alleviate oedipal dynamic between siblings; the much younger siblings are perceived as belonging to the next, younger generation and, as a result, are sometimes ignored. Subjects who did not have biological siblings felt this as a kind of deficiency. The following excerpt can be used as an example of some of the described dynamics:

"At first I thought that someone else might have had something better. This can be connected with a particular image of me coming in the afternoon, when my therapist is already exhausted, because she gave more to the others; this was a strong impression. I thought that others must have had been there already, as my sessions were in the afternoon — and I did not want to know anything about those others."

Answers to our final question — concerning the experience of participating in the interview itself — pointed to a very high intensity of feelings derived from talking about siblings (both biological siblings and their "therapeutic" counterpart). Subjects stressed that this was a difficult experience that surprised them and stirred their conflicts and dilemmas.

We should like to end with an excerpt from one of the interviews, which — in our view — illustrates some of the above-mentioned conclusions.

"I can't remember situations in which I would discuss with my parents anything concerning my siblings; I find it hard to talk about it. It seems that I had experienced the special place of my older siblings — they had been on this world longer than me, it was something else. Because of my role in my family it would be inappropriate if I had said that my siblings get on my nerves. I can't remember complaining about my siblings — or my siblings complaining about me. But in my psychotherapy there were moments that put my judgement of my therapist to the test. I had to touch upon those issues in the light of my doubts concerning my therapist's competence. It was very unpleasant, because I didn't want to hurt my therapist — I needed to get him back."

Acknowledgements

The authors are grateful to the subjects that decided to participate in this project. We also thank Ms Beata Łaszczuk for her technical help.

References

Frosh, S. (2006). *For and Against Psychoanalysis*. London: Routledge.

Joseph, B. (1985). Transference: the total situation. *International Journal of Psychoanalysis, 66*: 447–454.

Joyce, A. (2011). Why the Ugly Sisters and Cinderella? EFPP & PTPP Conference, Cracow, 2011.

Kruchowska, E. (2010). Metoda wielostopniowej analizy i interpretacji hermeneutycznej materiału empirycznego [The multi-stage hermeneutical method of analysis and interpretation of qualitative data]. In: M. Straś-Romanowska, B. Bartosz, M. Żurko (Eds.), *Badania narracyjne w psychologii* [Narrative Research in Psychoanalysis]. Warsaw: Eneteia.

Larmo, A. (2007). Sibling rivalry and the structuring of the mind. *Scandinavian Psychoanalytic Review, 30*: 22–30.

Pope, K. S., & Vasquez, M. J. T. (2010). *Ethics in Psychotherapy and Counseling: A Practical Guide*. Hoboken, NJ: Wiley.

Rusbridger, R. (2004). Elements of the Oedipus complex: a Kleinian account. *International Journal of Psychoanalysis, 85*: 731–747.

Wellendorf, F. (2001). Sibling rivalry, psychoanalytic aspects and institutional implications. EFPP & PTPP Conference, Cracow, 2011.

CHAPTER THREE

Therapeutic group—almost like a family: a few comments on siblings

Ewa Bąk

Theoretical introduction

In his clinical works, Freud rarely referred to the meaning of experiences related to the relation with siblings. One of such examples is the case of Little Hans (Freud, 1909b), where the arrivals of siblings are one of the key factors influencing the birth of neurosis. Another example is the case of Wolf Man (Freud, 1918b), where the choice of a sexual object in the patient's adult life is understood as the reversal and transference of the early, traumatic relation with his siblings who were sexual objects, which contributed to the development of neurosis. In another text describing the dynamics of transference in the patient–doctor relation, Freud claims that this phenomenon does not need to take the form of a paternal transference, but can also be a maternal or a brotherly one: "But the transference is not tied to this particular prototype: it may also come about on the lines of the mother-imago or brother-imago" (Freud, 1912b, p. 99). By this, he admits that the relation with siblings might be of importance for the development of personality and pathology in an individual.

Freud presents a much more detailed and broader description of the sibling relation and its dynamics in his social writings. In *Group*

Psychology and the Analysis of the Ego (1921c), he describes how jealousy, rivalry, and jaundice turn into the need for social equality and justice. He calls it a herd instinct and explains its ontogenesis in the following way:

> Something like it first grows up, in a nursery containing many children, out of the children's relation to their parents, and it does so as a reaction to the initial envy with which the elder child receives the younger one. The elder child would certainly like to put his successor jealously aside, to keep it away from the parents, and to rob it of all its privileges . . . in consequence of the impossibility of his maintaining his hostile attitude without damaging himself, he is forced into identifying himself with the other children. So there grows up in the troop of children a communal or group feeling . . . Thus social feeling is based upon the reversal of what was first a hostile feeling into a positively-toned tie in the nature of an identification. (Freud, 1921c, pp. 118–120)

The described emotional constellation is a source of unceasing peer rivalry and what follows, social rivalry. In order to avoid bearing destructive emotional costs, functioning in such a condition requires the development of a number of interpersonal, social, or political competences, which allow one to diminish the ambivalence.

What is the nature of the process of "identification with other children", what developmental mechanisms are responsible for equality and justice? In other words, what factors permit the negotiation of the balance between the conflicting mechanisms of rivalry and co-operation? It seems that Freud's description suggests that a mature relation with siblings consists in a transition from the order of emotions to the order of reason. If such a transition does not happen, neurotic mechanisms appear—those similar to the ones described in *Totem and Taboo*: ". . . taboo has grown up on the basis of an ambivalent emotional attitude" (Freud, 1912–1913, p. 60).

To gain better understanding of the nature of the processes conducive to the creation of the "mental order" of equality and justice, I shall refer to the thought of Lévinas (Bauman, 1997), a philosopher whose majority of considerations focused on the nature of the ethical relation between "Myself" and the "Other". The philosophy of Lévinas, to a large extent, stemmed from his reaction to the dread of the totalitarianism of the Second World War. In his search for a remedy, a key for a better future without wars, he focused on the ethical relation in a couple, fiercely supporting the idea of a profoundly responsible and involved attitude of tolerance and getting to know the alterity of the "Other". To Lévinas, the "Myself–Other" relation is of a transcendental, spiritual nature, it comprises the sensational and emotional dimension. The essence of this relation is responsibility, understood as care, mutuality, or devotion. Lévinas emphasises the exceptionality and irreproducibility of such closeness, as an ethical relation cannot be extended to other relationships without any harm to itself. An ethical relation is a state of mind free of rationality, judgement; it also seems to be free of aggression and violence. What happens when, in the world of the Lévinasian "Couple–the Others", the "Third One" appears? Lévinas writes very little about it, and usually only when asked by other authors. Unwillingly, and with much reluctance, he answers that the appearance of the "Third One" enforces a social or political relation; there appears a new quality which makes it necessary to refer to reason. In order to take control over the newly established relation and to reorganise previous reality shared only with the "Other", one needs a reason and its function: judgement, comparison, valuation, negotiation, etc. The mechanism of comparisons (threatening the idealistic absolute acceptance proposed by Lévinas's ethics) in closeness with the "Others" is enforced, and some divisions (into classes or categories) are justified. Mental mechanisms of comparison, judgement, and classification acting between the "Others" bring us excessively closer to the dread of totalitarian ideologies, from which Lévinas's tendency to stay within the borders of a couple might originate. It seems that the "Third One" is rather a sibling than a father, as the closeness of a mother or a father is a closeness of a care-giver (in a child's experience, parents sometimes operate as a joint object), and only the closeness of a brother or a sister becomes different.

Contemporary developmental psychology sets out a similar scheme of the relations between siblings. According to the scheme, the relations are deemed relatively independent structures. The interactions between siblings are a factor conducive to the process of becoming aware of the separateness of Myself–Others (Mitchell, 2003).

Proper development will then be dependent on the successful passage from the order of emotions to the order of reason, which conditions the ability to tolerate ambivalence. Below, I shall present three examples of disturbances of this process, resulting in "withdrawal of thinking", "apparent unity", and "denial of existence". The examples come from my clinical experience with therapeutic groups.

Clinical examples

The elder must leave: withdrawal of thinking

Maciek is a thirty-year-old man who started therapy because of panic–fear attacks transforming into intrusive thoughts about catastrophes. The thoughts, which usually pertained to imaginary threats to the life of Maciek or those close to him, escalated into divagations of a global character, including the end of the world. The fears started to threaten the stability of his marital relation, and, moreover, the patient was afraid that he would transmit his "fearful attitude towards life" to his children.

When Maciek was ten years old, his younger brother was born. Maciek was then ill with an infectious disease, so, in order to protect the newborn baby from the infection, Maciek was moved to his grandmother's house, where he spent around two weeks without seeing his parents or his younger brother. His brother was never his playing companion; a bond between them was never established, as if the younger brother could never have been seen. The situation was repeated in the adolescence period, when Maciek lost his peer friends. After failing to pass final exams in secondary school, Maciek could not follow his educational path in the company of his friends. He pursued further education alone, lacking involvement and deriving no pleasure from it, establishing no closer relationships, and he studied for as long as eight years. He chose a job below his professional qualifications, denying his ambitions and his need for rivalry. In the whole process of the patient's development, one could clearly notice deterioration of his mental functioning. In peer groups, Maciek played the role of a jester—a person who makes others laugh, is the object of jokes and malicious comments, and, at the same time, cannot feel the emotional context of such an attitude.

For over two years of group therapy, the patient was not able to accept any interpretations indicating a link between his problems and his life story. He denied attaching any emotional importance to the situations described above. He wanted to perceive his problems only as a kind of a disease, a flaw, or some inherited inclinations. He did not establish any meaningful relations with other patients in the group. At the same time, he participated in the sessions regularly, although no clear benefits derived from the therapy could be noticed. I was perplexed by the fact that one can be blind to such obvious dependencies, not to be able to understand them. This was until the day when a new patient joined the group. He was of a similar age to Maciek's, but, taking his "therapeutic age" into consideration, he was much younger than him. At the session directly following the one where the "younger brother" appeared, Maciek showed up, different than usual. Confidently, he informed me and the group that he was feeling much better, he had thought his situation over, and he had calmed down because he understood that he must accept himself the way he is. He wanted to end the therapy because he had already learnt a lot about himself; he wanted to leave and just live, to focus on his work and family. He realised that it was time to finish the therapy so that someone else could take his place in the group.

I understood that until then the analysis of Maciek's problems had not been possible, because his mind had not been available. It stemmed from his personal experience, that in the situation where reason was indispensable for establishing the new order, all its functions became blocked. Thinking about something that could not be a direct experience, that was out of sight, did not make sense. Similarly, in the situation of the countertransference, Maciek could not/did not want to look at his "younger brother", and neither could he think about what he was experiencing. Instead, he applied the only social order he knew, which commanded him to disappear, give way, and stay inconspicuous, at the same time denying the emotional context of withdrawal. In complying with such an order, he organised his functioning in the family, at work, with his friends, and, eventually, in the therapeutic group.

An interpretation referring to the social or political order, showing withdrawal from making comparisons, judgements, rivalry, objectifying, and negotiating, allowed the patient to "move from his place". It seems that, after having discussed the situation that appeared within the therapeutic group, Maciek started thinking, he became inquisitive and curious, asked questions, denied, formulated hypotheses concerning both his own problems and the problems of other members of the group. He also started to change at the behavioural level. He joined a sports team at work, where he could experience rivalry, making comparisons, and the fight for primacy. He started to think about finding a new job and he dared to travel by plane for a holiday with his family (which before had been inconceivable).

A brotherly conspiracy: the illusion of unity

This group worked for only a year; it was homogenous, all its members being young people between twenty-four and twenty-seven years of age (which could significantly intensify the tendency to compete and to rival). For them, the developmental step of leaving their parents' home, building a relation, and starting an independent adult life was difficult. The ambivalence they experienced was expressed by somatic symptoms, emotional instability, difficulty in maintaining a relation with a partner, holding a job, or inability to finish their studies.

Over the whole year, the dominating subjects of discussion were current events. I had an impression that the patients were not interested in any deeper analyses, and contented themselves with conversations about "what's up" and how they understood what happened. They carried on discussions, they were comparing themselves with one another, they were judging one another, and they were giving advice. Usually, the sessions were very dynamic, full of emotions and impulsive behaviours, and the patients seemed to have fun. They frequently repeated how good they felt in the group, how well they fit together, which was confirmed by their 100% attendance at almost all sessions. Frequently, when listening to my patients, I would think that what happened there did not apply to me, that I did not understand what they found so exciting. I was slightly irritated that no therapeutic work was being done (from my point of view), and that the group became a support group. I was wondering whether the group members were developing a transference relation and sometimes I had an impression that apart from merely noticing my presence by means of asking a rather "courteous" question, nothing more was happening. Two months before the planned summer holiday break, the patients informed me that they planned to finish therapy just before the beginning of the holidays. I had an impression that they had devised something behind my back. At that time, one of the patients told us about her dream:

> "I was a waitress in some restaurant, the restaurant was at an apartment, I guess, everybody was sitting at one table, a round table, and I was to attend them. Then I realised that my clients were all old people, I didn't like it that I had to serve food to them, and moreover there was no toilet there. I was afraid and disgusted with the whole situation. I jumped out of the window, although I didn't know whether it was high above the ground and whether I would survive this jump."

The dream displayed a broad emotional context that the group had denied until then. By creating an idealisation of a perfectly selected group of matching people, while having a good time, the patients totally denied comparisons (we are all the same) and rivalry (there is no therapist you could rival). When these feelings were to be admitted, there appeared a nightmare, as in the dream: magnified age differences, serving others, unbearable tension one cannot ponder upon, one that you can only escape from. The advent of the summer break confronted them with the fact that the superficial character of an idealised buddy relation had not actually created a bond that would allow the group to go through the holiday separation. They had to part with one another.

To me, the decision made by the group was a surprise, but then what seemed more important to me was the fact that the group came into agreement, and not that they were doing something against my desire to keep them in therapy. Proposing an interpretation underlining the value of the agreement, and respecting their decision, I let them establish their social order. We terminated the group. Today, I think that I yielded to the common group idealisation, like a parent who finds it convenient for the children to take care of themselves. Moderating peer arguments full of aggression and jealousy takes a lot of effort, so a group of young people perfectly understanding one another was subconsciously a very convenient situation for me. I think that we all participated in a solution which allowed the avoidance of realising the importance of the fact that one of us was getting something someone else did not receive, that there was a figure whose interest was desired and, at the same time, limited, unevenly distributed. Taking into consideration the core problem common to the patients, which was related to their separation from the family of origin, and entering a real situation of peer rivalry, one could say that the group created a utopian social order that allowed them to avoid this problem instead of exploring it. Mutual differences and the meaning of the therapist's presence became taboo.

At the family table: denial of existence

Another example comes from a group from the day-care ward, where the therapy is very intensive. The group was heterogeneous with regard to sex, age, education, and pathology. One of the patients' dominating common traits was large families of origin. More than half of the group members came from families with several children. None of the patients had good relationships with their siblings—their relations were most frequently very weak or aggressive, with elements of violence.

Such a group created a working style that allowed them to avoid the subject of their siblings' existence: unconsciously, they "dedicated" particular portions of the sessions to individual participants, shifting their attention from one patient to another. What they discussed together were their life situations; topics connected with the relations within the group did not appear at all. It could be noticed that the patients' expectations were directed solely at the therapists, whom they had to share somehow. The situation escalated as a result of a conflict between two young patients, which ended with one of them leaving the group. This drop-out was experienced by the group as a repetition of the experience of peer violence, both in the aspect of conscious identification with the victim, and the contact with their own aggressive impulses.

Apart from this "incident", the group was surprisingly disciplined. Both my co-therapist and I had an impression that the group blocked aggressive and rivalrous impulses in an unnatural way. The reason for this could be the fact that the transference between siblings was much stronger than the transference relations with the therapist, yet not overt. This hypothesis is confirmed by the inconsistency that could be observed between the content of the patients' statements and their behaviours. When describing their relationships with siblings, they most often talked about fear, humiliation, physical or psychological violence, or parental overprotectiveness on the verge of incapacitation (the youngest and middle children in the family), anger, remorse, emotional burden, and prematurely entering the role of a care-giver, or the feeling of guilt for siblings' mistreatment (the eldest children). We can say that in their case establishing a friendly social order, agreement, and support between siblings ended in failure. These relationships, often very emotional, contrasted with a surprisingly good mutual understanding within the group, giving concessions to each other and focusing on assuring every group member sufficient care and time. The group unanimously put much effort into not giving rise to any conflict. This attitude of the group and individual patients was interpreted as manifestation of resistance, fear of their own aggression and destructiveness, and excessive conformism resulting from the fear of authority or a stringent superego. However, such interpretations had no influence on changing the group's vibe. The patients denied having siblings, and they focused on their own parents or played the role of parents to other patients.

This situation lasted until the day when the group worked without the therapists. It was left under the supervision of two interns who had participated in the group sessions since the very beginning. It was a session of art therapy, which consisted of watching a film and then discussing it. After seeing the film, the patients started a heated discussion about it, cutting each other short and trying to convince others to agree with their viewpoint. It appeared that they perceived the attitudes of particular characters of the film in very different, extremely different, ways. Tension was rising around these differences, and the patients started to shout out their opinions. The heated discussion lasted until the end of the session. Having finished the discussion in such excitement, the patients parted for four days—because of a holiday the weekend break was longer than usual.

The dynamics of group work during a few consecutive days after the break were the results of emotions unleashed during the therapists' absence. Without expressing it directly, the group seemed to feel remorse, anger, and regret towards the therapists who had left the group, and, as a result, the group sank into chaos, the atmosphere became overwrought and dangerous. The patients were talking about helplessness and weakness and their desire to escape from these feelings into addictive substances. In the following days, aggression, jealousy, and rivalry were overtly expressed. During a break between therapeutic sessions, one of the patients, intending to manifest positive feelings, hit another patient in the thigh so hard that that she burst into tears. Their comments to each others' statements became more confrontational and there were remarks such as: *you're talking bullshit; you're stealing our time; the things you're saying have no therapeutic value; I don't care about it.* The patients started to compare and judge one another. Positive and negative inclinations of particular group members towards one another started to become visible, and resulted in creating subgroups.

The analysis of the "here and now" situation that appeared in the group allowed discussion of the feelings of rivalry, jealousy, and jaundice which the patients felt in their own families towards their siblings. These feelings were incited not only by the problems related to access to the parents' attention and affection, but also by the attributes, skills, or achievements of older siblings or the privileges their younger siblings enjoyed. The patient who had behaved aggressively admitted that in the group she could not stand each moment when the therapists focused on someone other than herself; that she envied others for practically everything—attractive appearance, intelligence, spontaneity, etc. When summarising the treatment of a person who was leaving the group ahead of time, the patients very precisely and insightfully showed how she was avoiding a real, emotional contact with the group. They were also able to analyse their own "strategies" for not seeing their siblings.

We (the therapists) had then an impression that the functioning of the group was changing from dependent and controlled to being more liberated and rational. Conscious acceptance of aggressive desires allowed the patients to experience the feeling of guilt and, in a further perspective, let them experience depressive feelings related to the impending end of therapy and parting. At the behavioural level, it manifested in the form of apologising to the patient who was "beaten" and removing piercings. The patients started to pay attention to late comings and absences, to comment openly on behaviours such as abandonment, disregard, or unwillingness to help others. At that time, one of the patients recounted a dream which illustrated the immensity and intensity of feelings related to siblings, both the real ones and the transference-based ones:

> "I was somewhere at war and I was a victim of gang rape. Then I felt as
> if I were standing aside, I was watching the suffering of somebody close

to me, but I couldn't help her; I was helpless . . . I heard therapists say that it may end up with a baby and that they had to take it out. And these men started to pull the baby out of me using a wire. It was horrible, there was chaos around me, lots of strangers . . ."

I think that this dream depicted the whole drama that took place in the "nursery" while the parents were absent. How terrifying and painful the experience of a relation with a sibling must have been (this was the actual experience of the dreaming patient). The dream also shows the changes in the state of mind of the patient, but also the group, over the several days described above. From dismay, the feeling of depersonalisation and psychopathic fragmentation, to the return of testing the reality and concluding that the people around me are not my close ones (bully brothers), but strangers. Only after settling mutual relationships, ridding them of projections, were the patients able to co-operate, giving one another support and encouragement with various activities out of the group: for example, moving out of the family home, assertive behaviour during a divorce case, starting studies.

Final remarks

The situations described above show how the change of the viewpoint of seeing "social" relationships and the transference related to siblings allowed the individual patient or the group as a whole to find a way out of the dead-end. In each of the described cases, the failure in establishing social order, the lack of a successful transition from the order of emotions to the order of reason had another basis: an unfortunate state of things coincidentally accompanying the appearance of younger siblings, which makes it impossible to establish a relation with them, insufficient strength of internalised support and co-operation, which does not allow going through a separation process, and domination of aggressive and envious feelings in the ambivalently experienced relation with siblings, which makes it impossible to develop friendliness, care, and love for the sibling.

Freud perceived a bond between individuals in a group as being of libidinal nature. According to Bion, the libidinal component of the bond is characteristic only for certain stages of group work, driven by primal or primitive functioning mechanisms. In a Bionese working group, the bond is of co-operative character (1961). To Bion, when a group is a working group, thinking, scientific exploration of reality and rationality dominate. A working group is a group where the order of reason prevails, which allows the negotiation of the internal ambivalence of the processes of rivalry and co-operation.

Both Freud and Bion focused on clinical work with individual patients. A quite depressing vision of social reality emerges from their theoretical works on groups—a vision of fragile balance between strong, contradictive tendencies. Freud claims that a symbolic "brotherly conspiracy" offers safety to the society, in exchange for relinquishing a portion of freedom. In his comments on Freud's works from the viewpoint of postmodernity, Bauman (1997) shows that nowadays it is the expansion of personal freedom that is responsible for diminishing the scope of safety. We are left with no choice but to renew the old contract. *Others* do exist, and how Bauman formulates it

> Now there are "they". They, those various others, do things to each other, may harm each other, make each other suffer. "This is the hour of justice."' The uniqueness of the Other, incomparable when constituted by moral responsibility, will not help much now; one needs to appeal to a force one could do without before, to Reason – that allows one, first, to "compare the incomparable", and – second – to "impose a measure upon the extravagance of the infinite generosity of the "for the Other". (Bauman, 1997, p. 49)

References

Bauman, Z. (1997). *Postmodernity and its Discontents*. Cambridge: Polity Press.

Bion, W. R. (1961). *Experiences in Groups*. London: Tavistock.

Freud, S. (1909b). *Analysis of a Phobia in a Five-Year-Old Boy. S.E., 10*: 3–149. London: Hogarth.

Freud, S. (1912b). The dynamics of transference. *S.E., 12*: 97–108. London: Hogarth.

Freud, S. (1912–1913). *Totem and Taboo. S.E., 13*: 1–161. London: Hogarth.

Freud, S. (1918b). *From the History of an Infantile Neurosis. S.E., 17*: 1–124. London: Hogarth.

Freud, S. (1921c). *Group Psychology and the Analysis of the Ego. S.E., 13*: 67–143. London: Hogarth.

Mitchell, J. (2003). *Siblings, Sex and Violence*. Cambridge: Polity Press.

CHAPTER FOUR

The intransience of the sibling bond: a relational and family systems view

Michael D. Kahn

This chapter has four foundational goals. First, to counter the assumption that siblings have a negligible influence on self-development. Second, to offset the premise that siblings are inherently rivalrous. Third, to offer evidence of the biological utility of having a sibling. Fourth, to better understand the phenomenology of siblings through the analytic endeavour.

The sibling relation is usually life's longest lasting intimate relation, longer than those with friends, parents, spouses, and children, and is valued by many precisely for that fact. Predictions of the nature of one sibling's impact on the brother or sister, or the sibling group's influence on one another in their varied configurations, can usually only be best understood on an in-depth, case by case basis. The relationships are multi-dimensional, reflecting shifting self-states over important developmental time, a veritable reflection and a chiaroscuro of the self, captured in memory, possessions, rituals, photos, turning points, and varying degrees of self-coherence. Highlights and lowlights throughout childhood and adolescence of shared experience with a brother and a sister create a moving set of configurations and memories for each person. Siblings are self-objects, sometimes mirroring, merging, and twinning permanent companions and confidants, and sometimes reviled and rejected repositories of the "not-me", the other, the disaffected and the disavowed aspects of one's own self. Pointed family reminders to be, or not be, like the other, coexist with the private and shadow world that siblings inhabit, that I call the "sibling underworld". As such, some of one's most private and intense experiences might have been with a brother or sister.

How can we hope to understand this complexity? As relational analysts and self psychologists, we are best suited to explore the depths of this important subsystem, unlike classical analysts, social psychologists, and historians, who examine birth order effects or conduct large-scale surveys (e.g., Sulloway, 1996). We accomplish this with assumptions of non-linearity in cause and effect, by considering the developmental scaffolding of experience that occurs for every child (Guidano, 1987) in relation to their brother or sister, by juxtaposing the inner and outer worlds as each individual ontologically unfolds within their sibling framework, and by examining the rhythms of a child being both subject and object in sibling interaction. We attempt to understand the depth of ambivalence, and the shifts in self-experience over time. Except in the extreme instances of total parental absence or death (see Bank & Kahn, 1982, 1997), sibling influence with one another always occurs concurrently within the mediated vortex of parental influence. With a heightened sensitivity about sibling dynamics, we can attempt to use the immediacy of guided, informed enquiry about such matters, examples of which will follow in this chapter, and we can also try to capture the evanescent aspects of our own sibling experiences in the enactments that take place as we open up analytic space with our patients. Unfortunately, some of this consciousness never transpires, even in the lengthiest of therapies. We need to understand why this occurs.

Black (2003), a relational analyst, gives a beautiful illustration of sibling sensitivity as she describes holding imagery, affect, and experience of her own as a patient of hers suddenly becomes critical and dismissive of Black's previous participation in having laughed with the patient, who had just told a bizarre story involving the patient's brother. Almost immediately, in her reverie, Black recalls a dinner scene of her own past, in which her silent parents are sitting with her and her brother, the father's bad mood is palpable, the brother sniffles, asks to leave the table, and returns, with a twinkle in his eye, glances at his sister, and then, spontaneously, brother and sister start laughing. Black writes,

> The laughter is infectious, impossible to contain. My father is outraged. "Control yourselves, or leave the table!" He finds us rude and disrespectful. We can't stop. We don't stop, and we are sternly dismissed from the table. (p. 640)

Black notes that the experience of laughter she and the patient had shared was deeply evocative of the laughter she and her brother shared, and the subsequent dismissiveness by the patient nested with the memory of her father's dismissiveness. Black further writes,

> . . . but there was something even more important about the laughter my brother and I shared. It generated a deeply meaningful and enduring connection between us, intimately joining us in revitalizing insurrections, throwing off what we felt was the deadening tyranny of my father's control. We were not laughing at him, but we were certainly laughing around him. The laughter functioned as a kind of in-your-face rebellion, an internally regenerative release, a flaunting of feeling that was once more alive, responsive. (p. 641)

We can only speculate about the vitalising impact that such experiences, repeated enough, had had on that analyst, subsequent to that actual, remembered occurrence, but the incident is strongly suggestive that her sibling relation had some regularity, predictability, and enduring aspects to it, that it follows Thelen's (2005) characteristics of dynamic living systems, possessing stability, flexibility, continuity, and epigenesis. How different the scene would have been if Black were an only child, and had not had a brother to protectively join with.

Multiple examples abound. I am in Mexico sitting at the edge of a children's play area and swimming pool watching two of my grandchildren, Max (eight years old) and Theo (four years old). Suddenly, I am aware that even though Max has gone off on his own, his younger brother starts to follow, not completely, but to stay in his proximity. Theo goes down the water-slide, he looks around to see if Max is within visual range, he looks away, then back again, as he walks to the ladder. The sequence repeats, over and over. His older brother reciprocates, looking back, the dance continues with multiple variation of younger brother checking on the proximity, is it also approval?, of his older brother, who casts glances towards his young brother, is it care-taking and protection? Neither seems particularly concerned with looking at me. And then I notice other groups of children who appear to be siblings by their physical similarities, youngers and olders, who are maintaining proximity, visual contact, physical engagement, agonistic contacting, as social anthropologists (Suomi, 1982) would call it, all of it enhancing the children's experience of experimentation, mastery, and play. This is not rivalry, not contrasts between the black and white of extreme differences, this is not binary demarcation, but forms of attachment, support, and caring, characterised by nuance and subtlety. In such scenarios, we can see siblings using one another in the service of two of Lichtenberg's (1989) primary motivational systems, attachment and exploration. Some of this becomes interiorised in the mind, and some of this remains as part of the body ego.

An epistemological stance

As we move from outer observations to inner reflections, we can see a shifting kaleidoscope of images of sibling relatedness. While there are some invariants of fixed roles and frozen identities which attach to some children in families without change (the binary splitting of them into the one who is smart, the other dumb, talented and unable, sick and well, criminal and innocent (Bank & Kahn, 1982, 1997), which can haunt them, or create an indelible print for life, more usual are the part identifications which stem from self–selfobject connections which the children create on their own. Read the poignant poem by a fifteen-and-a-half-year-old sister about her fourteen-year-old brother, on the eve of the boy's psychiatric hospitalisation:

Jonathan

> He was older than I in mind. Younger than I in heart.
> He understood things I would never understand.
> But, could he feel for things in his heart?
> He was like a stone on a beach, one among many,
> But he was different. He shone in the sun.
> I loved him. I often wondered if he loved me.
> Behind his doors there was a small child crying.

No one could cross the wall of his guilt, pain, and sorrow.
In the dark of the night I cry for him.
I turn away from the pain in his eyes. (His beautiful, yearning eyes.)
I ask myself, am I just like the rest?
One who shuts out the light of the sun?
Oh! How I want to help him!!!
I'm a woman with a heart.
One who tried and tried to reach the light.
I wish I understood what goes through the tunnel that leads to the
complicated puzzle in a beautiful gold statue.
                                        (Bank & Kahn, 1997, pp. 67–68)

Children's emerging identities, filled with dualities and contradic-
tions, as we can see in the poem, are contained in the consciousness
we have of the other, the sister's experience of herself as a child/
woman in her compassion for her brother, the brother's self as envi-
sioned in the memory and experience with him that she had had.
Coates (1998), citing Fonagy and Target's (1998) infant research, states
that the perception of the self that exists in the mind of the other
becomes the representation of the child's experience, a representation
of the world of representation. "My brother or sister holds the
memory of who I have been."

Given the intensity and duration of sibling experience for many,
once we are beyond the infant and early childhood years of rudimen-
tary representation and primary parental influence, we are compelled
to consider just what the effects of siblings are to one another. A non-
linear, dynamic, developmental systems paradigm seems best suited
as we listen for, and to, sibling dynamics. Generalisations about
sibling phenomena, of which rivalry is the foremost, have been shown
to be insufficient and often prejudicial. Interviews with many hun-
dreds of individuals, in and out of therapy, by this author, reveal clus-
ters of important, surprising, and often-life-altering effects. In a recent
article discussing non-linear dynamic systems, Piers (2005) has stated,

. . . a non-linear, dynamic system is a system whose evolution is
discontinuous, nonproportional and unpredictable. Breaking it down,
this means that, under certain conditions, nonlinear systems change in
sudden, abrupt, and discontinuous way . . . changes made in a component of a system do not necessarily have a corresponding proportional
effect on the outcome. In other words, there is not always a clear and

proportional link between cause and effect; small changes often have a profound effect ... even when armed with full knowledge of the current state of the system, we are unable to predict the future states of a non-linear system. (p. 231)

We have concluded that sibling phenomena often require a Janusian perspective. We require a sensitivity to the liminal, the ways siblings become important to each at critical junctures of developmental change, and how they can be enduring in their relating and in their self-representations. We also need to understand why previously vital connections between siblings fade and self- and object-representations become slippery, tangled, and confused, subject to repression or obfuscation.

Psychoanalysis's omission of the sibling

Even after forty plus years of intense and concentrated study of sibling relationships and sibling dynamics, I am still struck by how unnoticed and neglected sibling effects have been in the psychoanalytic canon. Repeated observations in the consulting room and daily life underscore how varied, sometimes intense, sometimes of lasting significance, and sometimes developmentally discontinuous, sibling phenomena are, and continue to be, in the lives of certain individuals. Highly experienced clinicians share some of this bewilderment, often approaching me with the same question and reference, "My brother(s) and sister(s) have been very important to me; why has our field had so little to say about these matters?", of which this conference offers welcome relief.

First, classical theory and perspective, with its emphasis on hierarchical arrangements in families and in the transferential dynamics between patient and analyst, held sway in our field for a very long time. Freud, himself a surviving and entitled eldest son, disparaged his own sibling relationships, resented John, the son of his older half-brother, was disturbed and subsequently guiltily haunted by the death of his baby brother, Julius, when Freud was nineteen months old, and dominated his five sisters in place of his weak father. With the exception of cultivating the dutiful idealisation of his ten-year younger brother, Alexander, there is evidence (Bernays, 1940; Jones,

1967; Roazen, 1975) that Freud as a brother and a brother-in-law was competitive, jealous, prone to envy and anger, and intolerant. Such themes are carried forth and evident in such major writings of his as *Analysis of a Phobia in a Five-Year-Old Boy* (1909b), *Totem and Taboo* (1912–1913), and *From the History of an Infantile Neurosis* (1918b). Freudian sibling theory could, and did, prevail in the paternalistic and hierarchical climate of early and mid-twentieth century Europe and America, and we know that Freud's insecurity and intolerance of competing views to his, and influence among his colleagues, caused him dismay and great conflict.

Second, classical analysts, buttressed by such canonical dictates, seldom delved into enquiry of sibling dynamics. Older patients have confessed to me, almost sheepishly, sometimes indignantly, that their previous therapists and analysts seldom, if ever, asked about their siblings, only surmised about birth order, ignored obvious clues, bypassed major sibling events such as the death of a brother or sister, sibling incest, eroticism, fluctuations in aggression, identification, attachments, the events surrounding parental divorce, physical and emotional disabilities—none of it (see Bank & Kahn, 1982, 1997; Kahn & Lewis, 1988). Could it be that such blatant avoidance has had its roots in countertransferential and unexamined dynamics by those analysts, labouring and, one might say, compromised by the neglect of this important aspect of psychological life? It has also been speculated that there is an overrepresentation of first-borns among analysts, or a wide age-spacing between such analysts and their siblings. Oedipus, an only child, was valorised. Antigone, his daughter and sister, who, in a supreme act of sibling loyalty, sacrificed her life for her brother Polyneices, was ignored. And rivalry, only one aspect of the sibling dynamic, was continually assumed as its pre-eminent feature, an Old Testament derivative of the ancient struggle for one's survival. In some analyses, there can certainly be echoes of rivalry and aggression, the product of the analyst and the patient's working dynamics, one seemingly more powerful, the other less powerful, which can also be a recrudescence of the sibling history of either participant. However, more often than not, clinical interviewing reveals that such feelings are capable of fluctuating, and can coexist with affection, attachment, reciprocal byplay, and identification.

Third, we now begin to assert that ignoring the sibling dynamic, to repress, dissociate, or deny it within oneself, is to unconsciously sidestep the juggling of the part-whole phenomenon that is an aspect of the acquisition and building of a cohesive self. Pre-oedipal children can quickly attain fixed identities, binary splits which are representations of parental and sibling projections, but post-oedipal children can, and often do, transcend these and, to reference Benjamin (1998), a characteristic of post-oedipal complimentarity in one's mind, in that it can include paradoxical rather than oppositional formulations. Thus, viewing one's sibling, and self-in-relation, as, for example, well–sick, clever–stupid, slow–fast, favoured–defavoured, inhibits the freedom of psychological movement in the self, and might take the form of fixed identities and frozen roles as life moves along. Benjamin, in discussing gendered phenomena, but applied here, states,

> . . . in the post-oedipal complimentarity, one can tolerate the tension of opposing desires and identifications. In effect, accepting the very incompleteness of each position makes multiple positions possible: not precisely identifying with all positions at once, but aware of their possibility. This awareness allows a fuller symbolization, one that operates in transitional area, bridging rather than splitting opposites such as active and passive. From this standpoint, true activity does not take the defensive form of repudiating passivity. Activity predicated on the activity–passivity split, directed towards a passive object, is merely actions; it lacks the intersubjective space of a potential other. Such space, as we have seen, is the very condition of symbolic activity; in other words, the condition of the representational activity of the subject is always a representation of the other subject . . . Characteristically, such activity can embrace receptivity to that other, responsive recognition of the other's impact on the self, and hence, participation in the reality of two subjects. (pp. 33–34)

How descriptive this is of the paradoxical feeling of similarity and difference many individuals carry within themselves as brother or sister.

Fourth, much of early sibling experience is unformulated (Stern, 1997). Conducted only partially within parental purview and their limited descriptions (e.g., *Our parents have no idea that we're doing this,* or, *I really hate him, secretly, inside myself*), it is heavily weighted to the motoric, unmodulated, imagistic, and right hemisphere mediated (Schore, 2003). Statements by patients such as, *I feel my brother is part of me; I can sense it when she is in trouble; When we're together it's like we're*

back there, reliving what we both went through; He reminds me about myself
in some uncanny ways I'd just as soon forget; I can't stop arguing with her,
but she's my sister, she's my family, that's all that's left, are a smattering
of the unformulated and affect-laden representations of the part of the
self. In situations of early and middle childhood where the family context is conflicted, troubled, or traumatic, siblings use each other, and
are used by parents (e.g., *Don't bother me, go and play with your sister*)
to be the affect-laden containers for each other's toxic and burdening
projective identifications. Simultaneously, they are turning to each
other for the attunement and responsiveness as selfobjects lacking in
the misattuning parental environment. The resultant ambivalence to a
brother or sister can be a *mélange* of self- and object-representations
which accrued during such periods of personal and family crises. In
close-in age siblings, four or less years apart, there is an unspoken *quid*
pro quo to use and need each other, but conscious and unconscious
confusion can reign, with unmediated affects ricocheting off one
another. The good boy–bad boy, good girl–bad girl dialectic can swirl
inside each child and between them as well. With siblings with a
wider age range there is less intensity, but the eldest can become an
unheralded place-holder of the strained emotions of the younger, a
parentified child, a care-giver, a few of whom work this through by
becoming therapists. Unlike Freud, the entitled and superior eldest
child, who brooked no interference and gave no particular solace that
we know of to his younger siblings, this newer generation of relational, self-psychological, interpersonal, and intersubjective psychoanalysts can more readily, and are beginning to, less defensively,
acknowledge how the myriad forms of care-taking of their siblings
influence their therapeutic experience (e.g., Cooper, 2006). When,
however, reactions to these early-in-life experiences become reactions
of done and done to, enacted primarily in affect storms, rather than
being adequately mediated, each child could subsequently experience
intense shame, and, consequently, they might grow to shun each
other. Hence, a disinterest in sibling experience.

As Morrison (1989, 1994) has pointed out, early-in-life experience
with misattuning parents who create ruptures in self–selfobject bonds,
create pervasive feelings of unworthiness and insignificance in a child,
partially defended against by grandiosity and idealised strivings.
Such dialectical tensions, in my experience, often find partial resolution in experiences with the near-at-hand sibling, the brother or sister

who might be experiencing similar disillusionment and disregulation. Siblings turn to each other, or are turned to each other, as compensatory selfobjects: *When no one else was there, I could always count on my sister*—a conscious self-awareness, but sometimes infused with guilt over reactions to the muted realisation that the original idealised objects of desire, the mother or father, would never rematerialise. One patient said, "I recall my mother being warm and kind to me, but after we moved, she must have become depressed, she took to her bed a lot, and things were never the same. I played a lot with my brother, we used to go out into our backyard and neighbourhood, and we hung out a lot. Some of my most vivid adventures were with my brother. It's strange, but we now only see each other once or twice a year, and sometimes months can go by before we talk on the phone."

Shame can also surround the acting out of impulses by the child with their sibling, contrary to the idealised representation of the self or the mirrored, internalised phantasy of being Mummy or Daddy's good girl or boy. In such instances of unresolved and unintegrated self-states, there is a dissociative process, an expulsion of memories, irreconcilable with the self-representations later, carefully, and fragilely constructed (Bromberg, 1998), or rationalised (I was just being immature). A result can be that the co-enacting "partner-in-crime", this other of the *folie-à-deux* of siblings, will be actively shunned. A number of women patients come to mind who were incestuously involved with their brother, and who now purposefully avoid them, and in therapy, initially shunned/dissociated these memories of themselves (Bank & Kahn, 1982, 1997). Or the male patient, a sensitive and dedicated health care professional, who was startled and initially repulsed at his sudden recollection of pummelling his younger brother with his feet in their separate beds every night, sadistically expressing his displaced rage at his parents whose marriage was teetering, and whose attention to their children was now seriously compromised. Such a faded, but now recalled, remembrance was at total odds with his current view of himself as helpful, compassionate, and without hostility to family members.

Clouded and confused representations can also be tinged with mourning, a grieving for the faded memories of the self and selfobject tie of sibling enactments of old. Carefully asked questions about such issues can often reveal a sadness that this, what was for the patient such an essential part of their childhood, is gone, or that it is a painful reminder of a period of parental deadness, unavailability, or narcissistic preoccupation, factors which promoted or compelled the sibling dependency. There was one woman, whose memories of her deceased older sister, whom she had loved and admired, were comingled with the embitterment over her father's alcoholism and mother's emotional disappearance, contextual matters deeply affecting her and her sister, who eventually committed suicide in her late twenties. The surviving sister came to understand that part of herself had died as well, and that she carried this unrequited grief, always, as testimony and witness to what each of the sisters had had to endure.

Fifth and last, sibling effects are beyond the chiaroscuro and have defied easy comprehension, because of the obvious fact that sibling constellations come in enormous permutations; two children, five children, twins, all boys, all girls, varying gender combinations and age spacings, deceased siblings, disabled ones, one-parent families, siblings separated or pushed together by crucial developmental and historical events, moving, immigration, divorce, war, step-siblings, half-siblings, and so on (Kahn & Lewis, 1988).

Generalisations become difficult. It is simply easier to extrapolate the effects on children from the dyad of mother and father than from the non-linearity and aggregate of sibling effects. As well as simpler narratives, the telling of parental effects on the construction and development of self is more easily grasped, and these effects can also be comprehended in the transferential dynamics between patient and analyst. Conversely, in most cases, sibling phenomena will not just spring forth. More active questioning of sibling effects is usually needed, given the shroud of confusion, the aggregate effects, the previously unformulated complexity of the sibling world, the shame and guilt previously referred to, and the developmental thrust, unsynchronised with one another, of each child's trajectory of experience. One can love and idealise a sibling, can cherish that individual and collective history as part of the self, only to have it fade, or be transformed as life events move us along, and the memories move into a shadow-land of the implicit. Then, it can be held in suspension, its derivative effects barely palpable, until a life event occurs, a parent falls ill, a brother dies, a sister is in crisis, and the patient comes into the consulting room. All of a sudden, a quantum stance is required by patient and analyst, on whether or how this brother or sister is important. We must however, not fall into a sibling "romance", assuming that with a heightened sensitivity to sibling dynamics, all siblings matter. Wide age-spacing, a "non-shared" environment (Dunn & Plomin, 1990), and varying life events, impacting on each child in qualitatively different ways, might render sibling effects negligible, phenomenologically expressed as, for example, *I've never been close to my brother, we're just so different, he left home when I was young. I've never really known him, nor does he know anything about my life.*

Sibling countertransference phenomena

Just as sibling effects might need to be coaxed out of the shadowy Herbartian "apperceptive mass" (Bellak, 1950, p. 11) of the patient, the analyst, too, needs to listen carefully to their own sibling reverberations. In instances where the analyst has suffered the impact of a seriously compromised brother or sister (Safer, 2002), countertransference phenomena can be more easily grasped. One therapist, the older brother of a repeatedly hospitalised schizophrenic younger sister, can acknowledge the myriad feelings he often experiences when confronted with a similarly highly troubled patient, or when he has to deal with such a patient's family. He feels empathy, fear, frustration, anger, despair, a compulsive desire to rescue, a strong pressure to help, or do anything effective. What he admits he is not initially aware of are the more subtle effects around the sobering and saddening realisation that the little sister that he once enjoyed playing with, and who was bright and idealised him, had disappeared gradually into a psychotically disorganised woman, who was refractory to help, homeless, and helpless. He admits these effects are buried, confused, wrapped around the despair he felt for his grieving parents and their collective loss. He admits their confusions, and the turning to him for increasing solace, was a direct catalyst to his seeking answers to his sister's dilemma and then becoming a therapist.

Another highly experienced therapist had a two-year-younger sister whom he had delighted playing with as a child. He remembered her as a pretty little girl who became heavier, and more disregulated and disorganised as she moved into her teenage years. The brother, who excelled academically and socially, became progressively more ashamed of his fat younger sister, and that he could easily dominate her for family affection and esteem. She remains, to this day, under-functioning and emotionally restricted. In his work with his patients, he is haunted by the shadow of his sister's failures, a *fingerprint* of himself as he experiences it, evident in myriad forms. He expresses shame at feeling ashamed of this sister, the *I still shouldn't have this feeling*, this visceral dislike of himself, *my DNA*, when he sees an overweight woman. He is aware that in the inevitability when working with women patients, who, at times, permit his views to become dominant during the therapeutic process, and who look to him for certainty and surety, he experiences an intense ambivalence at this power, remembering the echoes of himself dominating, excelling, transcending, as his sister, year by year, regressively slipped into a confused shadow of her former self.

I have my own version of sibling countertransference effects, owing to an uncommonly over-determined interest in siblings. I am an only child of two only child parents (approximately 15% of adults in the USA are only children.). No sibling stories were ever handed around. What was palpable in my early growing-up years was my quest for a sibling, a restitutional selfobject among my boyhood friends, simultaneous with a twin-like yearning for an alter ego within myself, to partly offset the intensity and over-responsibility of being an only child of distressed parents. My curiosity had been exteriorised early, with questions to my mother — "Why don't I have a brother or a sister?", which she always perfunctorily dismissed, saying, "It was the war. You don't know how much we suffered." I am reminded of Carl Whitaker, an old teacher of mine, who once stated, "What every family needs are rotating scapegoats." It can become nearly insufferable if one child becomes the prized container for everyone's unmetabolised and toxic projections. Better to share the pleasure. And it is hardly inescapable to me why my first publication was entitled, "The adolescent struggle with identity as a force in psychotherapy" (Kahn, 1968–1969).

In one-person psychoanalytic theory, only children were often characterised as privileged, successful, entitled, and self-satisfied, and with differing oedipal dynamics, in comparison to those forced to share the parental environment and to vie for parental favour (e.g., Arlow, 1972). What has not been stressed until now is the self-experience of struggling with what is "not there" in the sibless child's experience, rather than "what is". Under conditions of the always less than optimal capacity for holding, mutual regulation, and sensitivity by the parents, one's conscious and unconscious capacities for sustaining self-regulatory capacity often includes what Stern (2004) has characterised as the "yang" principle of reaching and probing for the relational world, and the "yin" principle of self-containment and receptivity, in complex and dialectical tension with one another. Restitutionally, the sibless child cannot compensate with, or attach to, a near-at-hand sibling. He or she must rely more on self-containment and self-regulation, while simultaneously struggling for the yearning of what is "not there". The emerging dialectic within the self can become overstrained, blunted, shame-filled, and conflicted. On the other hand, a heightened awareness of the subjunctive, what might have been, or what is not, can also occur. Being sibless and dealing with what is "not there" also leads to what Anderson and Goolishian (1992) refer to as a "not-knowing" approach in formulating questions, hypotheses, and speculations in the conduct of therapy. Since the self often contains a dialogue of multiple inner voices (Rober, 2005), the sibless analyst can discipline himself, or herself, to listen to what might "be" or have "been" as a sibling, not-knowing, not prejudging, but appreciating what the patient reveals about their life as a brother or sister. To be without a sibling is a different experience, requiring a heightened sensibility to shared, dialectical, not fully formed phenomena in the development of self.

What would it have been like if I had been a brother who had meted out aggression, or received it from my brother or sister, and then have to reconcile such memories and constructions, with later, more elaborated experiences? Would my own struggles with competition, envy, or aggression have taken a different hue or tone if I had lived in an intense world of sibling companionship, hostility, envy, betrayal, competition, identification, and love? It would certainly, I believe, have been different.

References

Arlow, J. (1972). The only child. *Psychoanalytic Quarterly*, 41: 507–536.

Anderson, H., & Goolishian, H. (1992). The client is the expert: a not-knowing approach to therapy. In: S. McNamee & K. J. Gergen (Eds.), *Therapy as Social Construction* (pp. 25–39). London: Sage.

Bank, S. P., & Kahn, M. D. (1982). *The Sibling Bond*. New York: Basic Books.

Bank, S. P., & Kahn, M. D. (1997). *The Sibling Bond* – (15th anniversary edn). New York: Perseus/Basic Books.

Bellak, L. O. (1950). On the problems of the concept of projection. In: L. Abt, & L. O. Bellak (Eds.), *Projective Psychology: Clinical Approaches to the Total Personality* (pp. 7–32). New York: Alfred A. Knopf.

Benjamin, J. (1998). *Shadow of the Other: Intersubjectivity and Gender in Psychoanalysis*. New York: Routledge.

Bernays, A. F. (1940). My brother, Sigmund Freud. *American Mercury, 51*: 336–340.

Black, M. J. (2003). Enactment: analytic musings on energy, language, and personal growth. *Psychoanalytic Dialogues, 13*: 633–655.

Bromberg, P. M. (1998). *Standing in the Spaces: Essays on Clinical Processes, Trauma and Dissociation*. Hillsdale, NJ: Analytic Press.

Coates, S. (1998). Having a mind of one's own and holding the other in mind. *Psychoanalytic Dialogues, 8*: 115–148.

Cooper, S. H. (2006). Surviving as a real object and transference/counter-transference enactment: wiggle room in relational theory and practice. Paper presented at the International Association for Relational Psychoanalysis and Psychotherapy, Boston, MA, 28 January.

Dunn, J., & Plomin, R. (1990). *Separate Lives: Why Siblings Are so Different*. New York: Basic Books.

Fonagy, P., & Target, M. (1998). Mentalization and the changing aims of child psychoanalysis. *Psychoanalytic Dialogues, 8*: 87–114.

Freud, S. (1909b). *Analysis of a Phobia in a Five-Year-Old Boy. S.E., 10*: 3–149. London: Hogarth.

Freud, S. (1912–1913). *Totem and Taboo. S.E., 13*: 1–161. London: Hogarth.

Freud, S. (1918b). *From the History of an Infantile Neurosis. S.E., 17*: 3–122. London: Hogarth.

Guidano, V. F. (1987). *Complexity of the Self: A Developmental Approach to Psychopathology and Therapy*. New York: Guilford Press.

Jones, E. (1967). *The Life and Work of Sigmund Freud* (Vol. 1). New York: Basic Books.

Kahn, M. D. (1968–1969). The adolescent struggle with identity as a force in psychotherapy. *Adolescence, 3*: 12.

Kahn, M. D., & Lewis, K. G. (1988). *Siblings in Therapy: Life Span and Clinical Issues*. New York: W. W. Norton.

Lichtenberg, J. (1989). *Psychoanalysis and Motivation*. Hillsdale, NJ: Analytic Press.

Morrison, A. P. (1989). *Shame: The Underside of Narcissism*. Hillsdale, NJ: Analytic Press.

Morrison, A. P. (1994). The breadth and boundaries of a self-psychological immersion in shame: a one-and-a half person perspective. *Psychoanalytic Dialogues, 4*: 9–35.

Piers, C. (2005). The mind's multiplicity and continuity. *Psychoanalytic Dialogues, 15*: 229–254.

Roazen, P. (1975). *Freud and his Followers*. New York: Alfred A. Knopf.

Rober, P. (2005). The therapist's self in dialogical family therapy: some ideas about not-knowing and the therapist's inner conversation. *Family Process, 44*(4): 477–495.

Safer, J. (2002). *The Normal One: Life with a Difficult or Damaged Sibling*. New York: Bantam Dell.

Schore, A. N. (2003). *Affect Regulation and the Repair of Self*. New York: W. W. Norton.

Stern, D. B. (1997). *Unformulated Experience: From Dissociation to Imagination in Psychoanalysis*. Hillsdale, NJ: Analytic Press.

Stern, S. (2004). The yin and yang of intersubjectivity: integrating self-psychological and relational thinking. *Progress in Self Psychology, 20*: 3–20.

Sulloway, F. J. (1996). *Born to Rebel: Birth Order, Family Dynamics and Creative Lives*. New York: Pantheon Books.

Suomi, D. (1982). Sibling relationships in non-human primates. In: M. E. Lamb & B. Sutton-Smith (Eds.), *Sibling Relationships across the Life Span* (pp. 329–356). Hillsdale, NJ: Laurence Erlbaum.

Thelen, E. (2005). Dynamic systems theory and the complexity of change. *Psychoanalytic Dialogues, 15*: 255–283.

CHAPTER FIVE

Moses, Aaron, Miriam: integrative sibling relation

Chava Yanai-Malach

The presence of siblings has an important influence on the psychic development of the individual. This issue connects to the relational theory that emphasises the transition from an authority relation between therapist and client to a more mutual relation, from a vertical relation to a relation that is conducted also on the lateral axis.

Psychoanalytic theory emphasises the parent–child relation as the main family drama. However, interestingly, storming dramas occur between siblings and enable further understanding of the formation of the human psyche. The presence of siblings enables mechanisms such as splitting, projection, and projective identification to exist on additional levels, and, through them, contributes to the growth of an integrative and mature psychological state, including shaping and establishing of self identity.

In this chapter, I argue that every individual must go through states of jealousy, competition, love, identification, and concern in the sibling relation on his or her path to integrative personality. I propose to examine the problematic sibling relation as a reflection of internal elements that remain split, as opposed to a normal relation, which indicates better personal integration.

I consider the role of sibling interactions through biblical stories. Examining the biblical texts, as well as the *Midrash* (homiletic inter-pretations of the Bible written by the greatest scholars of Jewish philosophy), I will present two thoughts. The first thought is that the succession of biblical stories portrays an orderly developmental process with a parallel to human personal development. The book of Genesis is abundant in sibling stories full of bitter and painful compe-tition, jealousy, hatred, pretence, arrogance, murderous desire, and actual murder. The story introducing the theme of siblings in the Bible—that of Cain and Abel—ends in an actual murder motivated by a primordial drive. In contrast, the subsequent stories which are my focus—centred on Moses, Aaron, and Miriam—are integrative and complex with fluid mobility among all the vectors: kinship, identifi-cation, uniqueness, separation, attraction, jealousy, and aggression. I offer a second thought as well, which is that, in contrast to the para-digms of Freud and Klein, where siblings are cast mainly in a nega-tive role, they could also play a positive one, supporting and nourish-ing, not only as a sublimate process, but as an important need. This role can be discerned in the biblical story of the three siblings.

In his development of psychoanalytic theory, Freud used charac-ters from Greek mythology to describe human phenomena. Oedipus and Narcissus are two central myths that received deep and wide-ranging theoretical treatment. But why did Freud ignore the biblical characters of the Jewish myths? Did he ignore these characters for the same reasons on account of which he rarely dealt with the presence and significance of siblings? However, it is possible that the difficulty to relate to the biblical mythology resulted from the fact that it is clearly loaded with sibling mythology—after all, Genesis and Exodus deal mainly with sibling stories.

Ignoring the topic of siblings is the claim of most writers in recent decades with regard to Freud. The claim is not that he completely ignored the issue of siblings, and many of the writers actually cite texts in which Freud did address the said issue. However, the major-ity of writers are of the opinion that Freud did not emphasise the deep significance of sibling relationships to the structural development of the human psyche.

Rosner (1985) assembles the references of Freud, Klein, Mahler, Kohut, and Finchel—undoubtedly leading theoreticians—on the topic of siblings, but is careful to note that

Sibling relationships have been largely neglected in the psychoanalytic literature. Little has been written about the impact of siblings upon ego development. Where they do occur, references to sibling relationships relegate them to a secondary position in which they are cursorily dismissed as rivals for mother's love or as parent surrogates. (p. 457)

Most authors agree with this statement in their attempts to deal with the deep meaning of sibling relationships, not only as a parent surrogate, but in their own right - both theoretically and in their clinical significance in practice, in transference and countertransference, and in their impact on the establishment of object relations and object choice (Abend, 1984; Bank & Kahn, 1980–1981; Coleman, 1996; Coles, 2003; Houzel, 2001; Lesser, 1978; Mitchell, 2003; Sharpe & Rosenblatt, 1994; Vivona, 2010).

Support for the view that the founding event in Jewish tradition is the murder of the brother rather than the murder of the father may be found in the writing of Rosenberg (1989, 2004). He argues that Freud developed his psychological theory based on one of the central characters of Greek myth. The myth of Oedipus, and the Oedipus complex that followed, represent the multi-dimensional rivalry between generations, between fathers and sons. Indeed, the intergenerational conflict and the struggle against authority exist in the Bible, but, despite this, Genesis presents us with a different pattern, the Cain complex, a sibling murder.

On first reading, it is possible to say that the stories in Genesis are compatible with Freud's position that love relationships between siblings are nothing but a reaction formation of hostile and jealous feelings (Coles, 2003). However, a closer look makes it possible to discern a developmental continuum in sibling relationships across the different stories. The story about Cain and Abel begins with Cain being unable to tolerate the rivalry over the love of God and, hence, murdering his brother. This story is compatible with Freud's notion as presented by Coles: "Hate as a relation to objects, is older than love" (Freud, 1915c, p. 139, cited in Coles, 2003, p. 53). Coles further comments that Klein agreed with Freud: "It is chiefly impulses of hate that initiate the Oedipus conflict" (Klein, 1932, p. 135, cited in Coles, 2003, p. 53). In Coles' opinion, it is for this reason that Klein viewed sibling love as a counter-balance to oedipal hatred. Indeed, in the following stories, we shall see how hatred is softened and the murderous instincts are replaced, first with splitting and separation, and later on by reparation, reconciliation, and integrative sibling relationships.

In the later stories, however, there is no murder. Abraham needs to decide between Yitzhak and Ishmael. Ishmael is sent to the desert and Yitzhak continues the lineage. Jacob, with his mother's assistance, pretends to be Esau in order to obtain Yitzhak's blessing. These stories involve splitting and separation. The unbearable part is sent to the desert with the visionary outlook of fathering a new nation.

We then encounter the story of the arrogant Joseph and of the brothers who plot his murder—a group context rather than rivalry between two siblings. Here, the group decision is overruled by Reuben and Joseph survives. Years later, the brothers are sent to Egypt to ask for Joseph's help, not knowing his identity. As Jacob is old and exhausted, the drama is actually driven by the brothers. They are the ones who go down to Egypt, they are the ones who need to deal with the abandonment of Binyamin, and it is they who make the association between the jailed Binyamin and Joseph who was left in the pit, and who express their regret among themselves. This regret moves Joseph so much that he reveals his true identity to them. In the story of Joseph and his brothers, we find a process of reparation and reconciliation instead of separation.

A further development that can be seen in the sequence of the Genesis stories is the transition from the vertical to the lateral dimension. In her important books about siblings, Mitchell (2003) is the first to propose that sibling relationships be considered along different dimensions than parent–child relationships. She proposes a two-dimensional psychology: the vertical dimension, in which the main drama is the parent–child relation, with the sibling relationships also affected by the parental context, that is, the rivalry over the love of the parent, and the lateral dimension, in which the main drama is among the siblings themselves. This parallels the sequence of stories: at the beginning, Cain and Abel facing God, Ishmael and Yitzchak facing Abraham and Sara's intervention, Jacob and Esau *vs.* Yitzchak and Rivka. In all of these stories, the plot is both cross-generational, that is, on the vertical dimension, and within a generation, on the lateral dimension. In the story of Joseph and his brothers, the central occurrence is on the lateral dimension, within the generation, although, at the beginning of the story, Jacob rouses the brothers' jealousy. After the story of Joseph and his brothers, we come to a positive sibling story and, to my mind, the most impressive story of all: the story that ends with the formation of the Jewish nation and with the acceptance of the laws, the Ten Commandments, as a symbol of the development of consciousness, social order, and culture. In this story, the parents play a very minor role and are hardly mentioned. The *Midrash Tanhuma* states,

> ... yet you find that all brothers hated each other. Cain hated Abel ... Ishmael hated Isaac ... And the tribes hated Josef ... But in this instance the Israelites asked of the Holy One, blessed be He: Do you mean like Moses and Aaron, of whom it is said: 'Behold how good and how pleasant it is for brethren to dwell together in unity' (Psalms, 133:1)? They loved and cherished each other. At the time that Moses took the kingship and Aaron the priesthood, they bore no resentment toward each other. In fact they rejoiced in each other's exalted role. (*Midrash Tanhuma*, Exodus: 27, pp. 347–348)

Vivona (2010) addresses psychological development through processes of identification along the lateral dimension. In her opinion, in the same way that parental identification is the solution to the oedipal conflict, so sibling identification softens the rivalry. However, this is complex, since, in contrast with the need for identification, there is also the need for uniqueness. Hence, Vivona points to three vectors in sibling relationships which are not easy to achieve:

> The triad of difference, sameness and closeness is difficult to achieve ... More specifically, the childhood tendency to equate difference with distance and similarity with closeness is likely to figure in the child's attempts to resolve the challenges of development ... Thus, the processes of identification and differentiation yield distinct compromises among the demands of the lateral dimension. (p. 13)

In my view, the story of Moses, Aaron, and Miriam presents a sibling model that optimally contains the tension between the three vectors pointed out by Vivona. In these relationships, as I shall later expand, we can discern the differences in the sibling personalities and roles, the similarity and identification that allows them to lead an entire nation, and conflicts, even deep ones, that are ultimately resolved, as well as love and caring.

Freud was deeply attracted to the character of Moses, but denied him his Jewishness in *Moses and Monotheism* (1939a) and ignored the two most significant persons in his life—his sister Miriam and his brother Aaron. This is the claim of all present-day writers about Freud's avoidance of the sibling's role in human personal development.

Now, let us enter into the biblical story of Moses, Aaron, and Miriam. The beginning of the story, often lost in our collective memory, deals with Moses' sister, Miriam, and takes place prior to his birth. The Maharal from Prague writes in his book, *Nezahk Israel*, that Miriam was one of the three saviours of Exodus (Moses, Aaron, and Miriam) and that she had a special role—to express the longing for, and bond of, the children of Israel to God.

It is interesting to note that this is also the first story in which a sister appears as a significant character. Mitchell (2003), in her important book, *Siblings*, begins her introduction to the book by noting the absence of a woman from the brotherhood of men. Thus, the idea that Miriam is given an equal role is ground-breaking and provides further evidence that this is a mature and integrative, almost contemporary, sibling story.

The story begins with Miriam the sister prior to the birth of Moses. The biblical story gives her the amazing role of ensuring his birth and, once he is born, keeping him alive. The sister, and not the mother, is the "life keeper" of Moses. Bialik and Ravnitzky (2000) in *Sefer Ha'aggada* present an engaging story (from *Tractate Sotah*) in which Miriam challenges her father, Amram, who has divorced his wife following Pharaoh's ruling that all male babies be killed.

> And there went a man of the house of Levi. Where did he go? R. Judah b. Zebina said that he went in the counsel of his daughter. A Tanna taught: Amram was the greatest man of his generation; when he saw that the wicked Pharaoh had decreed 'Every son that is born ye shall cast into the river', he said: In vain do we labour. He arose and divorced his wife. All [the Israelites] thereupon arose and divorced their wives. His daughter said to him, 'Father, thy decree is more severe than Pharaoh's; because Pharaoh decreed only against the males whereas thou hast decreed against the males and females. Pharaoh only decreed concerning this world whereas thou hast decreed concerning this world and the World to Come. In the case of the wicked Pharaoh there is a doubt whether his decree will be

fulfilled or not, whereas in thy case, though thou art righteous, it is certain that thy decree will be fulfilled, as it is said: Thou shalt also decree a thing, and it shall be established unto thee! He arose and took his wife back; and they all arose and took their wives back. (*Tractate Sotah*, Folio 12a)

Klein wrote about murderous wishes towards siblings, both the born and the unborn, who have the potential to be born through the sexual intercourse of the parents. This topic is developed by Houzel (2001) in his paper "The 'nest of babies' fantasy". He quotes Klein (1955):

> This anxiety is particularly strong in youngest and only children because the reality that no other child has been born seems to confirm the guilty feeling that they have prevented the parents' sexual inter-course, the mother's pregnancy and the arrival of other babies by hatred and jealousy and by attacks on the mother's body. (Klein, 1955, p. 138)

Is it possible that Miriam begins to struggle with primitive aggression, to fight murderous wishes and a primordial death drive the moment death becomes concrete and real through the cruel ruling of Pharaoh? Does she understand that the murderous drive must be processed and resolved? Does she receive a sublimatory role that lies at the foundation of all culture? Can the role of Moses emerge only from such a place?

Moses grows up in Pharaoh's palace and, seeing his people's suffering, kills an Egyptian who has brutalised a Jewish slave. Pharaoh receives word of this and wants to kill him. Moses escapes to the desert where he lives as a shepherd and where God is revealed to him and chooses him for the mission of setting the people of Israel free from Egypt. Moses, out of concern for Aaron, feels uncomfortable at the prospect of taking this mission upon himself. He says "Oh Lord, send, I pray Thee, by the hand of him whom Thou wilt send" (Exodus 4:13).[1] This means: all these years Aaron, my brother, was a prophet and I will now enter his domain and this will sadden him. God replies, "Is there not Aaron thy brother the Levite? I know that he can speak well. And also, behold, he cometh forth to meet thee; and when he seeth thee, he will be glad in his heart" (Exodus 4:14).

About this, Rabbi Shimon Bar Yokhai said, "The heart that rejoiced in the greatness of his brother Moses, shall wear the Urim and

Thummim' as it is written: 'And thou shalt put in the breastplate of judgment the Urim and the Thummim; and they shall be upon Aaron's heart'" (Exodus 28:30). Following that, he continues, asking,

> And how do we know that Moses was happy in the greatness of Aaron? Because it says, 'Like the precious oil upon the head, coming down upon the beard; Aaron's beard' (Psalm 133:2). Said R Eha: Had Aaron then two beards, that it should say, 'upon the beard; Aaron's beard'? The fact is that when Moses saw the oil of the anointment descending upon the beard of Aaron, it seemed to him as if it was descending over his own beard and he rejoiced; so it says, 'On the beard, Aaron's beard'. (*Midrash Rabbah*, The Song of Songs, 1983, 1–10, p. 73)

In psychoanalytic language, this is a mirroring process with a strong empathic experience (Kohut, 1984). Moses feels close kinship with Aaron and he feels that Aaron's success is his as well.

Moses accepts God's will and returns to Egypt. Aaron welcomes him and kisses him and Moses shares with Aaron the mission that he has received. Later in the story, Aaron and Moses, when coming before the people and Pharaoh, are referred to as one entity.

> 26. These are that Aaron and Moses, to whom the LORD said: Bring out the children of Israel from the land of Egypt according to their hosts. 27. These are they that spoke to Pharaoh king of Egypt, to bring out the children of Israel from Egypt. These are that Moses and Aaron. (Exodus, 6: 26–27)

One time, Aaron comes before Moses, and one time Moses comes before Aaron. Rashi says about that "There are places where Aaron precedes Moses and there are other places where Moses precedes Aaron—thus they are equivalent" (Rashi, Exodus, 6:26, *Midrash Rabbah*, 1983).

Rabbi Shlomo Ephraim from Luntshitz (1602) in his book, *Keli Yakar*, interprets according to the content of the sentence.

> The first part of the sentence emphasizes the nomination of Moses and Aaron to the mission. So we will not think that Moses is central to the mission and Aaron is secondary, the writings put Aaron forward, to instruct us that both are of equal importance. On the other hand, the second part of the sentence, describes the meeting of Moses and Aaron

with Pharaoh. And so we will not think that Aaron is the central speaker, and Moses, who was 'tongue-tied,' was just an adjunct to Aaron, here the writing puts Moses prior to Aaron—again to demonstrate to us that both were of equal importance in front of Pharaoh. The writing intentionally puts forward the less important player to emphasize to us the equal importance of both Moses and Aaron. (*Keli Yakar*, Exodus, 6:26)

There are additional references to equality and balance between Moses and Aaron. In the *Midrash Rabbah* there is a discussion as to by whom was the Torah given. "Thy Two Breasts: these are Moses and Aaron . . . Just as one breast is not greater than the other, so it was with Moses and Aaron . . ." (*Midrash Rabbah*, 1983, The Song of Songs: 4–5, p. 198).

Long before psychoanalysis, before Melanie Klein, Moses and Aaron are metaphorically compared to two breasts—these are the breasts from which the people are nourished, both their spiritual nourishment as well as their material food. Two breasts are needed, since each serves a separate function—slightly different, but complementary. It should be noted that in some interpretations, Moses is perceived as aggressive, hot-tempered, and able to kill—the bad breast—while Aaron is moderate and soft-hearted—the good breast. But both are needed: Moses will become a leader and Aaron a grand priest.

Miriam reappears only after the crossing of the sea, when Moses praises God in the song of the sea: "And Miriam the prophetess, the sister of Aaron, took a timbrel in her hand; and all the women went out after her with timbrels and with dances" (Exodus, 15:20).

It may be asked why Miriam is mentioned only as the sister of Aaron, and Nachmanides Ramban interprets this as follows: "It is because in the song Moses and Miriam were mentioned, and Aaron was not—hence the writing wanted to remind us and said—Aaron's sister" (Nachmanides, Exodus 15:20, *Midrash Rabbah*, 1983). Once again, the motivation of retaining positive balance between the siblings is evident.

According to the prophet Micha, God sees Miriam as an equal messenger to Aaron and Moses in Exodus: "For I brought thee up out of the land of Egypt, and redeemed thee out of the house of bondage, and I sent before thee Moses, Aaron, and Miriam" (Micha, 6:4)

Similarly, the Chronicles, written at a later time, reveals the importance of Miriam by making an exception and mentioning her in the genocidal list, contrary to the habit of noting only the sons: "And the children of Amram: Aaron, and Moses, and Miriam" (Chronicles 1, 5:29).

There are numerous *Midrashim*, legends and interpretations that emphasise mainly the positive relation between the siblings, but the text does not ignore conflicts and tension between the siblings. Three main conflicts are described: the role of Aaron in the incident of the golden calf; Aaron's wish to mourn his sons against Moses' will; Miriam's mockery of the Negro woman and jealousy regarding the choice of Moses as leader.

In the first incident, after Moses disappears, Aaron is unable to resist the will of the people and builds the golden calf. Moses is angry with him for this crime, but Aaron asks Moses for understanding of the people's emotional state, with which he has had to deal. It should be noted that this complex incident does not undermine the stature of Aaron in the eyes of the interpreters. Weiss (2006), lecturer in Talmud and Mikra, in her book *Committing my Soul*, quotes Yochanan Grinshpoin, a researcher of Hinduism:

> When Aaron made the calf, he acted according to the mercy principle, he saw the people in terrible agony, a people of slaves that was set free not long ago, and was left without a leader. The people are frightened, experience a sense of loss, and Aaron chooses to help the people. Aaron tells the angry Moses 'Let not the anger of my lord wax hot; thou knowest the people, that they are set on evil' (Exodus 32:22). Moses is angry at Aaron but forgives him nonetheless. (p. 208).

The second incident is a painful one for Aaron. At the inauguration of the temple, after Aaron and his sons are chosen to be priests, two of Aaron's sons, Nadav and Avihu, sin by burning alien fire in the altar. This same fire burns them to death as a punishment. Moses orders Aaron not to mourn his sons, since they sinned, and to continue with the ceremony. "Let not the hair of your heads go loose, neither rend your clothes" (Leviticus 10:6). Aaron is unable to comply and conflict develops. Aaron explains to Moses,

> Behold, this day have they offered their sin-offering and their burnt-offering before the LORD, and there have befallen me such things as

these; and if I had eaten the sin-offering to-day, would it have been well-pleasing in the sight of the LORD? And when Moses heard that, it was well-pleasing in his sight. (Leviticus, 10:19–20)

Thus Moses accepts Aaron's arguments.

Dr Lea Mazor, from the Hebrew University, has written about the third incident in her paper "Moses Aaron and Miriam: siblings, leaders and rivals" (2001). She argues that the story describes an open conflict over the leadership. It begins with Miriam and Aaron being jealous of Moses and challenging his leadership:

And Miriam and Aaron spoke against Moses because of the Cushite (black) woman whom he had married; for he had married a Cushite woman. And they said: 'Hath the LORD indeed spoken only with Moses? hath He not spoken also with us?' And the LORD heard it. (Numbers, 12:1–2)

Putting Miriam's name before Aaron's tells us that Miriam was the initiator and dominant force in the rebellion against Moses. We can infer this also from the rage that was directed towards her and from the magnitude of her punishment. Miriam and Aaron raise two arguments against Moses: one is the issue of the negro woman, and the other is the issue of equality in the prophet role. The issue of the negro woman is against Moses' leadership, since fault is found in him. The equality claim is against Moses' stature as having sole right to speak in the name of God. Miriam's punishment is instantaneous: "And when the cloud was removed from over the Tent, behold, Miriam was leprous, as white as snow; and Aaron looked upon Miriam; and, behold, she was leprous" (Numbers 12:10)

Miriam was against the black (the negro woman) and was punished by white (leprosy). Aaron is described in the story as close to Miriam. He joins her against Moses; when he sees her punishment, he confesses to his role in the crime and comes to her aid with an emotional appeal to Moses to save her. Moses responds with a short prayer: "Heal her now, O God, I beseech Thee" (Numbers 12:13).

In all three incidents, we can see that a dialogue takes place in which the siblings try to resolve a conflict, to understand each other, to forgive and to spare one another. All three suffer a common fate, dying in the desert. None is allowed to reach the Promised Land, the country of Israel. Even at the moment of death, equality prevails.

At the beginning of the medieval period, an unknown author collected all of the traditions concerning the death of Aaron and integrated them into a short pamphlet: "Midrash over the death of Aaron". This is a dramatic story of Aaron's last day, of Moses' difficulty informing his brother of his impending death, and of the refusal of the people of Israel to accept it. "Take Aaron and Eleazar his son, and bring them up unto mount Hor. And strip Aaron of his garments, and put them upon Eleazar his son; and Aaron shall be gathered unto his people, and shall die there" (Numbers, 20:25–26). The Midrash tells us that when God commands Moses to tell Aaron about his death, Moses objects that it is not appropriate for him to tell his brother about it, since Aaron is older than he. How can Moses tell him to go to the mountain and that there he will die? God suggests that Moses use only hints, hoping that Aaron will grasp the situation. Moses cries and is saddened but embarks on the difficult mission. First he tells Aaron: "There is something God commanded me to tell you", but he refuses to elaborate on what this is and invites Aaron to accompany him out of the camp. As they go out of the camp, Aaron says to Moses: "Tell me what God told you". Moses replies that he will tell him only when they arrive at the mountain. Moses continues to walk, delaying the bitter announcement, until they reach a magical cave at the top of the mountain. There, Moses asks Aaron to remove the vestments of the grand priest so that they will not be contaminated by the cave. Only when they enter the cave and in it are a made bed, a set table, a lighted lamp, and ministering angels, only then does Moses reveal to Aaron that his time has come. Moses comforts Aaron: "Shall my death be as yours, that you die and I bury you, while when I die, no brother will bury me. You die, and your sons inherit your place, while I die, and others inherit my place". This is how Moses succeeds in comforting his brother. "And Aaron climbed to his bed and God received his spirit, Moses left the cave, and the cave immediately disappeared and no creature in the world knew about it" (Otsar Hamidrashim, Aaron, *Midrash Rabbah*, 1983).

This is a moving description of the closeness between the brothers at the moment of Aaron's death, a moment of empathy, love, and comfort. They are careful not to hurt one another and bid each other farewell, having shared the long trek through an exciting and significant period in the history of the people of Israel.

I conclude by offering the opinion that this story provides us with an alternative to sibling relationships immersed in jealousy, rivalry, and murderous phantasies. I do not deny that such emotions and drives exist, but I argue that the idea that this is the only option, an idea that has dominated professional psychoanalytical thinking, is too narrow.

Bank and Kahn (1980–1981), in their paper "Freudian siblings", analyse three works by Freud (*Analysis of a Phobia of a Five-Year-Old Boy, Totem and Taboo,* and *History of an Infantile Neurosis*) and show how, according to Freud, all sibling influence is negative: one controls the other, they painfully compete with each other, somebody always loses in the rivalry over the parent's love, they often sense a prolonged mutual rage under the surface.

Abend (1984), in "Sibling love and object choice", considers the alternative that interactions with siblings during development might contribute to the integration of the self:

> The importance of sibling rivalry and its consequences in mental life was one of the earliest discoveries of psychoanalysis. In contrast, the love ties which exist between siblings have commanded far less interest, no doubt because it was readily observed that the appearance of such material in patients' associations primarily served defensive functions. There are circumstances, however, in which the libidinal bonds between siblings come to assume a powerful and lasting significance in the development of certain individuals. (p. 425)

The story of Miriam, Aaron, and Moses starts in the book of Exodus with the sentence: "Now these are the names of the sons of Israel" (Exodus, 1:1). A name is an acknowledgment of the subject—a complex subject, mentally and emotionally developed. The transition to a people, as described in Exodus, in contrast to the spirit of Genesis, necessitates a step forward in spiritual development and in constructive relations between siblings.

In summary

In examining the sibling stories in the Bible and their relation to psychoanalytical thinking, it occurred to me that one fascinating aspect of the stories is the evolutionary nature of their sequence. Each story brings with it another layer of emotional working through at a higher organisational level: from a solution by murder, through splitting, and then to repair, integration, and reconciliation. It is possible to see this sequence as paralleling individual development, with severe sibling rivalry reflecting a personality where there are split internal structures as opposed to a "good enough" sibling relation which demonstrates improved personal integration.

In a parallel process, these stories are also a story of the evolution of a people and a nation. It is possible to see that, alongside this personal evolution, the sibling stories progress to the development and formation of a people whose apex is in the complex and dramatic manner in which Moses offers the Ten Commandments. It is interesting that the subject of the formation of enlightened society was present in Freud's thinking, but, as mentioned previously, he chose, in *Totem and Taboo* (1912–1913), to describe remote primitive tribes which, in order to become human, revolted against the great father and murdered him.

The precise time of the writing of the Torah is intensely debated: however, it is fairly agreed upon that the stories of the Bible reflect the consensus and belief system during those times. This raises the question as to whether the Bible, written approximately 2,500 years ago, presents the sibling stories, intentionally and consciously, as an evolutionary process, a continuum leading from permittivity to enlightenment.

Acknowledgements

First, I want to thank my friends Roni Amiel, Orly Fisher, and Simi Talmi, from the Tel-Aviv Institute for Contemporary Psychoanalysis (TAICP), with whom I worked together on the topic of siblings. I want to thank Yorm Kansler, who opened for me the wonderful and rich world of the Bible and *Midrash*. I thank Dr Gila Ofer from TAICP for her continuous encouragement throughout the process of publishing this work.

Note

1.   All Bible texts were taken from: *A Hebrew–English Bible According to the Masoretic Text* and the JPS 1917 Edition © 2005, all rights reserved to Mechon Mamre for this HTML version.

References

Abend, S. (1984). Sibling love and object choice. *Psychoanalytic Quarterly*, 53: 425–430.

Bank, S., & Kahn, M. D. (1980–1981). Freudian siblings. *Psychoanalytic Review*, 67: 493–504.

Bialik, C. N., & Ravnitzky, Y. C. (2000). *Sefer Ha'aggda*. Tel-Aviv: Dvir (in Hebrew).

Coleman, D. (1996). Positive sibling transference: theoretical and clinical dimensions. *Clinical Social Work Journal*, 24: 377–387.

Coles, P. (2003). *The Importance of Sibling Relationships in Psychoanalysis*. London: Karnac.

Freud, S. (1912–1913). *Totem and Taboo. S. E.*, 13: 1–161. London: Hogarth.

Freud, S. (1915c). Instincts and their vicissitudes. *S. E.*, 14: 111–140. London: Hogarth.

Freud, S. (1939a). *Moses and Monotheism. S. E.*, 23: 3–137. London: Hogarth.

Houzel, D. (2001). The 'nest of babies' fantasy. *Journal of Child Psychotherapy*, 27: 125–138.

Klein, M. (1932). *The Psychoanalysis of Children*. New York: Dell.

Klein, M. (1955). On identification. In: *Envy and Gratitude and Other Works*. London: Hogarth, 1975.

Kohut, H. (1984). *How Does Analysis Cure*. In: A. Goldberg & P. Stepansky. (Eds.), Chicago, IL: University of Chicago Press.

Lesser, R. (1978). Sibling transference and countertransference. *Journal of the American Academy of Psychoanalysis and Dynamic Psychiatry*, 6: 37–39.

Mazur, L. (2001). *Moses Aaron and Miriam: Brothers, Leaders and Competitors*. Nhardah: Parsha pages of the Hebrew University of Jerusalem Hebrew University of Jerusalem. Institute of Jewish Studies. Center for Judaic Studies (in Hebrew).

Midrash Rabbah (1983). The Song of Songs, S. Maurice (Trans.). London: Soncino Press.

Midrash Tanhuma-Yelammedenu (1996). A. S. Berman (Trans.). Hobokon, NJ: Ktav.

Mitchell, J. (2003). *Siblings. Sex and Violence*. Oxford: Blackwell/Polity.

Rosenberg, S. (1989). Oedipus and Cain: Midrash Bereshit. *Apirion*, 14: 19–22 (in Hebrew).

Rosenberg, S. (2004). Cain and Yehuda: Midrash Bereshit (bhol.co.il, in Hebrew).

Rosner, S. (1985). On the place of siblings in psychoanalysis. *Psychoanalytic Review*, 72: 457–477.

Sharpe, S. A., & Rosenblatt, A. D. (1994). Oedipal sibling triangles. *Journal of the American Psychoanalytic Association*, 42: 491–523.

Vivona, J. M. (2010). Siblings, transference, and the lateral dimension of psychic life. *Psychoanalytic Psychology*, 27: 8–26.

Weiss, R. (2006). *Committing my Soul: Commitment Readings in Talmud*. Tel Aviv: Yediot Aharonot Books and Chemed Books (in Hebrew).

PART II

GROWING UP WITH A SICK
OR DISABLED SIBLING

The disabled child's siblings and parents: dealing with the impact of the birth of a disabled sibling: a case study

Marie-Ange Widdershoven

Introduction

During her conference discussion about "Siblings in development", held at the London Centre for Psychotherapy in 2007, Juliet Mitchell stated: "When the mother is expecting another baby the child feels this baby as a reproduction of itself, like a narcissistic birth" (Mitchell, 2009, p. 84).

Reading this, I started to think about, and perceive in another way, my clients who grow up with a disabled sibling. How does the child feel about the birth of this sibling? Does it feel that this narcissistic birth is like a reproduction of itself, and how does it cope with it?

It has been found by a large number of authors that the birth of a disabled sibling generates a multitude of different feelings, such as rage, isolation, uncertainty, resentment, embarrassment, envy, and guilt. Anger and guilt are the most often mentioned and are found to be the most damaging (Atkins, 1991). The loss of the ideal sibling evokes feelings of guilt about being the normal child and strengthens the struggle between the life and death instincts.

The sibling might try to deny these feelings in order to protect itself and its family and this can lead to feelings of depression (Atkins,

1991). On the other hand, the sibling might create rescue phantasies in an effort to repair the narcissistic quality of sibling love. Subsequently, the sibling will have to grieve for the ideal image of him or herself as a family rescuer so that he or she can develop a healthy self-image able to cope with the narcissistic loss (McKeever, 1983).

The clinical picture that emerges could be that of a prolonged mourning process. Bowlby (1963) describes, as features of childhood mourning, the unconscious insistence to recover the lost object and the denial that the object is permanently lost. The loss of the longed-for healthy child and the narcissistic wounds it evokes will have to be worked through in the process of mourning.

As a result of the narcissistic pain, the parents of the disabled child can develop unrealistic expectations of the healthy child, who has to compensate for the disappointment, frustration, guilt and/or feelings of failure in the family. A consequence of these expectations might be the emergence of narcissistic pain, conflict, and ambivalence, resulting in the development of a harsh and punitive superego. The healthy child might attempt to please the parents, protect them, and cheer them up in their narcissistic pain, depression, and bewilderment (McKeever, 1983).

The healthy sibling might try to maintain the approval of other adults by keeping thoughts and feelings to him or herself, as he or she sees the parents do, resulting in a generalised "web of silence". The birth of the disabled sibling might change the communication in and outside of the family. The family's emotional climate changes and this might endanger the overall development and general well being of the healthy sibling (McKeever, 1983).

A case study

For the purpose of this presentation, I focus on the therapy process of an adolescent girl with an autistic sibling and try to highlight the complexity and difficulties in the transference and countertransference that emerged during therapy. When I first met this adolescent and heard about her difficulties, my thoughts went immediately towards more primitive anxieties of abandonment and primary fear of separation. Later on, I understood what a tremendous effect the birth of her autistic sister had made on her mental state of mind and I was startled by her denial of any negative feelings towards her sibling. In this presentation, I elaborate mainly on the mental impact of having a disabled sister, although her primary anxieties, as a result of growing up with a depressed mother, and the oedipal anxiety in relation with her emotionally abusing father, clearly should not be underestimated in the expression of her psychopathology.

Furthermore, in concordance with findings in the literature, I was really startled by the "silence" in the therapy process with regard to the adolescent's sibling during the first part of therapy. Because of her denial of accepting any comments from me about her feelings for her sister, I myself started to "forget" that she had a disabled sister for many months. After my decision to present a paper to this conference, I realised how this "web of silence" had engulfed her and, consequently, me.

However, first let me give you more information about my client.

Maria is the first child in a family with two children. When she was twelve years old, her sister was born. She was diagnosed with autism when she was two years old. Her parents come from a high socio-economic background and have a high level of education. Her father is Greek and her mother English.

Maria was referred when she was seventeen years old because she had hypochondriacal symptoms and disturbances in the psychosomatic sphere. She was a very bright student, managed extremely well in her studies, and was to become a junior student in medical school. She felt all the symptoms started when she finished high school and her mother decided to leave, together with her autistic sister, for her homeland, where she felt her daughter would have better treatment. It was decided that the father would be travelling to and from Greece and the UK until he received his pension, which would enable him to settle down in the UK. However, soon after the mother and sister left for the UK, the parents decided to divorce, and one year later the father remarried.

Mother is a secretary, but has been unemployed for many years. She was described by Maria as passive, depressed, hypochondriacal, and inert. It was obvious that Maria had an insecure attachment to her mother and she described her first contact with kindergarten as a traumatic experience that triggered primitive anxieties of fear of abandonment and separation. When she was an infant the mother sometimes neglected her and at other times spanked her, because she used to cry a lot. Maria had bitter feelings towards her mother. She felt she always had to support her mother and not the other way around. Her father was described by Maria as authoritarian, aggressive, competitive, narcissistic, and demanding. Maria remembered that he began having extra marital affairs from the time she was still an infant and that he abandoned home, her mother, and her several times. He was a well-educated medical doctor, both admired and feared because of his austerity. The father was twenty years older than the mother.

Maria was twelve years old when her sister was born and they lived together for five years. After her mother and her sister left Greece, Maria felt abandoned and had anxieties about living alone. On the other hand, she reminded herself that she was seventeen, almost eighteen, and almost a grown-up, so why could she not live by herself without being anxious? From then on her difficulties started. She cried a lot and she could not cope with the anxiety the separation from her mother provoked. She had her first anxiety attack when her father remarried. Her fears and concerns became hypochondriacal and she felt afraid of illnesses and of being alone. She was vulnerable to pervasive anxieties, especially those connected with illness or death. In the meantime, she also felt guilty about being far away from her sister. Feelings of envy, jealousy, and ambivalence towards her sister emerged more intensely.

When her sister was two years old, she was diagnosed with autism. Maria remembered that her sister cried a lot and she used to exhibit uncontrollable and aggressive behaviour. As a kind of substitution, a defence, Maria felt she had to be the perfect daughter, with a perfect body, responsible and flawless.

The therapy process

From the first moment we met, Maria gave me much food for thought because of the positive, almost massive, therapeutic alliance she created, and I felt almost suffocated by the way she tried to "glue" herself to me. From the beginning of the therapy, she became completely dependent and attached to me, something that made me feel I would never be able to miss an appointment, or go for holidays, or end the therapy. She had great difficulties with the normal breaks in the therapy and felt them to be traumatic because they triggered

primitive anxieties of abandonment. During these first months of therapy, she was not able to talk or think about her sister; she felt abandoned by her mother, her father, and, consequently, me during our
first holiday break. The "web of silence" engulfed us both.

After the holiday break and her visit to her mother and sister, she
returned with the following dream:

> "I had a baby in my belly, not a normal baby, but something like a bat,
> ugly with wings and bones only. I did not want it but it was too late to
> terminate the pregnancy. I started to smoke and drink so as to hurt the
> baby, because I felt it had hurt me, but I could not get rid of it."

She thought about this dream with feelings of repulsion, terror,
and fear. She realised how difficult it was to think about her sister and
to cope with the anxieties of the narcissistic wounds she had brought
about. On the other hand, she tried to identify with her depressed
mother and feelings of guilt about her sister emerged.

Maria realised that she lost her mother not at seventeen, but when
her sister was born and her mother was trying to cope with her feelings of terror and rage and her own depression, due to the narcissistic injury. After the birth of her sister, Maria had numerous symptoms
such as eating disorders, depression, fear of death, and suicidal
thoughts at the beginning of adolescence and during it, but they were
never recognised by her parents as psychic pain. The birth of a disabled sibling while she was in her early adolescence gave rise to
highly disturbed feelings about her own body and mental health.

She identified with her sister's disability, looking all the time at her
body and phantasising that there was something wrong with her. If
her skin showed marks, she felt this would result in cancer and she
would die soon. Her breath would become irregular and she thought
she would die in panic. On the other hand, she was afraid she would
become crazy with all these weird thoughts and she would end up in
an asylum, as she phantasised her sister probably would. Her sister
became the reflection of herself through the unconscious process of
mirroring. Her mirror reflection became a narcissistic trauma
(Mitchell, 2009).

I felt the psychic pain she experienced at having an autistic sibling.
I was wondering how it must feel to be the healthy sibling, because
she tried to project her healthy parts on me, while she felt left only
with the crazy, disabled parts. I became an idealised therapist, whom

she phantasised as omnipotent, with a healthy body and a healthy family, while she felt like a crazy, sick adolescent, unable to cope with her "mad" thoughts, her sister, and her parents. She identified with her disabled sister, feeling autistic, withdrawn, and afraid I would judge and reject her, as her father and her mother judged and rejected her sister.

She started to talk more and more about her sister and said she always felt uncomfortable with her because of her stereotypical movements (hand flapping), her bizarre rituals, and the fact that she masturbated continuously. On the other hand, she identified with her; she felt she was not well and she could become crazy. She felt vulnerable and she succumbed easily to having temper tantrums in which she would bang her head on the wall uncontrollably. She experienced her emotions and behaviour as devastating and uncontrollable. She was not able to study and she felt she was could not materialise any good ideas about her studying because they would congeal. She was afraid she would always be insignificant like her mother or her sister and never famous like her father.

Feelings of anger and guilt coincided and intertwined. She felt lost in the complexity of her own emotions. "It is like there is a little animal inside me, I can't talk, I feel anxious, angry, but it is not other people's fault. It is like there is something wrong with me, I feel trapped, confused, stuck and I do this to myself all alone. I feel like ice at a moment like that and no one can reach me. Like my sister who locks herself in her room and I ask her what is wrong and she answers: 'I can't talk, I can't tell you, you will not understand'." It took us a long time to work through the mourning process she felt because of the loss of the ideal sister, the ideal mother, and the ideal father.

Later on in the therapy, she brought the following dream:

"... on the doorstep of my house sat a homeless female, dirty, crazy, but also very young, like a little girl. She was sitting on the stairs of my house. I felt ashamed that she was there but I said 'never mind, she is not a bad girl, she will do no harm ... she is quite cute'."

She still seemed confused about her mixed and ambivalent feelings towards her sister, but she started to make movements towards reparation and, therefore, was able to experience her as a cute little girl at the end of the dream. Her bad, aggressive, "homeless", and "dirty" feelings did not damage her (or the therapy) any more and she could cope with them without losing her self-esteem to herself and her sister.

During the same period, she said, "I am not afraid of the future any more, but still unsure of having a child myself. My whole family is crazy: my sister has autism, my mother walks around like a zombie, and my father acts like there is nothing wrong. Often I feel I am the only normal one in the family, but to have my own child, with this burden? A good solution might be to adopt a child." It seemed as if she became able to compensate for the loss of the ideal sister through a phantasy of having her own perfect, healthy child, but that this could be realised only by adopting a child, as the burden of the disabled sister weighs heavily on her.

Maria's final dream seemed to close the circle and to allow her to hope for the future and to become independent. She dreamt that I (her therapist) decided to leave Greece (and her) with my husband and I told her that we could communicate through Skype if she wanted to stay in contact with me. At first, she felt betrayed and angry with me, and her friends told her that I was not allowed to leave her. Afterwards, she started to think about the end of the therapy and she felt that I could leave, that she could keep in her mind all the work we had done together, and she could continue with that.

In conclusion

I end this presentation with a short extract from Atkins (1991):

> ... the sibling may become dependent on the therapist as the hope arises that she may be able to risk truly experiencing living. As this evolves it is important to rework and recall past failures. Clinicians must be aware of and use their counter transference in such a way that they too, can have made mistakes that can be recalled and reworked, with all the transferential feelings involved. The goal is to allow the sibling to take a risk and possibly fail, without risking loss of self-esteem to herself and her family. (p. 532)

I am aware that the clinical material I have presented can be commented on and worked through (as has been done during the therapy) within a more oedipal framework. However, for the purpose of the conference and this chapter, I tried to focus on the sibling complexity that emerged from the clinical material, which preceded a more oedipal reflection.

References

Atkins, S. P. (1991). Siblings of learning disabled children: are they special too? *Child and Adolescent Social Work, 8*(6): 525–533.

Bowlby, J. (1963). Pathological mourning and childhood mourning. *Journal of the American Psychoanalytic Association, 11*: 500–541.

McKeever, P. (1983). Siblings of chronically ill children. *American Journal of Orthopsychiatry, 53*(2): 209–218.

Mitchell, J. (2009). Siblings in development, towards a meta psychology. In: V. Lewin & B. Sharp (Eds.), *Siblings in Development: A Psychoanalytical View* (pp. 77–99). London: Karnac.

CHAPTER SEVEN

The disabled child's siblings and parents: the ghost sibling

Nancy Taloumi

his chapter refers to the way the existence of a diseased child affects the psychic development of his brothers. In the case examined, the healthy child identifies with the diseased brother and in his phantasy is persecuted by him to become the same.

Identification with the sibling plays an important role in the mental development of the child. It allows the child to approach his parents and this facilitates the identification with them. The sibling functioning as the mediator of the mental identification procedures, a passage through the identifications with other objects, constitutes the basis for the mutation of further identifications for reaching out to others and to society.

Kaës (2008) argues that the sibling complex is not only a displacement for the avoidance of the Oedipus complex, and neither is it limited to the complex of the intruder, which could be its paradigmatic form. It is characterised not only by hatred, envy, and jealousy, but also includes these dimensions and many equally important others, such as love, ambivalence, and identification with the other as both one's double and different from one. The sibling complex is a transformation of the Oedipus complex. The rivalry triangle within the sibling complex differs from the oedipal triangle through the objects that comprise it (love and hate relationships among them, the emergence of jealousy, envy, and violence, and the channels that are open within the relationships, including prohibitions and their violation). The identification process that is associated with the Oedipus complex can be compared to the process of the sibling complex, whose specificity lies in the possibility of mediation and opening to other objects and other structures. The sibling relation plays a protective role in understanding the primal phantasies of sex difference and castration anxiety because the generation difference is not an issue, as it is in the relation with parents.

Kaës (2008), in his study of the sibling complex, suggests that it consists of two opposing forms: the first, the archaic, where the subject has part object relationships with his brother and sister (imaginary maternal body or his own imaginary body). The second form is where the subject is found in a triangle of rivalry, pre-oedipal and oedipal. Here, we encounter the first forms of the double, the narcissistic homosexuality and mental bisexuality.

In families with a disabled child, as in the case I will mention below, it is observed that the healthy children undergo a painful and puzzling experience. Children who have a disabled brother often regress, for example, to fragmentation anxiety, or to reactions related to castration anxiety. This depends on the conflicts, intrapsychic and intersubjective, of each child and on his cognitive and psycho-emotional development. Scelles (2008) argues that identification with a physically disabled person can result in the risk of a narcissistic trauma in his siblings.

The experience of people who support families with disabled children shows that only rarely do members of the family express how each one of them experiences this pathology. It is possible to refer to diagnosis and symptoms, but rare to talk about their feelings and how they experience this particularity. If this difficulty is associated with defences, especially defences of the parents, sometimes siblings might have the potential to transform these defences.

The way each child understands the pathology, at each stage of the life of the siblings, results from a complex process of many aspects of reality itself.

In the case I describe, although it is a treatment in its initial phase, I attempt to highlight that the burden of the trauma of the disabled sibling is involved in the mental functioning and the identification process of the healthy child, expressed through fears of loneliness, emptiness, breakdown, and total annihilation.

Clinical example

Orestis, an eleven-year-old boy, asked his parents if he could visit a psychologist because he suffered from intense fears.

Orestis, a child desired by both parents, the third-born after two older brothers, was, at the age of two, suddenly abandoned by his mother because, during that very period, the eldest son was diagnosed with autism. The mother became upset by this and turned all her attention to the disabled child. The father was also upset, and did not find it easy to be near him.

Orestis grew up in a well-educated family where the mother was the desired object to the four men of the family, while the father, even though he was a lovable person, was considered likely to have autistic symptoms by the mother and, thus, by the children.

Orestis came to the first meeting and, like an adult initiated in psychoanalysis, he referred to his problem, which consisted of waking up at nights with a need to go to mum and dad's room. He insisted that despite his efforts to resist that, he could not avoid doing it as he was overcome by his fear of being alone.

To my question about what he was afraid of, he answered that he was afraid that someone could enter the house, but mostly afraid of his loneliness. When he woke up, he felt very lonely and embarrassed about it, because he was old enough to be on his own and he thought of what his friends would say about it. What embarrassed him most, however, was that he was coming between his parents, who had their private life, and so his daddy would get angry when he went to their room.

In that moment, I thought that Orestis was regressing and seeking a relation with the pre-oedipal mother of whom he was deprived because of his brothers.

Then, he referred to his interests and his extracurricular activities, where he wanted to succeed and be the best, and the fact that he became scared when someone criticised him. He connected the fear of the night with his fear of the teacher and, although he was the best student, he was afraid of being criticised by the teacher, a thing that he could not stand. The fear appeared in his first school year, and since then it had been getting worse every year.

Orestis's case attracted my interest: first, because he invested in the treatment and, second, because of his contradictory image. His physical development and his external appearance reminded me of a younger child, while the contrasting development of speech, thought, and behaviour gave me the impression of an older child.

I thought that the contradictory image that he brought to treatment included both sides, the most childish side seeking care, which, in a magical way, could relieve him from his torment, and, at the same time, his pseudo-mature side used intellectual investment to defend a fragile self.

In subsequent sessions, he mainly referred to this fear and to the only moments he was not scared, which was when there was an adult close to him and when he was in their country house. He often referred to competition and rivalry issues with both his best friend, whom he resembled a lot, and his second brother, whom he admired and had been jealous of since his early childhood, because he thought that *mummy and daddy loved him more*. He seemed to try to establish his ego through jealousy and the double and to assimilate from the other as much as possible in order to differentiate from his mother and to ensure his personality and objectivity. This model seemed to be provided by the healthy brother (the second). He never talked about his eldest brother.

According to Lacan (1938) the firstborn, to the extent that he is more integrated, provides the archaic model of the ego. In Orestis's case, this brother was covered with a veil of mystery and could not provide him with an adequate model. In one of my questions regarding his feelings about the first-born, he answered that, owing to his problem, he was never jealous of him, because they were not close and then immediately talked about something else.

As treatment progressed, he talked about the fears that came mainly from any questioning of his perfection. He wondered himself why he was so sensitive to criticism, since neither of his parents was strict.

He was taking care to be the best at school, in his extracurricular activities, and in his behaviour, while the slightest adverse remark easily hurt his vulnerable ego.

I thought that in transference I played the role of a mother that could be trusted and perceived as capable of containing his anxiety. However, the fact that he interrupted almost all the sessions, especially when he expressed his difficulties, by going to the toilet, showed that, at the same time, I represented a devouring mother-imago, as well as a sibling one, who threatened him so that he needed to be alone with himself to confirm his existence. To my intervention that what we say here might cause him some concerns, he replied, "I am not scared here."

Often, when he felt vulnerable with regard to me, he identified with me defensively (identification with the aggressor), playing the role of the therapist.

During a session, while talking about his fears, he suddenly said that he was afraid of the eldest brother when he was young, while now he pitied him, and then he immediately changed the subject of conversation. I felt that he did not want to say it; he gave me the impression that he said it accidentally, that it was a lapse. After that, he talked about his first nightmare. There was a man who shouted at him, threatened him in English and he did not understand him. I think that his eldest brother remained, at a deeper level, a stranger, and he was felt to be threatening by Orestis. Although, in this family, the issue of disability had been discussed extensively by all its members, the deeper feelings of this child had not been expressed in words.

The fact that he expressed his fear of his brother resulted in the occurrence of many dreams, which he drew, and I thought that these were the means of expressing and processing the conflicting feelings towards his brother, since we do not choose our dreams; they come unconsciously, and we do not have responsibility for what they signify.

The return from the Easter break and his separation from the country house, which symbolised the maternal hug, revived separation anxiety that induced the emergence of a non-integrated self-image, which was depicted in his drawings.

Dreams brought to the surface feelings of emptiness, loneliness, and self-loss. The relationships with the others were threatening and there was a lack of trust. In one of these dreams, he came out of his house and, while the day was sunny, a heavy rain started to fall. Afterwards, he returned to his house, which was small and empty. Or, in another dream, he found himself at a crowded party and the very next moment he was alone in the middle of the sea.

During this phase, I avoided interpretations that could possibly have disrupted his defences and could increase his fears, and I resorted to holding, which he seemed to need.

Approaching the summer holidays in one of the last sessions, he said that it was strange that while holidays were coming, he was more scared and felt bad, but in fact he was having a nice time. The previous Sunday he had been at a bazaar for children of African countries, where he had a lovely time.

At the time he referred to his visit to the bazaar, I was thinking it was fortunate we had not met, because I had gone there, too. My thinking was interrupted by Orestis asking to go to the toilet. On his return, he said, ". . . on Sunday, at this feast, I think I saw you." "It is likely, because I was there, too," I replied.

Later, while, he was referring to disturbing critical comments made by his father and his second brother, he talked about a dream where people on the street disappeared as they walked and he ran to hide in order to survive. Before I could comment on something, as if he did not want me to make any comment, he went on, saying, ". . . now I've remembered an old nightmare where I was being chased by a leper. At first, I thought he was old but then I realised that he was young. He caught me but he did not hurt me."

The fact that at the feast my attention was turned elsewhere and I did not see him led to the revival of annihilation anxiety that he had felt in the past, when his mother was preoccupied with his eldest brother. At an age where the phantasy of sibling unity, as well as unity with the mother's body, prevails, he perceived the sibling as a partial object and, in his case, a threatening one (a leper).

In the course of the treatment, he brought his second brother to the fore. He recounted a dream where he was standing on the bank of a river with someone who was his double and they tried to cross the raging waters of the river. The other said he would go across, but he himself would not make it and would drown. Recollecting this dream, he talked about how much he was jealous of his second brother when he was little and how much he wanted to resemble him. I suppose that now the realisation that he was different from his second brother threatened his integrity, because if he was not the double of the second brother he could become the double of the firstborn.

Over time, I realised that he had started to exist for Orestis. I considered that the revival of past feelings in transference led to the illumination of the dark side of this relation. Dreams were equally nightmarish. However, they were different now. The nightmare was more specific: it looked like a ghost hiding its face, leading him to an icy landscape where there was nobody. He said, "Probably what is chasing me is the anxiety inside me." When I associated this with what he had mentioned in a previous session, that when he was little he was afraid of his first brother, he denied it, and said, "On the contrary, now I have more in common with the first than with the second." From that moment, and after he talked about the eldest brother, I felt that there was a psychic movement. The fear remained, but he seemed to differentiate himself, to become more confident and to be able to confront this nightmare with his own resources, which were reasoning and magical thinking. This appeared in a dream where he was alone, looking at a tree whose top was missing. He was sitting on a bench and felt that the tree hypnotised him. Orestis started staring at it and then a branch fell. "I did that with my mind," he said.

In a later session, he was very sad because of the death of his beloved cat. He described how all the family was grieving together for the cat and then he went to sleep in his mother and father's room, *not from fear but from sorrow*, as he indicated.

This incident provided the whole family with the opportunity to proceed to the symbolisation of loss, which had not taken place in the case of the disability of the brother.

Conclusion

In Orestis's case, we are witnessing a reversal. The intruder is not the younger brother, who comes and dethrones the eldest, but, on the contrary, the intruders are the two older brothers. Bion (1970) considers that the level of anxiety of the child who has been displaced verges on existential anxiety and might represent for the child a period of catastrophic change.

The mother, according to Cooper (2005), strives to create an internal space for each child once she understands the importance of the position of the child in respect of identifications. It seems that Orestis's mother, due to the narcissistic trauma and guilt caused by the problem of the older child, could not provide an internal space for Orestis.

Through the therapeutic process, Orestis tried to fill the emotional void created by his parents because of the disability of his brother, and to symbolise the consequent trauma in order to get rid of the ghosts chasing him and to form his own identity.

Finally, I must stress that the subjectification of a sibling's disability by children is promoted by its verbal expression within the family context. This means that the sharing of thoughts and concerns about the problem of the sibling is the best way to mentally integrate an external threatening reality, succeeding, at the same time, in keeping the fraternal bond in life.

References

Bion, W. R. (1970). *Attention and Interpretation*. London: Tavistock [reprinted London: Karnac 1984].

Cooper, H. (2005). The sibling link. In: J. Magagna, N. Bakalar, H. Cooper, J. Levy, C. Norman, & C. Shank (Eds.), *Intimate Transformations: Babies with their Families* (pp. 42–56). London: Karnac, 2005 [originally published in the *International Journal of Infant Observation and Its Applications*, 5(3): 69–82].

Kaës, R. (2008). Le complexe fraternel archaïque [The archaic fraternity complex]. *Revue Francaise de Psychanalyse*, 72: 383–396.

Lacan, J. (1938). Le complexe de l'intrusion. Les complexes familiaux de la formation de l'individu [The intrusion complex, according to Lacan's article for the family]. *Revue Psychanalytique*, 20: 33–51.

Scelles, R. (2008). Dire ou ne pas dire en famille, processus de subjectivation du handicap au sein de la fratrie [To tell or not to tell in the family, the process of subjectivation of the handicap at the source of siblinghood]. *Revue Française de Psychanalyse*, 72: 485–498.

CHAPTER EIGHT

The disabled child's siblings and parents: their predicaments

Maria Papagounou

Therapists, in their clinical practice with parents of autistic and psychotic children, listen to the parents gradually unfold the story of their relation to their child. They express their difficulty in talking about this relation and even in finding ways to broach this subject. Therapists also face the various ways in which parents do, or do not, present their healthy child in the sessions.

> For the child it is the words spoken by those around him about his 'illness' that assume importance. These words, or the absence of them, create the dimension of the lived experience in him. At the same time, it is the verbalization of a painful situation that makes it possible for him to bestow a meaning on what he is living through. (Mannoni, 1987, p. 61)

This difficulty in putting "illness" into words is not limited to the sick child, but often spreads to the healthy sibling, the parents themselves, and their social relations.

In this chapter, I discuss the impact that living with an autistic or psychotic child has on the parents and the siblings and the vicissitudes that arise in their family relations. I provide some examples and vignettes from my clinical work and I wil present how the healthy sibling's presence is portrayed—or not—in the parents' sessions. It is important to note that these vignettes come from sessions with the parents that concern the "sick" child, who is in psychoanalytic psychotherapy with another therapist.

The birth of a "sick" child creates a new psychic reality and demands the formation of new, or the adjustment of old, psychic functions. The relation between healthy siblings and its dynamics will facilitate the understanding of the dysfunctions of the relation of a "sick" child and its siblings. Margaret Rustin writes,

> The single child who has to share parents with a new arrival in the family does have to deal with rivalry, but at the same time gains a partner, and this mitigates the loneliness that a singleton can also experience . . . We might think of [the siblings] as a sort of 'we' ego. This is a very important function of siblinghood. (Rustin, 2007, p. 28)

> Long-term intimacy between siblings can be a preparation for both later friendships and love relationships . . . the opportunity provided by siblings for multiple identifications and for the expansion of psychic life. (Rustin, 2007, p. 34).

An important aspect of siblinghood is the sharing of a common family history, no matter how this is inscribed in the child's psyche, for the rest of his life.

Autistic and psychotic children have emotional and affective deficits. Their relation to other people, be they parents, siblings, teachers, therapists, is characterised, quite often, by an absent or limited ability to relate, to engage in and sustain meaningful relations. The psychotic child bears a deep anxiety and panic and is often fragmented, confused, and overwhelmed by internal and external excitations. His body image is confused and becomes entangled with outside objects; there are no distinct boundaries between reality and the world of phantasy. He is full of omnipotent phantasies and has a low tolerance of frustration. The autistic child is mainly withdrawn from interactions with other people. There is a lack of expressive language and a need for the preservation of sameness and bodily sensations. Further, "the absence of a needed person is experienced as a 'hole' which can be filled immediately with an Autistic Object" (Tustin, 1981, p. 107). As Meltzer, Bremmer, Hoxter, Weddell, and Wittenberg (1975) describe, the self lives in a two-dimensional world.

The autistic child has no transitional area, as described by Winnicott, since there is an absence of the sense of primal identity which is a libidinal cathexis of the body, "not a sense of who I am but that I am" (Mahler, Pine, & Bergman, 1975, p. 8).

These children form fragmented and partial relations. The healthy sibling has to accommodate and adjust to this new internal and external psychic reality. This condition calls for the creation of a new type of relation, which is formed in a unique way for every child. There is, however, a common ground in this relation. The children are exposed to paradoxical behaviour in respect of the spectrum of this pathology. Additionally, parents, being devastated, cannot contain the healthy siblings' anxieties, questions, fears, etc. The absence of this containing function of the parents, as Bion (1984) claims, causes the psychic burden of the healthy child to stay unmetabolised and, thus, does not help to make the burden bearable and possible to live with. Furthermore, the parents often expect the child to help out, but, in actuality, they wish the child to comply with the special needs of the sibling. The healthy child occasionally becomes bewildered by the pathology and the inconsistency of the relation.

I shall illustrate the above with a vignette.

A nine-year-old girl came to my office, accompanied by her mother. She was worried about her six-year-old psychotic brother. She was extremely involved in his upbringing and she seemed very mature for her age. Towards the end of the session, she said, "You know, it is so hard, I do not know how to reach out to him. Sometimes he does weird and crazy things. I think they are funny and I laugh. There are times that we can even do things together and then all of a sudden—is it my fault? He does something and I am afraid. We are brother and sister, but not always, only sometimes." She stopped for a while, and just before leaving, she said, "It is like a crossword puzzle; there are some letters there but the others are missing."

Feelings of guilt, fear, anger, and loss over the things siblings cannot share and do together are prevalent at this stage. Ambivalence is present in siblinghood and, as it is with contradictory feelings, it is more intense in the case where one of the siblings is disabled.

Healthy siblings often carry the psychological burden to please their parents and to compensate for their sibling's inability. The healthy child might be in a position where excessive parental projections and desires must be fulfilled. This could lead to the formation of a harsh superego and to a false premature psychic growth. A therapist often hears parents say that they want to have another child who would take care of their disabled one when "they are gone". Despite these difficulties, parents also talk about the compassion, the empathy, and the protectiveness of their healthy children as well as their ability to set limits for their sibling. Parents are amazed, first, by the ability and the effectiveness of the healthy child's interventions and, second, by the ability of the other child to abide by the rules. The therapist can work with the parents in order to understand this function. Sometimes, it is the case that the parents' observations aid the therapist in helping them to understand their children. I think that if the parental figures are not severely traumatised and weak, they can facilitate, to a certain extent, the bonding between the siblings.

The family's functions revolve around the sick child, whose existence changes the ordinal position of the siblings since he is treated as the youngest. These families provide an image of normality. Family dynamics often impose enormous stress and feelings of fear. ". . . communication in these families is quite disturbed and insufficient— if not non-existent" (Maratos & Alexandridis, 2000, p. 102). "Turk has observed that this pattern of diminished communication spreads to other aspects of family life, producing a generalized web of silence" (Turk, 1964, cited in McKeever, 1983, p. 211).

Many therapists, however, consider this silence as part of the pathology of autism. Silence seems to function as a "protective shell", as if to protect the parents from feelings of guilt, narcissistic pain, and shame resulting from being considered responsible by others. It is as if parents believe that the "unspoken" is also non-existent. In clinical practice, we have numerous examples that illustrate the parents' inability to put into words their child's illness, not only to outsiders, but to their other children, who live with this illness as well. It is, therefore, understandable why they sometimes do not ask questions concerning their brother's or sister's illness. In a way, it is as if they want to protect their parents from overwhelming emotions caused by their questions.

An example of this function is a mother who told me that when her son asked her why his brother acted the way he did, she answered, "You were exactly like that when you were his age." The mother was pleased with her answer and thought that the matter was settled, since her son stopped asking her. I think that she might have expressed her unconscious hope that her autistic child, as he grew up, would be cured, or she expressed "the struggle going on in mother's mind to make a space for each child" (Rustin, 2007, p. 26). The mother was also unable to listen and contain the anxiety and answered him with a distorted image of himself.

Although the detailed presentation of the work with parents of autistic and psychotic children is not the subject of this paper, I need to mention the parents' emotional reactions, which depend on the structure and the complexity of their psychic apparatus. Parents live with a chronic narcissistic trauma and they are in a mourning process for the loss of the ideal child they expected to have. This leads, in some cases, to depression. This constant feeling of loss evokes anger, enormous frustration, guilt, and hostility, death wishes for the disabled child as well as destructive and self-destructive phantasies. I want to stress the parents' feeling of shame which Engelse Frick (2000) claims: "As shame can be regarded a narcissistic affect, the parent can experience the need to seek help for the child as a narcissistic violation" (p. 76). She also states,

> when people are feeling shame they perceive others as contributing to the shameful situation by their judging position. To reduce the importance of the other one may therefore attempt to deny the shameful situation or to deny the significance of the other by not interacting. (p. 77)

This might be a reason that makes these families withdraw from social and family relations. The parents' chronic severe trauma has serious intrapsychic repercussions and new adaptive processes are formed. These processes "are aiming at adaptation by regression (in the service of the ego) to fixation points gathering energies from them and trying out old abandoned ways" (Tischler, 1979, p. 31).

I would like to turn my attention to the role of the father in the families of disabled children since, in clinical practice, we observe that he is mostly absent. We have also observed that the father's active presence can have a mediating and regulatory role in the amelioration of the condition of the psychotic or autistic child. He might disentangle the mother–child relation and facilitate the psychological development of the healthy child by setting the structure and the rules in the family. We often see that the father is excluded from the mother–child relation. Thus, this relation cannot become tripartite. He cannot set the necessary distance between them and establish the connection with external reality. Tustin writes "the autistic children's lack of a normal differentiation from the mother in early infancy means that the 'father elements' have been shut out of their awareness" (Tustin, 1992, p. 182). In families with a disabled child, the actual and the symbolic presence of the father is minimal or non-existent. He is ignored by the mother, he usually gives up very soon, and he is left out. "As Margaret Mahler so well puts it, 'the father cuts the umbilical cord'. In autistic children the psychic umbilical cord has not been cut" (Tustin, 1992, p. 182). The necessary limits were never set in order for the child to bear the frustration of sharing the mother with the father.

A clinical vignette illustrates the above. Recently, a mother came to her appointment alone. I was surprised, since the father wanted to discuss the relation between his psychotic son and his older brother. When I expressed my surprise over his absence at this session in which we were to discuss what was on his mind, the mother replied, "Oh, do not worry. I can do that. I know what he wants to say, anyway. What he knows, I know. It is the same being here together or just me. Anyway, when I go home, I will tell him. I know best. It is better for him to rest."

An omnipotent, archaic, controlling mother that knows everything excludes the father because she knows what is best for her husband, the children, and the therapist. It is common in clinical practice for fathers to miss their appointments, but not to be excluded by their wives.

I end this chapter with a clinical vignette that illustrates functions that were discussed earlier, as well as the psychic movements in the family.

I have been working with the parents of a five-year-old autistic boy who has a seven-year-old brother. The mother attended regularly, but the father was mostly absent at the beginning. Gradually, he would appear more often and, although he was not always there, I felt that there was therapeutic continuity in our work. The father is a high-school teacher working long hours and the mother has a university degree and stopped working when the child was diagnosed. Now, she is a housewife and spends most of her time with her autistic son. They tried to give the impression of a "normal" family, but I felt the setting was lifeless. They live in a very nice but distant, as they said, suburb of Athens. They described the neighbourhood as a deserted and isolated place, projecting their own feelings of despair and loneliness from living with a distant and silent autistic child. They seemed unable to enjoy their living conditions. We had been working on this matter for some time and they expressed the shame that they had both felt. They did not want other people to see them. They did not take their children out for a walk and they would not let the disabled boy out in the fenced garden because *somebody might take him away*. I thought that this was an unconscious phantasy that had to do with aggressive feelings towards the child. As for the older son, he made them very happy, but he was forbidden to talk about his brother's problem. They both described him as an excellent boy who is their "relief". He is a very good student, quiet, undemanding, and he does everything alone.

The parents used to talk mostly about the autistic child's everyday problems in a distant, superficial way. When something painful was discussed, they immediately brought up their healthy son. This was a sign of their fragile narcissism. At times, they would get notes from the older son's teacher to go and see him at school. They ignored them. They kept saying to me that their son was all right, as if they needed to put my mind at ease or efface my thinking which was placing them in their paternal and maternal roles. When they finally went to see the teacher, he told them that the child had been doing his homework regularly, but he would forget it when asked in class. They were infuriated, and the father spanked the boy and sent him to his room. There was an overflow of emotions, anger, disillusionment, and no room for thought, as they kept saying over and over, "Now we have another problem." The world turned upside down. They wondered whether *he was losing his mind*. I thought that this overflow of emotions was related to their phantasy that their older son might also become autistic and lose his mind. I felt that the anger towards their son was a displacement of the anger towards his autistic brother. His failure at school elicited their narcissistic trauma and the idealised child was no longer invested in; he was a bad object and had to be punished.

In my countertransference, I also felt that they were angry with me for making them see the teacher, thus exposing them, especially the father, to another teacher and making him feel more humiliated. My understanding of their feelings of disappointment in their son was not sufficient to contain their anger. It was a very intense session and there was no room for thought and reflection. When they left, my thinking process could recover from a lifelessness caused by their projections and anger. I thought that a new space was formed by the symptom of the child in a process of differentiation. A rupture was created in the preservation of sameness in this family: hostility and aggression came to the fore. It also came to my mind that a couple of months ago the mother described a feeling of suffocation. The parents needed time to understand why the boy was forgetting at school what he had learnt at home. I think that since he was told to forget his autistic brother at home, he also forgot the things he learnt at home. The tremendous pressure he was under to please his parents and the heavy burden that represented, as well as his need to make his presence felt, created this symptom, which could have been an unconscious expression of aggression towards his parents, particularly towards his father, who was a teacher. Jacobs writes ". . . failure to remember what he has learned, can also be unconscious expressions of hostility toward parents and serve as a kind of mockery of the injunction to forget" (Jacobs, 1980, p. 35).

I also connected the feeling of suffocation that the mother had felt and thought that maybe the older boy was "suffocating", too. When the parents worked through this experience, they understood the meaning of the symptom. Later on, they were able to talk to their child and the symptom disappeared. This was experienced by them as a reparative function which they had accomplished.

A year later, the mother said, "As I was parking the car, I saw my older boy looking out from the window. I felt he looked sad and thought maybe he was lonely and wanted other kids to play with." I thought that this mother was gradually forming the ability to observe him with insight and reflect on her son's needs and feelings as well as her own. She was more capable of opening up to a new dimension, the outside world, to see the connections they, as a family, could have with this world. After five years of working with this couple, we will finish the therapy shortly. They seem more capable of coping with their everyday life and using the insight they have gained. Probably, they will have a better life than they did before. This is very precious for every family with an autistic or psychotic child.

Healthy siblings grow up in a family environment with many pathogenic functions, but with parents who also have healthy sides. These sides can be further used in the care of the healthy child, in the sense that the early relation environment is crucial not because it shapes the quality of subsequent relationships but because it serves to equip the individual with a mental processing system that will subsequently generate mental representations, including relation representations. (Fonagy, 2001, p. 31)

In the work with each family, the presence or the absence of the healthy child in the words of his parents has a different meaning. Parents often need the session as a safe place to demonstrate the healthy, mature, and parental side of their personalities to the therapist and to themselves. At other times, the presence can be used as a defensive mechanism in order not to touch upon the pain and the aggressive phantasies that the disturbed child might elicit in their discourse. It also serves to avoid the feelings that their lost dreams of the ideal child will not come true. Since the psychotic child does not have a place of his or her own, the healthy one has to fill the void and assuage the fear of the autistic emptiness and silence. In our work with parents, we try to understand the meaning of the presence or the absence of the healthy child connected to the psychic function that it serves.

References

Bion, W. R. (1984). *Learning from Experience*. London: Maresfield Library, Karnac.

Engelse Frick, M. (2000). Parental therapy—in theory and practice. In: J. Tsiantis, S. B. Boethious, B. Hallerfors, A. Horne, & L. Tischler (Eds.), *Work with Parents. Psychoanalytic Psychotherapy with Children and Adolescents* (pp. 65–92). London: Karnac.

Fonagy, P. (2001). *Attachment Theory and Psychoanalysis*. London: Karnac.

Jacobs, T. J. (1980). Secrets, alliances, and family fictions: some psychoanalytic observations. *Journal of the American Psychoanalytic Association*, 28: 21–42.

Mahler, M. S., Pine, F., & Bergman, A. (1975). *The Psychological Birth of the Human Infant. Symbiosis and Individuation*. London: Maresfield Library.

Mannoni, M. (1987). *The Child, his "Illness" and the Others*. London: Karnac.

Maratos, O., & Alexandridis, A. (2000). Work with parents of psychotic children within a day-care therapeutic unit setting. In: J. Tsiantis, S. B. Boethious, B. Hallerfors, A. Horne, & L. Tischler (Eds.), *Work with*

Parents. Psychoanalytic Psychotherapy with Children and Adolescents (pp. 93–114). London: Karnac.

McKeever, P. (1983). Siblings of chronically ill children: a literature review with implications for research and practice, *American Journal of Orthopsychiatry, 53*(2): 209–218.

Meltzer, D., Bremmer, J., Hoxter, S., Weddell, D., & Wittenberg, I. (1975). *Explorations in Autism. A Psycho-Analytic Study.* Strathtay, Perthshire: Clunie Press.

Rustin, M. (2007). Taking account of siblings—a view from child psychotherapy. *Journal of Child Psychotherapy, 33*(1): 21–35.

Tischler, S. (1979). Being with a psychotic child. A psycho-analytical approach to the problems of parents of psychotic children. *International Journal of Psychoanalysis, 60*(1): 29–38.

Tustin, F. (1981). *Autistic States in Children.* London: Routledge & Kegan Paul.

Tustin, F. (1992). *The Protective Shell in Children and Adults.* London: Karnac.

CHAPTER NINE

A family under a microscope: about the influence of family ties through DNA

Françoise Daune

Introduction

W innicott (1957) believes that life is a series of experiences of great intensity. Freud (1914c) noted that the individual finds himself divided between two necessities: to be at once himself and, at the same time, to be a link in a chain in which his will is superfluous.

These two needs have been particularly evident to me over the course of my many years working with cancer patients and their relatives. A positive diagnosis of cancer and the treatments it entails are potentially traumatic events in a patient's life. They shift the basis for identity, stir narcissism, and challenge relations to self and to others. Cancer and its treatments underline the patient's mortality—the human condition of being an end in oneself. But the patient is also a link in a chain, whether it be during the search for a bone marrow transplant donor or for the mutation gene in the case of the genetic transmission of some cancers.

Research reveals somatic bonds within the family, and in the context of this chapter I focus specifically on the relation among the siblings. The strength of such bonds will be put to the test by the more physical ones of the body. My investigations look at filiation and the place in the family from a biological point of view, but also raise the issue of identity and relational bonds.

Discovery of cancer plunges the individual into the depths of his somatic being, to the very centre of that intimate part of the self that is shared with siblings. However, this somatic bond is sometimes very much different from the relation bonds within the family. Disclosure of the illness can trigger self-questioning among and between siblings on issues of identity, similarities, differences, filiation, and place in the family. In addition, disclosure may reveal the randomness of transmission (compatible or not, carrying the genetic mutation or not) and of one's destiny, as Freud (1914c) notes, irrespective of one's will.

In such a context, the medical reality might serve as a trigger for resetting family relationships, and might, indeed, put them at risk. The following presentation will focus on the psychological impact of the microscopic biological investigation and the illness on the patient, his siblings, and the family.

Donor, where are you? Who are you?

A bone marrow transplant inevitably involves the relatives in the search for a potential donor. The similarity or otherness of siblings becomes an issue—brother, sister, donor, or not? While the transplant depends on the donor's acceptance, the medical success of the treatment depends on the biological and physiological acceptance of the stem cells by the recipient's body. As Ascher and Jouet (2004a) remark: "the donor: sought, selected, involved, validated clinically, biologically, and legally, but also informed and willing" (p. 89, translated for this edition). A relation of power comes into being for this much-prized donor whose cells are desperately needed. A very special, unusual existence overtakes this brother and/or sister relation, represented by this collection of stem cells. The transfusion is also experienced as an "emotional acme". This donation can be experienced as a miracle, producing the fantasy of being reborn. The marrow itself, so precious: a liquid gift that is immune to the anxieties of fragmentation and is renewable.

Family test results tensely awaited, hopefully awaited—even more so if there are many siblings—but . . . Such is the story of Mr R, a sixty-two-year-old patient diagnosed with myelodysplastic syndrome. A bone marrow transplant is under consideration.

Mr R is the second child in a family of seven: two boys and five girls. A sister and a brother died suddenly. An investigation was launched within the family. His four sisters agreed to be tested (which is not always the case). Unfortunately, none of them was compatible in terms of HLA (human leukocyte antigens, an individual's unique marker system allowing the body and its immune system to recognise what belongs to it or not). Then the search for a non-familial donor started. Mr R tells me of his disappointment at the failure of the research among his sisters. He will also tell me how convinced he is that his brother, who died a year previously, would certainly have been compatible and so a donor. As the other man in the family, his brother was the one with whom he had the strongest and most important ties. Mr R will tell me of his fear that, like his brother, he will die. He sees it as a sign: to join his brother in death is another similarity between them. He anticipates it will happen before a donor can be found.

His sisters also express a sense of failure: *so many siblings and not one can be a donor!* They, too, subscribe to the fantasy that either the deceased sister or brother could have been a donor. Both could have been donors, or just one of them, or neither. Functioning as one, the siblings see themselves as having been dispatched by disease, by death. Their strong ties have been knitted by family tragedy: both parents died prematurely, a mere fifteen days apart. In the absence of the parents, the siblings invested in their group identity. Now, in the face of biological reality, they have to admit their powerlessness and confront disappointment. The psychological power of the clan cannot help; the law of the physical prevails. A medical condition will rearrange the sense of identity among these siblings, where "I" had become "we".

It should be noted that the level of compatibility among siblings is twenty-five per cent. The number of children within the family increases the chances of finding a donor, but, as the story of Mr R shows, this is not necessarily the case.

In contrast, let us examine the story of a young man, Mr L, suffering from leukaemia, who had one brother. A major disagreement existed between them, as a result of which they had no contact with each other. The brother was seen as the black sheep of the family, a delinquent. None the less, at the parents' request, the brother agreed to be tested. There was sufficient compatibility—he could become a donor. However, Mr L refused to accept his brother's bone marrow—he would rather die than receive the bone marrow of this brother. Fortunately, another donor was found outside the family and the transplant could take place.

Goldbeter-Merinfeld (2004) reminds us that "relations among siblings are forged over time, through the forced or spontaneous sharing of toys, games, secrets, but also through betrayals and rivalries" (Goldbeter-Merinfeld, 2004, p. 95, translated for this edition).

Meynckens-Fourez (2007) also tells us, "brothers and sisters are people who have not chosen or decided to be the same family and cannot divorce, but sometimes we could say that they separate or get separated one way or another!" (p. 37, translated for this edition).

This situation shows how a related donor is solicited by the family, or by the medical staff. He could be said to be a designated volunteer, a designation of which it is difficult to divest oneself due to family pressure. The situation is different for the unrelated donor, who is always a volunteer. Whoever the donor may be, he is the one on account of whom the continuation of life will be possible, on account of whom a new future can be expected. As a provider of the cells necessary for the medical treatment, he might be exploited. I will not address here the problem of "medical babies", which merits its own workshop.

The cases described here show how the psychological links between siblings determine how the transplantation is experienced, as well as how the "gift" of a donation might provoke various fantasies.

A young man receiving marrow from his sister expressed the fear of becoming a girl, the fear of becoming a little bit like his sister. A crisis of identity is provoked by having another in one's self, in counterpoint to the experience of the donor, whose self is transferred to the other. The crisis of identity in the context of a bone marrow transplant involves a disturbing sense of alienation, not least because it is a cancer treatment. In the context of a family donation, we have here a kind of "uncanny brotherhood". One could go so far as to call it a sense of disturbing filiation.

De M'Uzan (2004) talks of the "psychological chimera" stemming from the encounter of the unconscious psychological activities of participants in an analysis. The effects of this "chimera" provide a means to discover the modalities of the psyche. The consequences of the "chimera" can be dramatic because they lead to the appearance of new and strange morbid identities, while the protagonists' identities become impossible to distinguish. The "psychological chimera", in the context of bone marrow transplant, materialises at a somatic level — we could, in fact, call the process a "psychological transplantation".

One type of somatic rejection is the physical rejection, or GVH (graft *vs.* host). This phenomenon reflects the compatibility of donor and recipient and manifests itself when the stem cells (the "Other") reject the organism into which they have been transplanted. With reference to this phenomenon, de M'Uzan wrote, "it is, so to speak, a reversal of the immunological defence: intolerance is no longer expressed towards the other *by the self per se*, but by the other towards the self inside the self" (de M'Uzan, 2004, p. 13, translated for this edition). This aberration appears to the patient, his relatives, and the care-givers, raising the question of who incorporates whom.

Another aberration has an antic-leukemic effect, constituting an immunological fight to the death involving self and non-self. This phenomenon is called GVL (graft *vs.* leukaemia). The family donor sees the effects of the transplant at first hand, effects which it is hoped are positive, but might also be negative, because a recurrence, a progression, or complications such as GVH cannot be prevented, and this might, in turn, leave the door open to a sense of guilt. On the other hand, when the treatment succeeds, the recipient will struggle with what Ascher and Jouet called "An imaginary debt, unbearable, indefinite, infinite" (Asher & Jouet, 2004a, p. 98).

My DNA, your DNA, for which mutation?

The foregoing treatments disturb the limits between self and other, between self and non-self. These links are also at issue in the case of oncogenetic mutations. Detection of such mutations can only be effected by a comparison with an afflicted, or formerly afflicted, family member. Out of necessity, one must communicate with this person, but such communication is not always straightforward.

One woman who came to me for consultation knew that her only sister had been diagnosed with breast cancer. She, too, wished to be tested, but had broken off her relation with the sister. She could not imagine contacting her, and even thought she would refuse to undergo the diagnostic procedure.

I met another woman, Mrs C, at the request of the geneticist who had just notified her that she was carrying the BRCA1 mutated gene. Mrs C was forty-six and had developed a (left) breast cancer ten years previously and a (right) breast cancer seven years previously. Cancer had occurred among family members over several generations; the need to search for a genetic mutation seemed obvious.

Mrs C is the eldest of a family of four (three girls and one boy). Most of her sisters had been to the geneticist long before Mrs C, because they were concerned and wanted to be tested. Mrs C had difficulty understanding her sisters' anxiety. None the less, under pressure from her sisters, she was encouraged to go for a consultation. The oncologist had long ago recommended it, but she herself did not see the point. She told me her belief that, as the eldest of the siblings, the fact that she had been ill would protect the others from cancer, and so they had nothing more to fear. She seemed to have a magical belief regarding herself and cancer: "I have looked after myself, I have been treated, everything is fine!!!" Nevertheless, she had had two cancers at a young age.

Eventually, the lasting side-effects of long-term treatment make her "take seriously" what had happened: "The treatments are demanding, I didn't do them for nothing." Originally unsure what she was doing in consulting me, in the course of our conversation, she surprises herself—her awareness of the presence of the gene makes her question herself. The verbal disclosure has an impact on her body: she becomes aware that something has actually happened.

She explains her reluctance to be tested as being due to her fear of unbalancing the unity (as she sees it) of her siblings—the results could show that they are not identical. As the eldest sister, she has to protect the cohesion of the sibling group. Yet, her attitude and her speech do not reflect those of her siblings.

She becomes aware during the discussion that if she carries the gene, her brothers and sisters could also carry it. Her image of the family is shaken by the realisation. Portraying herself as the protector of the family was a way of avoiding the thought that the disease could affect the ones for whom she acted like a mother (their actual mother died early) and whom she did not want to lose. This was her protection against an unbearable pain—an unspeakable one, because it implied a possible separation. Maybe now she could start to talk . . .

In fact, if it was discovered that one of the sisters was carrying the mutation, prophylactic measures could be proposed, such as an oophorectomy. However, there are no certainties. Carrying an onco-genetic mutation gives a statistical probability: the risk of developing the disease is increased, but not certain. Similarly, not carrying the mutation does not exclude development of the disease.

This notion of statistical probability has a huge influence for each person on the results of the medical analysis. Notification of the risk has a physical impact—a threatening knowledge is imprinted on the body.

The various prophylactic proposals will serve to highlight for the siblings the differences between them and, therefore, put their cohe-sion to the test.

Take the story of two sisters whose mother died of breast cancer at an early age. While both agreed to be tested, they each had a different attitude towards oophorectomy. For one of them, this should be done immediately after getting the results, if the result was positive. The second wanted to postpone the surgery and even consider a third pregnancy.

This difference was a source of tension between them, which almost led to rupture. Therapy focusing on their differences allowed them to prevent such a rupture, and to understand how they had dif-ferently experienced their mother's illness. A relational distance allowed them to overcome what Caillé calls "fratitude" and to achieve fraternity. Fratitude is, for Caillé, "a state of mimetic competition that involves many dangers . . . the experience of an imposed existential condition for which it is natural to anticipate individual conse-quences". He defines the link between siblings: "it is such as, in essence, acquaintance with and through a historical fact", that is, shar-ing one or two common parents. Fraternity requires "consideration and respect for each other's rights and needs" (Caillé, 2004, p. 12, translated for this edition).

While awaiting the results, the sisters realised that the results might not be the same for both of them—they could both carry the gene, or neither of them, or one but not the other. After several months, the results came back that they were both carriers. Both had an oophorectomy with little delay. For the second, the disclosure of the result materialised the reality of cancer and the need to take steps in order to avoid it.

Fédida, talking about genetics, wrote, "everything related to genetics and procreation constitutes a terribly sensitive inter-human zone, where the most archaic anxieties crystallise and the most enigmatic beliefs are voiced" (Fédida, 1982, p. 41). While the links between the narcissistic and fraternal identification are constantly in flux because of the passage of time, they are also suspended, questioned, and brought to the fore during the search for either a donor or an oncogenetic mutation.

A new aspect of reality—the expression of genetic variety—is revealed to the various siblings through the potential dissimilarity of their individual bodies. This new research-based consciousness that their bodies are not the same will affect them all differently, although the time will also come to put personal feelings aside.

Indeed, the search for an oncogenetic mutation affects the family in its broadest sense. It is more about the generational (vertical) connections than sibling (horizontal) ones, as the patients' questioning shows: who has transmitted it to me, and what have I transmitted? These questions highlight the unique anxieties of the afflicted, all their guilt, anger, and sadness . . . The search for a related donor is carried out among siblings, which means horizontally. It stays within the same generation, raising a less dangerous rivalry, but a more threatening one in terms of identity. That said, due to the mixing of populations, if a donor is not found among siblings, it is more difficult to find one within non-related donors. Consequently, a parent might be called upon, whose compatibility will always be only fifty per cent. In the case where multiple siblings are compatible, the choice of a donor follows a highly standardised procedure based on biological criteria.

In addition, the donor, as the name suggests, actively gives, while the same cannot be said for the transmission of genes. Certainly, there is a potential sharing of status, but does the question of who is incorporating whom apply? As I have already shown, the donation gives rise to anxieties and fantasies.

The search for a genetic match exposes similarities, differences, and raises the question of transmission. DNA becomes a somatic catalogue that emphasises each individual's uniqueness. The donor's uniqueness is queried while the stem cell recipient's is modified; the latter could well quote Rimbaud—"I is someone else" (Rimbaud, 1965, p. 250).

Ultimately, the search for oncogenetic mutation is not an emergency. There are no curative treatments available. As the term "genetic counselling consultation" indicates, the geneticist provides preventive proposals, not curative ones. In contrast, finding a donor is carried out with some urgency and is meant to be therapeutic.

Conclusions

A lot more could be said on this topic, given the complexity of the situations we have to face. A biological family portrait established by research is very different from the family narrative each member builds according to the singularity of his or her history, of the course of his or her family life. New knowledge concerning the body will change the relation the patient has with him- or herself, with others, and, particularly, with siblings during the search for a donor. Somatic bonds as well as the psychological bonds between the siblings will be questioned or even undermined. Revelations might lead the siblings to be seen as a source of danger. Enmity between brothers or within the clan show how relations are both somatic and psychological, but on both levels it is a matter of life and death.

References

Ascher, J., & Jouet, J. P. (2004a). Les mondes paradoxaux de la greffe de moëlle osseuse [The paradoxical universes of bone marrow transplantation]. In: *La greffe entre biologie et psychanalyse* [Transplantation Between Biology and Psychoanalysis] (pp. 87–118). Paris: Presses Universitaires de France.

Caillé, P. (2004). Fratries sans fraternité [Siblings without siblinghood]. *Cahiers Critiques de Thérapie Familiale et de Pratiques de réseaux, 32*: 11–22.

De M'Uzan, M. (2004). Préface. In: J. Ascher, & J. P. Jouet, *La greffe entre biologie et psychanalyse* [Transplantation Between Biology and Psychoanalysis] (pp. 7–15). Paris: Presses Universitaires de France.

Fédida, P. (1982). La clinique psychanalytique en présence de la référence génétique [Psychoanalytical practice concerning genetic issues]. In:

P. Fédida, J. Guyotat, J.-M. Robert (Eds.), *Génétique clinique et psycho-pathologique, hérédité psychique et hérédité biologique* [The Clinic and Psychopathology in Genetics, Physical Heredity and Biological Heredity] (pp. 36–50). Villeurbanne: Simep.

Freud, S. (1914c). On narcissism: an introduction. *S.E., 14*: 67–102. London: Hogarth.

Goldbeter-Merinfeld, E. (2004). Frères et sœurs au croisement des temps et des lieux [Siblings at the crossroads of time and place]. *Cahiers Critiques de Thérapie Familiale et de Pratiques de Réseaux, 32*: 91–104.

Meynckens-Fourez, M. (2007). La fratrie, le point de vue éco-systémique [Siblings, the eco-systemic point of view]. In: E. Tilmans-Ostyne, & M. Meynckens-Fourez (Eds.), *Les ressources de la Fratrie* [Siblinghood Resources] (pp. 37–68). Paris: Eres.

Rimbaud, A. (1965). Lettre à Paul Demeny, 15 mai 1871[Letter to Paul Demeny, 15 May 1871]. In: *Oeuvres completes* [Collected Works] (pp. 267–274). Paris: NRF de la Pléiade.

Winnicott, D. W. (1957). *The Child and the Family*. London: Tavistock.

PART III

LOSS OF A SIBLING

CHAPTER TEN

The transgenerational pattern of trauma transmission

Prophecy Coles

I have recently written a book exploring the unconscious transmission of intergenerational trauma, *The Uninvited Guest of The Unremembered Past*, published by Karnac in August 2011. One chapter explores the theme of an unremembered dead sibling. For instance, the death of Freud's mother's brother, Julius, one month before Freud's brother Julius died. Similarly, André Green's mother's younger sister was burned to death in an accidental fire at his birth. The impact of the unexamined losses of maternal siblings upon Freud and Green might add to Freud's concept of the death drive and Green's chilling landscape of the Dead Mother.

I explore the clinical case of a middle-aged woman, Muriel. When she was seven, her father died on his return from the Second World War. In her internal world, he is a stranger. We discover that she had lived in a "secret identification" with her father's dead brother, who had died a hero in the First World War. The fantasies that this dead brother had had upon Muriel are unravelled. Significantly, Muriel's father had lived under the shadow of this "heroic" brother. Muriel's grandparents had idealised their dead son and Muriel's father felt an angry failure in comparison. Gradually, Muriel's "secret identification" with her dead uncle wanes and she feels devastation when her father dies. Most movingly, an unconscious fantasy reveals that she believed that, by becoming the uncle, she could alleviate her father's pain at his sibling loss and comfort her grandparents for the loss of their son.

The trauma of a sibling death across the generations

In this chapter, I want to concentrate on a theme that emerged from my most recent book, mentioned above, which is the effect of an unremembered dead sibling upon subsequent generations. In my previous book, *The Importance of Sibling Relationships in Psychoanalysis*, I had wondered why, in the UK, but not, I hasten to add, in the USA, there had been an absence of interest in the importance of sibling relationships. As I pursued that question, I became convinced that sibling relationships help to structure the inner world and facilitate the growth of the infant mind.

Once I had argued for the recognition of the imprint of sibling relationships within the inner world, I began to wonder if there might be other figures who were jostling for a voice in the consulting room. As I thought about these ghostly figures, I became more alert to their presence both in my analytic work and in the biographies of some significant psychoanalysts. For instance, in reading some of the biographies and articles that have been written on Freud, I found the following facts (Krull, 1982). When Freud was a few months old, his mother conceived his brother, Julius, and Julius was born when Freud was seventeen months old. Julius died six months later (Gay, 1988; Jones, 1953; Krull, 1982). Various psychoanalysts have suggested that the death of Freud's brother has haunted psychoanalytic theory (Mitchell, 2000; Raphael-Leff, 1990). Raphael-Leff wrote that this death "remained encapsulated as an unprocessed wordless area of prehistoric deathly rivalry and identification" (1990, p. 325).

I want to suggest that another contribution to this "unprocessed wordless area of prehistoric deathly rivalry and identification" that has haunted psychoanalytic theory was the death of Freud's uncle Julius. This death was one month before the death of Freud's brother Julius. Freud's uncle was his mother's younger brother, and he was twenty. It is not hard to imagine that Freud's mother, Amalia, was shocked and depressed by these two deaths. We know that she had named her second son after her brother and this seems to suggest a close relation between the two siblings, Amalia and her brother, though I have no written record to confirm that intuition. It is this double sibling death, across two generations, which I believe haunts Freud's psychoanalytic theory: the death of Freud's mother's brother Julius and Freud's brother Julius, not just the death of Freud's brother. Furthermore, it is these two unexamined deaths that help in part to explain the absence of any theory about the importance of sibling relationships in the body of Freudian metapsychology.

The importance of the maternal state of mind upon her child is increasingly well documented (Gerhardt, 2005; Green, 1983; Murray, 1992; Schore, 2002; Stern, 1985; Trevarthen, 2008, to name but few). However, it was surprising to discover that an important contributor to the debate about the effect of the maternal state of mind upon her child, André Green, had suffered the same two-generation sibling death as Freud. In his paper, "The dead mother", Green describes in chilling detail the way a depressed mother entombs her child in a deathly universe for the rest of its life. In an interview in 1999 with Gregorio Kohon, Green tells him that at the time of his birth his mother's sister was burned to death in a fire. Two years later, his older sister had to be hospitalised in Paris—they lived in Alexandria—for four years and Green's mother would be frequently absent as she visited her ill daughter. Green suggested that his mother's absence when he was two probably played an important part in giving emotional significance to his theory about the effects that a depressed and absent mother could have upon her child. I want to suggest to you that his mother must have been depressed already when he was born, because of the death of her sister. In other words, it was not the loss of the maternal mind when he was two, but an already devastated maternal state of mind that haunts his theory of "The dead mother" and chills us to the marrow.

Why do I think these two sibling deaths are significant and need to be recognised? I am suggesting that these two sibling deaths have influenced the trajectory of the psychoanalytic theories of both Freud and Green and, therefore, of many others. In the case of Freud, he was led to postulate the idea of a death drive, or instinct, as an explanation for "prehistoric" and intractable mental states that psychoanalysis could not shift. That is to say, when analysis met an immovable resistance, then the death drive was the force that was creating this roadblock. For Green, we come up against a similar immobility in the unconscious mind. A depressed mother entombs her child in a deathless universe from which there is little escape. I want to suggest to you that a route can sometimes be taken around these road-blocks that we all meet in therapy if we allow ourselves to imagine there might be a ghost haunting the present impasse. This ghost, or unmourned death, might need to be recognised before there can be any further psychological movement within the therapy. In the case of Freud and Green, their mothers' dead siblings haunt their theories through the concepts of the death drive, or "The dead mother", and we are blocked.

It is the thought of the two dead siblings in Freud's and Green's families that leads me to a clinical example of a woman whom I have called Muriel. I came to believe she lived in an encapsulated "secret identification" with her dead uncle, her father's brother, whom she had never known. This "secret identification" with her dead uncle was, she imagined, a means of restoring her dying and depressed father to a state of well being, as well as comforting her for the loss of her father. However, as her presenting symptoms showed, she was blocked from a creative life of her own.

Before I detail the course of our therapy, I need to say that my understanding of Muriel's "secret identification" was influenced by the work of Kestenberg (1972, 1975, 1980; Kestenberg & Kestenberg, 1982) and many others who have written on survivors of the Holocaust, such as Bergman and Jucovy (1982), Grubrich-Simitis (1981), and Krystal (1978). They showed the way that children pick up their parents suffering, even if the parents never talk about their experiences. More important for what I am arguing today is the idea that children can set about trying to make their parents better by a "secret identification" with a dead relative whom the parents had lost and could not speak about. This "secret identification" is meant to serve as a comfort to the bereaved parent. It is as though the child believes it can really bring the dead person back into life, through becoming the dead person. This delusion is fuelled by a fantasy that in becoming the lost grandparent or lost sibling, the grieving parent would be restored to happiness. Of course, this "secret identification" has deathly consequences for the "heroic" child. Did Freud have a fantasy that if he could become his uncle Julius his mother might be comforted? Did Green believe that as a mere boy he could not comfort his mother for the loss of her sister?

To return to Muriel, she came to see me because, entering her forties, she wished to have a child but could not manage to form a close relation with a man. The transference experience with Muriel revealed an uneasy relation with her mother that in turn reflected her mother's early history. Muriel's mother, whom I shall call Ruth, was born in 1913, just before the outbreak of the First World War. She was the oldest child. There followed, quite quickly after the war had begun in 1914, a sister who was sickly and needed a lot of maternal care. Ruth's father—that is to say, Muriel's grandfather—signed up but did not return from that war. He was never referred to again in Ruth's family. So, here is the first death that I believe was secretly hidden in Muriel's inner world, a grandfather who had been left in an unmarked grave. Muriel's grandmother never spoke about her husband and, as a result, Ruth could not mention her father. The sibling death that we were to discover was still not near conscious thought at this stage.

I then learnt more about Ruth and the traumas that both she and Muriel had suffered. Ruth had married a soldier, and, two years after Muriel was born, the Second World War erupted. Muriel's father was captured early on in the war and survived the ferocious experience of a concentration camp in the Far East. He returned when Muriel was seven, a damaged man physically and mentally, and he died soon after. His photograph was hung on a wall, but Muriel could not find any emotional attachment to him. He was a stranger or an unknown relative whose lifeless portrait she passed each day.

In spite of all this historic knowledge about the traumas that had beset Muriel's family, the therapy was lifeless and dead. Nothing seemed to animate Muriel into a state of hope or expectation. I dreaded our "dead" sessions. Throughout this time, however, something outside the therapy was going on in Muriel's internal world, though as yet there were no words to describe what this might be. Muriel began to read Pat Barker's trilogy *Regeneration*, about the First World War, and our sessions were filled with Muriel's obsession with these books. I could not understand the extent of Muriel's passion for them. What was she really trying to tell me as she spoke about the heroes in these books? I found myself asking her one day if there was someone else who had been left out, unnoticed, in Muriel's own family. Muriel's reply was to bring a photograph of a paternal uncle whom she had never known, but whose portrait she had constantly looked at because it had hung on the wall beside her father. He was her father's much older brother who had been killed in the First World War.

This photograph had the most powerful effect upon the dynamics of the therapy. It was as though he had brought some life into the consulting room, or another way of putting it might be to say that the therapy woke up from its deathly slumber. Muriel knew that this uncle had been a war hero and that her father had lived under his shadow. However, what neither of us knew then was that in bringing the photograph, she was beginning to discover a lost bit of herself that had been identified in a "deathly embrace" with her uncle.

The new liveliness in the therapy heralded a sibling transference between Muriel and myself. We became like sisters—she was an only child—engaged in a fascinating task of understanding the older generation. I became in her fantasy the sister she had longed for, and with whom she could share the secrets of her family, out of earshot of her mother. It was this shift in the transference that helped me to think about the parallel sibling relation between Muriel's father and her uncle. We began imagining her father and his brother together and what they might have felt about each other. Gradually, Muriel came within reach of wondering about the impact of her uncle's death upon her grandparents and her father.

A new and enormously important shift in the therapy followed the sibling transference. Muriel became extremely angry with her family and with me. She said she was fed up with all her family and not least this seemingly heroic uncle. He had trapped them all and she hated her grandparents for idealising him. She shouted, "No one has been able to move from the hallowed ground he seemed to stand upon." In her mind, she wanted to wrench his portrait down from the wall where it hung beside her father's, and she wanted to leave therapy, for I was causing her extreme distress. This liveliness and passion that was displayed in the therapy for the first time encouraged me and led me to suggest to her that her intense feelings about her uncle showed us that her father was still alive in her mind.

Painfully and reluctantly, she began to wonder if she had blocked off any feeling about her father's death because of his abrupt departure. Once she could imagine she might have had some feelings about her father, she could begin to think about the sort of man her father might have been and eventually to wonder about the effect the death of her uncle might have had upon her father psychically. She could begin to cry as she thought about her father's grief at the death of his brother, and, from this circuitous route, she began to experience her hidden grief that had followed her father's death.

As we entered the foothills of Muriel's grief for her dead father, I had a disconcerting response to Muriel's material. I had seen the photograph of the dead uncle, and he was undoubtedly a handsome figure who had been tragically killed in the prime of his life, but I was now filled with a rage, similar to that which Muriel had brought a few sessions before, when she had wanted to tear up the photograph of her uncle and walk out of therapy. I also felt I wanted to tear his portrait off the wall. What was consuming me? Who was this uncle for Muriel? I thought about the work that had been done with Holocaust survivors and wondered if Muriel had filled the "hole" or "gap" in her psyche, as a result of her father's premature death with a secret alliance with her uncle. Was I wanting to crack open this secret alliance with my violent fantasies? Did the idea of a secret alliance with her uncle provide a clue to the difficulty she had in imagining she could be a wife and mother? Were they secretly entombed together, uncle and niece? As I tried to bring my intense feelings under control, I realised that one reason I wanted to tear the portrait off the wall was the fantasy that this would comfort Muriel's father. I felt sure that Muriel's father had died in a condition of defeat. Not only had he been defeated by the injuries he had suffered during the Second World War, but I could imagine he had died under the shadow of the portrait of his "heroic" brother. In his parents' eyes, he could never replace his "heroic" brother or even comfort them for their loss.

We were now entering the final stages of our understanding about the effect her father's dead brother had had upon the whole family. Her father had died depressed by his horrific injuries, but also in a more profound state of psychological despair. He had never been able to replace his "heroic" dead brother in his parents' eyes. Muriel had intuitively and unconsciously picked up her father's state of mind and, in her own "heroic" way, tried to find a way to console her father and, of course, herself. Like many of the children of survivors of the Holocaust, she carried an unconscious delusion that if she could find a way of becoming her uncle, then her father and her grandparents would be comforted. Muriel's secret identification with her dead uncle also, as we gradually discovered, protected her from her own grief, hence her rage with me and her uncle when this timeless fantasy began to crack apart. Her uncle had been her "safe" and eternal hero, and by "safe" I want to indicate that Muriel had invested him with a meaning that could remain secret from her mother. This uncle never left her. He lived eternally and unchanging in her mind until she began to tell me about him.

When Muriel ended the therapy, we both agreed that her unconscious identification with her dead uncle had imprisoned her. It had been a "heroic" act on her part, born out of her fervent wish to comfort her father. Understanding something of the complexity of this unconscious fantasy, she came to see that she had been held in a deathly embrace of unacknowledged grief and rage, occasioned by two world wars, that had stretched back at least three generations on both sides of her family. We were both grateful to the photograph of her uncle, for he had helped us to think about the place he held in her family and, in turn, this allowed Muriel to begin to feel the sadness of her father's early death. Her feelings about her mother shifted once she could imagine her mother's unacknowledged grief for her father—Muriel's maternal grandfather. Finally, she felt less angry with her paternal grandparents for their idealisation of their "heroic" son. Her family no longer needed rescuing from their suffering or protecting from her rage and she could begin to imagine a life of her own.

As I said at the beginning of this clinical example, I came to understand that Muriel had lived in an encapsulated "secret identification" with her dead uncle, her father's brother, whom she had never known. This "secret identification" with her dead uncle was, she imagined, a means of restoring her dying and depressed father to a state of well being, as well as comforting her for the loss of her father. However, as her presenting symptoms showed, this "secret identification" had blocked her from a creative life of her own. Had something similar gone on for both Freud and Green as they struggled to make sense of their mothers' minds?

References

Barker, P. (1993). *Regeneration*. Harmondsworth: Penguin.

Bergman, M. S., & Jucovy, M. E. (1982). *Generations of the Holocaust*. New York: Basic Books.

Coles, P. (2011). *The Uninvited Guest from the Unremembered Past*. London: Karnac.

Gay, P. (1988). *Freud. A Life for our Times*. London: J. M. Dent.

Gerhardt, S. (2004). *Why Love Matters*. London: Routledge.

Green, A. (1983). The dead mother. In: *On Private Madness* (pp. 142–174). London: Rebus.

Grubrich-Simitis, I. (1981). Extreme traumatisation as cumulative trauma: psychoanalytic investigation on the effects of concentration camp experiences on survivors and their children. *Psychoanalytic Study of the Child, 36*: 415–450.

Jones, E. (1953). *Sigmund Freud: A Life & Work. 3 Vols*. London: Hogarth.

Kestenberg, J. S. (1972). Psychoanalytic contributions to the problem of children of survivors from the Nazi persecution. *Israel Annals of Psychiatry and Related Disciplines, 10*: 311–325.

Kestenberg, J. S. (1975). *Children and Parents. Psychoanalytic Studies in Development*. New York: Jason Aronson.

Kestenberg, J. S. (1980). Psychoanalysis of children of survivors from the holocaust: case presentation and assessment. *Journal of the American Psychoanalytic Association, 28*: 775–804.

Kestenberg, J. S., & Kestenberg, M. (1982). *Generations of the Holocaust*. New York: Basic Books.

Kohon, G. (Ed.) (1999). *The Dead Mother. The Work of André Green*. New York: Routledge.

Krull, M. (1982). *Freud & His Father*, A. J. Pomerans (Trans.). London: Hutchinson.

Krystal, H. (1978). Trauma and affects. *Psychoanalytic Study of the Child, 33*: 81–116.

Mitchell, J. (2000). *Mad Men and Medusas. Reclaiming Hysteria and the Effect of Sibling Relations on the Human Condition*. London: Penguin Press.

Murray, L. (1992). The impact of post-natal depression on infant development. *Journal of Child Psychology & Psychiatry, 33*(3): 543–561.

Raphael-Leff, J. (1990). If Oedipus was an Egyptian. *International Review of Psychoanalysis, 17*(3): 309–337.

Schore, A. N. (2002). Advances in neuropsychoanalysis, attachment theory, and trauma research: implications for self-psychology. *Psychoanalytic Inquiry, 22*: 433–484.

Stern, D. N. (1985). *The Interpersonal World of the Child. A View from Psychoanalysis and Developmental Psychology*. New York: Basic Books.

Trevarthen, C. (2008). *Thought in Motion. Interdisciplinary Approaches to Mind and Body. Lecture at Tavistock Centre, 5–6 September*. New York: Analytic Press.

CHAPTER ELEVEN

A sister is being murdered

Sarah Mandow and Alison Knight-Evans

I n his seminal paper, "Mourning and melancholia", Freud (1917e) mapped out the terrain of the already disturbed or fragile mind when it is confronted with an experience of overwhelming loss. He clearly distinguishes this internal state of affairs that he calls melancholia from the process of mourning, a painful, energy-consuming, but ultimately life-orientated task. In melancholia, the response becomes inward looking, an attack on the ego that weakens rather than develops psychic functioning. Klein (1955) contributed the concept of projective identification, which can explain the way in which a fragile ego cannot face the damage done by the attacks to itself and its objects, splits off the bad feelings, and experiences them not as loss of a good object, but as the presence of something malign. This terrifying, unwanted part of the ego is projected into the other and controlled and defended against as if it were a completely separate entity.

The seeds of melancholia are sown in infancy and both theories recognise the centrality of the infant's tie to his/her maternal object to the ability to develop a robust enough capacity for taking in both good and bad experiences from the primary care-giver and for good to prevail. More recently, Mitchell (2000) has argued that just as important, but almost entirely neglected in psychoanalytic theory, is the relation to, and experience of, siblinghood and its centrality in forming identity. The child is faced with the annihilation of its place with the arrival of siblings.

Freud (1917e) describes the way the loss of the object is transformed into ego loss, a loss of the self, and is then subjected to not just a highly critical internal judge, but a cruel and murderous one. Although he is talking about the actual loss of an external figure, it is implied that at the root of all unmourned losses that are reactivated, it is the loss of the primary object, usually the mother, that is at the heart of it. In Mitchell's version, a murder symbolically happens when the child is no longer the special one and its place is taken by another. She argues that the arrival of the Oedipus complex, and the child's wish to kill the father who possesses the mother and is responsible for the sibling, is of secondary importance to the need to eliminate the usurper:

> On the advent of a younger sibling, the subject is displaced, deposed and without the place that was hers or his: s/he must change utterly in relation to both the rest of the family and the outside world ... Another baby replaces the baby one was until this moment. Henceforth, a craving for love together with a love/hatred of excessive proximity, construct a fragile psyche. (Mitchell, 2000)

In his paper, "Who is killing what or whom?", Bell (2000) makes the point that underlying all suicides and similar acts of self-destruction there is an attack upon the self that is a self identified with a hated object. The attack is simultaneously an attack upon the object and a punishment of the self for such sadistic and cruel attacks upon the object.

An assumption that seems to be implicit in all these ideas that we want to explore is that there is no significant difference in terms of the impact to the psyche between an actual external loss of a person through death and the psychic death that results from symbolic losses. Taking Mitchell's view of the sibling trauma into account means that the issue is not just loss, but murder: "The child who was the infant as baby had its emergent self annihilated – it is no longer what it had been: the baby. Its first response was not jealousy nor rivalry – but the wish to kill" (Mitchell, 2000).

On the other hand, the child is also excited by the discovery of someone so like themselves that there is also a strong wish for a replica self. Mitchell identifies this as the source of the powerful love–hate ambivalence and the tension between deadly rivalry and intense identification with the other.

This chapter explores some of these issues through the connecting theme of siblings and murder, but from two different sets of circumstances. The first is from work with two patients being seen in private practice, for whom the symbolic murder of the sibling is a constant theme in their internal worlds, where it has not been possible to relinquish the infantile grievance by growing up, where previous losses and murderous wishes prevail. They cannot resolve their ambivalent feelings towards their sister, and instead their impossible love–hate way of relating results in switching constantly between murderous rivalry and identification with the sibling (Bell, 2000). This dynamic split operates through the denial, which can sometimes be best described as "wilful" (to allow for the preconscious elements), rather than simply conscious, of the sister's existence.

The other set of circumstances derives from the somewhat unusual and arbitrary occurrence of three unconnected women in different National Health Service (NHS) inpatient settings, each of whom had suffered the traumatic loss of a sister—two through murder and the third through suicide. Although these bereavements are, in themselves, deeply traumatic, all three women and their siblings had backgrounds of systematic sexual abuse in childhood.

A comparison was undertaken of some of the key dynamics in these cases with those previously mentioned where the sisters are still living. The effects of trauma and loss related to the death of a sibling can be seen to have undergone subtle and sometimes dramatic changes to the psychic terrain of these already vulnerable patients, compared with those who have not suffered the ultimate loss, with some unexpected, contrasting outcomes.

The comparison of these two related, but quite different, sets of circumstances gave rise to the question of whether there are any distinguishing aspects in the dynamics of the theory outlined above when applied to symbolic and actual murder in loss of a sibling. While it would be beyond the scope of this chapter and the expertise of its authors to give an informed answer as to the importance, we took this opportunity to investigate whether there are any distinguishing features between the two situations and we found some interesting and not necessarily predictable differences. They are observations of a tiny handful of cases and, therefore, do not make any claims to generalise, or to give any definitive answers. All personal details have been altered to protect patient confidentiality.

Murder as phantasy

Anne was in her thirties and was in private psychotherapy for about a year. When her mother was pregnant with her sister, Beatrice, three years younger, Anne's father had left the family home and she had never seen him since. Another, much younger, man moved in immediately. Anne felt he favoured Beatrice and bullied Anne in quite a subtle, menacing way, with mind games. She believed there was no direct sexual abuse, but she felt miserable and uncomfortable around him. She had recurring dreams of being chased by him with nowhere to hide, suggesting a sense of the lack of containment she has experienced and her longing for a secure attachment figure.

Anne's phantasy was that *he* was the father of her sister. This phantasy wiped out her sister as rival and distorted the relation in her mind to maintain her unique position in her internal family. The Freudian view of murderous oedipal wishes is less salient here than Juliet Mitchell's argument that it is the sister, the usurper, who has to be eliminated. Murder is in the air, although it is her father who has disappeared.

She described her mother as very unstable, many men moved in and out of her life, and she saw her sister as the spoilt "princess" in the family. It seemed that little was expected of her, while Anne became the "parentified" child who felt responsible for everyone. She received recognition through this role, while feeling enormously resentful. She did well at school and continued to be successful in her working life, funding her mother and her sister when they ran out of money, compelled to meet their needs. This is an example of how her excessive emotional greed was projected into her sister and her mother, who were infantilised, and, thus, identified as the mother, she was no longer the displaced sibling.

She had issues around food and weight and described herself as manipulative. Her rivalrous need was to be perfect in all ways, thus to wipe out all other numerous Beatrices in her mind.

Her dreams often contained violence, fear of losing people, and of dying. She brought a dream shortly after being given the summer holiday dates and a change of day and time:

She arrived, unsure about the time and found no one at my consulting room. Then two people came out of the other room—then she was with me, but Beatrice was also there, playing on her mobile. She had interpreted the change of her appointment as someone else (Beatrice) being put in her place.

She became very angry and jealous towards Beatrice, who was going off on holiday but did not have enough money, so Anne was prevailed upon by their mother to give her what she needed. Anne longed for a holiday in the sun but was frightened of flying, convinced that the plane would crash. She had a dream at this time of urgently pushing Beatrice on to a plane. Knowing her own terror of flying, she recognised this as her own murderous phantasy—Beatrice had always got exactly what she wanted and Anne longed to be able to be as carefree and irresponsible as her sister.

While Beatrice was on her exotic holiday, Anne dreamt that she herself was in somewhere like Jurassic Park and that there were spitting dinosaurs all around her. Her T-shirt was drenched with their venom. She was amused by her interpretation of her dream and acknowledged her venomous feelings towards all women who might in any way displace her, and also towards me, who sees other patients besides herself. What was also apparent was her own drive towards self destruction—an identification with the sister who has to be destroyed.

A constantly recurring dream was of being in something like a war zone and desperately trying to rescue her mother and her sister, together with dogs and cats; she was trying to get them to a safe place and there was a huge red bomb chasing after her. This was clearly about her rage, of which she was unable to let go. She did express some of her feelings within the family, but controlled most of her anger for fear of its intensity and fear that it would destroy everyone and everything. She knew she needed her family until she had managed to create a family of her own, which would be very different from the one she was born into.

Anne's real longing was to have a baby. She found it very difficult to be around any woman who was either pregnant or who had a baby.

Her phantasy was that a baby of her own would belong totally to her and that somehow, through this baby, she herself could have the childhood she longs for. The baby would be a replacement for herself.

Beatrice was experienced by Anne as intrusive and greedy, the beloved baby gobbling up all the good that was available. Her solution was to have a baby of her own. This wished-for replica self can be seen as an attempt to resolve her ambivalence towards her sister. She was unable to mourn for what she had never had, and her envy of others together with her fear of losing them created a state of mind that felt unbearably unsafe. She attacked herself rather than risk destroying, and thus losing, others.

Cathy provides another example of unresolved ambivalence towards her sister, Diana, who was two years older. Cathy was in her early forties, married with two daughters and pregnant with her third child. She was seen in private psychotherapy twice weekly for about seven years. Cathy had been told she was "a mistake" and that her father had wanted her to be a boy. She described an anxious childhood. Her parents quarrelled a lot and her father would sulk for days, so that she had to tiptoe around him, terrified. They finally divorced when she left for university, but she was not told. She came "home" for the Christmas holidays to find her home gone and her parents separated.

She hardly mentioned her sister for the first few months in therapy and seemed to have had little to do with her while they were growing up, although she said they were quite close when they were little. She saw Diana as having grabbed all the goodness of the family while she, herself, was left out in the cold, although some of that had been of her own choosing: she had moved away rather than voice her needs, hoping that someone would have noticed her distress. She had been anorectic throughout her adolescence and later had more or less cut herself off from her family, her sister in particular. They had kept in touch by texting but this was a cover for Cathy's rage at how Diana had moved into the family environment with her two-year-old daughter and taken over—in particular, taken over their mother. Cathy felt displaced/eliminated and, in her rage, had eliminated her sister—an identification with the usurper who had deposed her.

She tried hard to avoid difficult feelings; for example, she rigidly reported the chronology of her week to maintain a safe distance from more threatening feelings. In her art class, she was encouraged to sketch every day spontaneously, but not to use an eraser. She found this almost impossible. This metaphor for rubbing out anything disturbing in her life seemed to originate in the sibling trauma.

The atmosphere in the consulting room with Cathy was like walking on eggshells. She was quick to pick up on any lack of attunement, leaving her therapist with an acute sense of having let her down, but also a feeling that there was space for only one person in the room. Her need for constant attention was overwhelming. She invariably arrived late for her sessions, which was understood to express the phantasy that there were no other patients. She made sure that whoever might have been before her would be gone, in order to eliminate any rivals. She brought a wish to have been a happy child, together with an almost unbearable anxiety and sadness, haunted by ghosts from the past. She was terrified of any awareness of her anger, so she turned it all against herself. She was afraid it would alienate people from her, and she was envious of others who enjoyed family warmth in a way she could not.

It seemed that she felt there was only room for one baby in her mother's mind and Diana had apparently claimed that place. Hence, she withdrew in a silent rage, as her father had done. She lived in a perpetual state of anxiety. She was adamant that, after she had had the baby, she would not bring it with her, as she would resent having to share the therapeutic space. So, she would "kill off" her own baby rather than risk losing her place with her therapist. She brought a dream in which

> . . . she was with others in a kind of fortress where a film was being shown. It contained a lot of very nasty violence, but the main character was wearing a mask. On the other side of the room real murder and torture were taking place, mirroring the film but "real". She fled, fearing either becoming a victim or a witness, but, perhaps significantly, not the perpetrator.

The infantile grievance could not be relinquished; her ambivalent feelings towards her sister could not be resolved, resulting in her impossible love–hate way of relating. She could only switch between murderous rivalry and identification with her sister, rather than recognise her need for her and allow the development of a healthy dependence.

Murder as fact

Three clinical examples are derived from psychoanalytic work in various inpatient therapeutic settings over a number of years.

Emma and Fiona had sisters who were murdered and the sister of the third woman, Geraldine, committed suicide, which is, of course, murder of a particular kind. Although the shocking nature of the losses had been prominent among the antecedents given by professionals making the referral to treatment centres, in all cases the patients themselves for a long time volunteered little or nothing about their dead sisters unless asked. An example of the extreme guilt associated with rivalry was evident in the case of Emma, who had been devoted and tireless in her efforts to find a publisher for her dead sister's manuscript. She was eventually successful and, when the posthumous novel was due to be published, she organised the launch party, meticulously planning to make sure it was a "perfect" occasion. She provided the food and drink, as well as comfort and solace afterwards. Then, when friends and family gratefully departed, she went back to her flat and attempted to take her own life.

She recalled in the therapy the feeling of utter abandonment that had come over her, that no one had asked her whether she was all right to be on her own; they had only been thinking of the dead sister, not the living one. She, too, had been merged with the dead sister and if she had succeeded in killing herself she would have "wiped out" the massive impact on the parents of the dead sister. She said that her parents had never been interested in the effect of the sister's death on her, only their own loss. In effect, she felt invisible, annihilated, and bereft.

The symbiotic nature of the identification, by which I mean the phantasy of two functioning as one ego, was also evident in the unthinking way she chose that particular occasion to try to kill herself, as well as elements of revenge and self-sacrifice.

Fiona began to talk late on in her therapy about how she had felt at the time that both she and her murdered sister were entering treatment. She was prone to trying to kill herself by suffocation, to the point of losing consciousness. This mirrored how her sister's husband had ended her sister's life, but was never consciously acknowledged by Fiona herself. Again, the murderous revenge is simultaneously an attack on the sister for abandoning her, an expression of a symbiotic identification, and an act of punishment on herself for still being alive, although the two-in-one aspect of her phantasy could later be understood as an unconscious denial of the reality of the actual murder.

For the third example, Geraldine, whose half-sister had committed suicide, the severe emotional neglect in the family had led to the sisters finding comfort in mutual masturbation. Geraldine had a close relation with her grandmother, with whom, in her late teens, she moved in, while her half-sister remained in the family home. The grandmother was seriously ill when Geraldine was admitted for treatment. She repeatedly said that if her grandmother died, she would kill herself. The significance of this came to light gradually, in that, prior to the suicide, Geraldine had, for the first time, stood up to her sister's demand for sexual gratification from her by putting her seriously ill grandmother's needs first. Tragically, her sister that night took an overdose and died. Geraldine's belief was confused: had she not tended to her grandmother instead, her sister would still be alive; her grandmother had been transferred to a specialist treatment setting that offered a small possibility of a remission, and this brought up a great many issues for Geraldine, not least that it let her off the hook in some ways. If her grandmother died, then she would face the wrath of the dead sister: there would be nothing between them except a rejection of the sexual body and she was consumed day and night by a primitive fear of retribution from her sibling.

This unconscious denial of the sister's death emerged more clearly late in treatment. For Emma, she described having created an internal split to deal with the trauma. She summed up the phantasy thus: "I was very good at behaving as if I was facing something and coping with it when actually a bigger part of me is still in a dream world where it isn't happening and therefore I feel safe."

I think it is worth noting the change of tense from past to continuous present, as in "it isn't happening". Cause and effect has been suspended, internal and external worlds are indistinguishable and a state of untested unreality has to be maintained at all costs. The purpose of "it isn't happening" is to avoid the reality of "it has happened", and the sister is gone forever. So, conversely, a sister is being murdered, which also means it can never be put in the past and, therefore, needs to be defended against continuously and forever.

Thus, a sense of safety is achieved by appeasing the guilt towards the dead sister by retreating into a state of being neither alive nor dead and this played a significant part in allowing these patients to take refuge in the inpatient treatment in the first place, but, once the ending of the treatment became palpable, then the enclave of false safety began to break down and often resulted in a brief acute phase before the recovery stage began. The ending of treatment can often serve as a very powerful therapeutic tool in itself. It is something known about by both parties—therapist and patient—from the beginning and, therefore, cannot be masochistically controlled through being distorted or perverted into a deliberate act of cruelty forced upon her.

For Geraldine, the crisis also coincided with her grandmother's illness becoming terminal. At the level of unconscious phantasy, this appeased the dead sister for whose death Geraldine felt responsible, so losing her grandmother was a punishment for that. Yet, because she had been the reason for rejecting the dead sister's sexual body, by losing the parental role of grandmother's carer, there was now no reason not to give her sister what she wanted. However, external reality was now impacting on her internal world and it was, at times, extremely moving to witness Geraldine's struggle to acknowledge her own wish to live and the internal crisis around her sister that it created. She became angry because staff and patients wanted to include her in a short holiday away from the Unit, but she had always gone on holidays with her sister. It did not take much to reveal that the anger was now because she wanted to enjoy the holiday with the others and resented the part of her that felt she "belonged" to the sister, although she was terrified of admitting it. So much so that for some while until this dynamic could be fully understood and interpreted, she suffered excruciating hallucinations of her sister at the foot of her bed, admonishing her or beckoning to her, she was never sure which.

As the more adult part of her grew, so the hallucinations diminished. She could then begin to talk about the sexual involvement with her sister and how it had served many purposes, not least to modify and control their envious rivalry over who got father's attention. Finding at last the courage to say clearly what did happen and what did not was an indication of giving up the mindless state in which she merged with her sister and lost touch with reality.

Fiona, at times, sank into a deep depression, but she also had a version of the merged state that serves to avoid or deny reality. Since her sister's murder, the event had been "untouchable", as she put it.

Nothing had meaning for her; any attempt by the therapist to offer meaning was forcibly rejected as crass and futile, or, if it did touch her, she felt subsumed by the interpretation. Her sister was "the only one", as she put it, and she continued to keep her sister's phone number on her mobile and would scroll through to her name for comfort.

When Emma reached the point of being able to accept her sister's death through the acceptance of the end of treatment, she had also begun police proceedings against the priest who had sexually abused her and her sister in childhood. She became more confident and articulate through the gruelling process of long police interviews and her recall of events and her sense of clarity grew substantially.

Geraldine was able to face the death of her grandmother in a thoughtful way, managing to say her goodbyes and to be present at her grandmother's bedside through the final hours. She had also gone to the police about a social worker who abused her when she was a child in care and was beginning to understand and show concern that she might have left many other young people at risk.

Fiona, whose bouts of depression and idealisation of her soulmate sister persisted, did not reach the same point of acceptance and after treatment she joined a team of laboratory technicians committed to developing more effective resuscitation instruments.

Conclusion

This chapter has tried to show and explain the observation of some transformations that take place in the fragile psyche when a powerful phantasy of murder of the hated and loved sibling has become a reality. Where the wish to murder the sister has been overridden by the act of murder having been committed, albeit by a third party, the tensions between rivalry and identification that we recognised as expressions of a love–hate ambivalence in the examples of the living siblings seem to have been subtly transformed through the further trauma into a dynamic where rivalry is replaced by guilt, and identification is expressed as symbiosis. The hate and love of the sibling who wants simultaneously to annihilate and have a replica-twin in the "murder as phantasy" group of patients can be distinguished under the guise of opposing pulls towards revenge and self-sacrifice in those of the "murder as fact" group.

Furthermore, the state of denial in the first examples was one of a "wilful" denial of the sister's existence—something that was vividly illustrated by patient Cathy's addiction to "rubbing out" anything that she did not like. In the case of the patients where murder has become a reality, so that a certain playfulness in the phantasies of killing off the rival is no longer possible, there emerged evidence of a deep, unconscious denial of the sister's death, something that was shown to serve many purposes.

Finally, the chapter sought to demonstrate a further difference in terms of the task the two groups of patients had to face in therapy. Both groups had to face a fact of life. For the "murder as phantasy" patients, there was a need to face the fact of a living sibling in order to allow a healthy dependence to develop. In the case of the other group, each had to face the hard fact of a sister's death, and once this was possible then the possibility of, or hope for, a healthy separation was achievable.

Given how much more psychologically damaged the bereaved siblings were in the first place, it is striking that they were able to make, within the time and resource constraints of NHS services, such significant shifts in their functioning. All three accepted that they no longer wanted to kill themselves, something that had seemed inevitable to them before treatment. Whereas the patients for whom death is only part of their internal reality, one can imagine that it will take long, painstaking work before they relinquish their grievance and accept their need for the sister. In some ways, it seems to underline the fact that life is infinitely more complicated than death; for those whose sisters are alive, it is an ongoing, ever-changing problem, one where being in the thick of it makes it hard to see the wood for the trees, so to speak. For the others, death brings clarity to the situation. It is an unchanging fact, like the ending of the treatment, and the simplicity and usefulness of it can be missed if we observe only trauma.

References

Bell, D. (2000). Who is killing what or whom? Some notes on the internal phenomenology of suicide. *Psychoanalytic Psychotherapy*, 15: 1, 21–37.
Freud, S. (1917e). Mourning and melancholia. *S.E.*, 14: 237–258. London: Hogarth Press.

Klein, M. (1955). On identification. In: *Envy and Gratitude and Other Works 1946–1963* (pp. 141–175). London: Hogarth, 1975.

Mitchell, J. (2000). *Madmen and Medusas: Reclaiming Hysteria and the Effects of Sibling Relations on the Human Condition.* London: Allen Lane Penguin Press.

CHAPTER TWELVE

Casting a long shadow: implications of sibling loss

Deborah Blessing

W hat happened? Why did you go? These and other questions took hold in my mind when my patient, Lynn, abruptly ended her four-year, twice-weekly therapy. A single professional woman of nearly forty, Lynn had come to see me for help with her long-standing bulimia. Her leaving—with no notice, no explanation—felt like a gaping hole where a presence should be. Perhaps she was unwittingly offering me a pale version of her own experience when, at age fourteen, her then eighteen-year-old sister, and only sibling, died suddenly in an accident. The unexpected, traumatic ending of her sister's life that had left its mark on her psyche, her life, seemed to have now insinuated itself into our relation.

Lynn is one of sixteen patients I have seen who is a survivor of a sibling death. While the circumstances surrounding these deaths varied considerably, they were primarily early losses, occurring most frequently in early childhood or adolescence. Most were sudden, unexpected deaths, though two followed a long illness and two sibling deaths preceded the births of my patients. Despite markedly different circumstances, there was one remarkable concordance: twelve of these sixteen patients had an eating disorder, and the remainder had subclinical food/weight issues or pathologies akin to an eating disorder, such as alcohol dependence. In this chapter, I hope to make the case that the indigestibility of sibling loss finds a ready pathway for expression in an eating disorder or related pathologies. I present two extended case vignettes that explore the link between a sibling death and a particular pattern of defensive manoeuvres often associated with eating disorders that the surviving siblings—my patients—also manifested.

The loss of a sibling/child shakes up the entire family. It inexorably shifts family dynamics, rearranging the internal landscape of each member. Life is simply never the same, and, for many young survivors, fault-lines are laid that remain potential sites for future disruptions. The sense of going on as usual, and expectations of who dies when, are turned on their head. Most importantly, the illusion that one is safe, that one's parents offer protection from harm, is shattered. Bumping up against the recognition of the fragility of life while they are vulnerable and dependent on parents leads them to take extreme measures to avoid their terror and overwhelming psychic pain.

Such measures clearly have an impact on therapy as well. Here, alliances formed and foundations laid might rest on shaky ground, and can result in collapse in the form of enactments, impasses, or, as in Lynn's, the above-mentioned patient's case, aborted treatment. Disturbances in the psyche's bedrock, especially if early parenting experiences were less than good enough, might work against gaining relief because the wall of protections erected is too hard to penetrate or too porous to sustain a boundary. The need to maintain an already unsteady equilibrium is great; the cost to the personality, enormous.

Understanding the particular ways in which siblings become part of our internal world and contribute to shaping our identity and identifications enables us to better appreciate the meanings attached to sibling loss and helps to explain why an eating disorder so readily provides the means to cope with and express its impact. While there are a number of psychoanalytic papers on sibling loss, I found none that makes a link specifically with eating disorders. Eating disorders are often a response to trauma—this is well documented—but the literature does not address sibling loss as one of those traumas. In drawing together what happened in the clinical setting as well as my understanding of it, I hope to discover whether others have encountered similar clinical findings.

As noted, psychoanalytic author Juliet Mitchell comments, "siblings are everywhere and nowhere"—everywhere in our consulting rooms, in everyday life, in literature and film, but nowhere fully elaborated in our theories (Mitchell, 2003). While parents are accorded central importance, neither parents nor siblings are experienced only as fully independent relationships. Part of our experience of our parents includes how we perceive them perceiving us, especially in the context of our siblings. In other words, there is a larger context for each relation within the family. The rivalries and triumphs, the passionate, intense love and hate (including moments of murderous impulses), the terrible fears of, and reactions to, displacements and exclusion that are part of the fabric of family life, mostly involve our experiences with siblings, even if they are closely aligned with what is taking place in relationships with parents, too.

Comparisons about and between siblings as well as the ways in which a sibling is "like me, but not me" contribute to individuation and to building a sense of identity as an individual and as part of a family. Siblings also enable us to partially separate from parents; love between siblings can soften the pain of exclusion from the parental pair. Siblings are especially well suited for playing out ambivalences. They are our companions, our competitors, our defenders, and the ones who taunt us. Knowing well what hurts or helps us, they can land a blow or lend a hand—whatever the experience, it can turn on a coin, register deeply, or be forgotten in an instant. When all goes optimally, when no one dies, when we are still loved in spite of how hateful we can be, we might come to acknowledge and tolerate our dark sides and to develop a helpful superego, lessening the extreme severity of the primitive superego common in children and in those who have not integrated their love and hate. Our sense of having a place and of being one among others—which some feel is a separate developmental line—grow out of sibling relationships (Dalal, 1998; Emde, 1988). All of these experiences, including the jockeying for position and the ubiquitous attention paid to who is getting what from whom, are ordinary, though difficult, parts of growing up; they facilitate development as well as being troublesome. Powerfully felt, these experiences enter into the child's internal world and phantasies and are later played out in the larger world of peers, and even spouses.

The degree to which a sibling's death takes over the survivor's internal world depends on a host of variables; the age of the child, the nature of the death, the relation to the sibling who died, and the stew of complicated relationships to parents—especially whether good experiences and good objects have found a home in the internal world early in life. When development is still fluid and when getting a bit older has not rounded the sharp edges of rivalries and concerns about displacement, the triumph of surviving can feel unbearable. As piercingly painful and guilt inducing as losing the other is, there is also an unconscious sense of triumph in being the one left alive. A kind of confusion about place in the family, including whether the dead sibling's position has been usurped, often follows. A concrete example: one young adult patient asked me, "Now that my sister died, do I still say that I am one of four? Or are there just three kids now that she is gone? Am I now the firstborn?" Identifications with the dead sibling are common, as are phantasies that the internalised dead sibling or internalised parents will seek retribution for any hateful or destructive feelings harboured when the sibling was alive.

Hostile feelings towards parents are quantitatively and qualitatively different from those directed at siblings. A small child will not physically or emotionally take on a parent in the same way they will hurt or be cruel to a sibling, especially if no one is watching. Being completely dependent on parents for survival works against any actions that would lead to losing their love and care. Alienating a sibling does not pose that same threat. The oedipal drama with parents is marked by the threat of castration, or, put another way, of being cut down to size, a narcissistic blow, certainly, but one that favours survival and development. Siblings, being of the same generation—or lateral relations, in Mitchell's terms (2000)—not only do not ensure our survival, they actually compete for parental love and resources and might well want us out of the way, just as we might wish to be rid of them, especially if we were there first. Sibling relationships breed the elemental fear that I am not central to those I need most and that my existence might not matter. I wish to underscore that the drama of sibling rivalry is created by the threat of annihilation— annihilation at the hands of the other who might lay claim to the place that I occupy (Mitchell, 2003). We need think only of Cain and Abel, and the many literary elaborations of this aspect of sibling relationships.

This fear of annihilation, or of being an annihilator, contributes to the development of an eating disorder as a response to a life-shattering event that is too much to take in, let alone digest. Central to the experience of those suffering from eating disorders—and those who have lost a sibling—is the question of whether they have a right to exist; can they dare to come alive, to become a separate, experiencing self. Many such patients appear robotic, as if occupying a nether region, poised on the edge of the dividing line between life and death. While actual deaths sometimes result from an eating disorder, I am referring more to the lively, feeling, thinking parts of the self—that which makes us most human—that have been killed off or have never come to life at all. Constricted participation in life, even in their internal life, where imagination or yearnings pose a threat, have been prominent features of patients whose sibling died as well as other patients with eating disorders. Any and all feelings are dangerous.

Yet, the eating disorder patient also feels an emptiness that is cruelly resistant to being filled. This obviously applies to anorexic patients, but also to those who are not starving themselves. When a bulimic patient, such as my patient, Lynn, for instance, binges, what is taken in is not intended to nourish or to remain inside. "No entry" defences, so named by eating disorder expert Gianna Williams (1997), ensure tight control over everything that is taken in or absorbed and refer not only to food, but also to food for thought. Helpful insights or relationships are refused; attempts to get through to the patient are experienced as trespass. Instead, pseudo self-sufficiency, shut-down thinking, and dissociated experiences prevail, preventing these patients from knowing about their emotional life or their dependency. Their intention is not to know about their painful experiences, not to let in the import and the impact. They do not know who they are— there is no "them" there. On the surface, eating disorder patients are often all too eager to please, but their refusals to take in tell another part of the story. Paradoxically, eating disorder patients also desperately want to be superlative: they want to be the thinnest, the smartest, or, if this is not achievable, they hope to be the worst, as long as they are the "most". This is a distortion of an ideal self and is strongly linked to both intense envy and the terror that unless they distinguish themselves in these ways, they will not exist. In their all-or-none precarious world, they are either everything and the only one, or nothing, no one at all. But they also torment themselves endlessly for their greedy wish to have it all, concretely connected to food. It is easy to see how the life-shattering event of sibling loss plays into these features of competitiveness, distorted identity, and, perhaps most prominently, guilt.

When a child dies, the ripples that spread across the waters of family dynamics crash up against the shore of oedipal dynamics as well. Even without a death, in families where one or more children develop an eating disorder or related pathologies, the couple in the family is usually *not* the parental couple, but the mother and a daughter, entwined with each other, fused, undifferentiated, and excluding the father. If the sibling who died was perceived as mother's favourite, one sure and tormenting way to engage a now depressed and withdrawn mother is to involve her in having to keep another child alive by developing an eating disorder. Unconsciously, the eating disorder fits the bill because it also expresses rage at the mother; it invites intrusive interventions while also rejecting the emotional and literal food that mother has to offer. When the oedipal triangle involves a sibling–mother couple, envy and rivalries are intensified between siblings. If the child who died was the left out sibling, the child enmeshed with mother feels responsible, as if she had taken possession of the source of nourishment, starving the others. Developing an eating disorder then serves as punishment, as well as an identification with the dead sibling.

In the light of these dynamics, it is not surprising that each of my survivor patients, as well as other eating disorder patients I have treated, suffered crippling guilt. The nature of this guilt is not concern about damage done and the wish to make reparation associated with more ordinary pricks of conscience when one has harmed another in actuality or phantasy. Guilt on that level presumes that the person can tolerate ambivalence towards others and maintain reasonable self-regard. It is usually time limited, modifiable, and an intrinsic part of mourning. What I have in mind is something more primitive and all consuming—extreme states of mind that destroy the connections to others or to loving parts of the self. Hate and aggression are defended and glorified as supporting continued existence—a kind of do or die. The reproaches levelled against the self are not only those felt towards the other; there is, instead, *confusion* between what is self and other.

In his ground-breaking paper, "Mourning and melancholia", Freud (1917e) foreshadows his theory of the structure and function of the superego as part of healthy or pathological mourning. Freud's superego houses the internalisation of parental representations and prohibitions as well as the ego ideal. In other papers from that period, he describes an unconscious sense of guilt—a repetitive need for self-punishment (Freud, 1924c).

In this chapter, I use superego more as an omnipotently punishing function related to terrifying and cruel internal figures than as a structure of the mind engaged with the ego. This so-called superego involves one or more pathological organisations that operate destructively and stand in opposition to the important positive aspects of a more ordinary superego. Even when harshly self critical, a reasonably healthy superego allows realistic judgements about good and bad, love and hate to be made, and reparation is felt to be possible. Not so in a pathological organisation, where ties to the object and to one's own mind are hated and broken and where any life-enhancing activity is prevented from bearing fruit. Many post-Kleinians—among them Bion (1959), O'Shaughnessy (1999), Rosenfeld (1971), and Steiner (1982, 1987)—have wrestled with defining these narcissistic and destructive forces that offer no genuine protection or safety, but only terrifying and persecuting experiences, projected from parts of the self to figures from without as well as from within.

Of the different concepts of pathological organisations that have grown out of the post-Kleinian group, O'Shaughnessy's "abnormal superego" and Rosenfeld's "internal gang" come closest to what I have observed in my patients and in my own countertransferences. Neither operates as "pure culture", but both join forces with "no entry" defences to wreck relationships and undermine progress.

Lynn

Lynn, the patient who abruptly ended her treatment, is an example of someone most often under the sway of an internal gang. The "stuckness" readily observable in many of my patients—a virtual arrested development keyed to the age the person was when the sibling died—highlights the traumatic, mind-invading aspects of sibling loss and is linked to the dictum that the survivor is forbidden to achieve or obtain whatever was precluded by the sibling's death.

Lynn presented as someone frozen in time. Other than in her professional accomplishments, she seemed considerably younger than her almost forty years. At five feet five inches, about twenty pounds overweight, her sandy-brown short hair, conservative clothing, and pale complexion unadorned by make-up gave her a colourless, drab appearance. She seemed to want to blend in and escape notice. Her struggles were that of early adolescence: she was uncomfortable in her body and with her sexuality. She blamed her social withdrawal on being overweight. Her sense of identity was constricted, largely unformed, consisting almost entirely of her earliest comparisons with her deceased sister, as if traits or talents could only apply to one of them but not to both. Lynn was the bright, awkward, and, in her view, unattractive one—intellectual success was her domain. She described her sister as pretty, sexy, popular with boys, and the apple of her father's eye. More arty than brainy, her sister shared common interests with their cultured mother, a difference that pained Lynn. Fun, liveliness, and love were her sister's exclusive province. Lynn perceived her sister as the hands-down favourite in the family and in life. She had deeply loved, envied, sometimes hated, but also quite idealised her. In death, as in life, her sister stood for a standard Lynn despaired of ever meeting. Rightly or wrongly, she imagined that her parents thought that the wrong sister died. While there is always more than one phantasy operating in the unconscious at any given time, and dynamics and motives are overdetermined, Lynn's phantasy of being the one who should have died was a core belief.

Overwhelmed by her loss, Lynn on and off tried to connect with her sister's boyfriend after her death. She and he shared the loss and the sadness, but she also harboured a conscious wish to have this boyfriend for herself, representing a complex layering of longing to be with someone who knew, loved, and had been with her sister; a wish to be her sister as well as to have what she had had. Other than her adolescent pursuit of this young man, at the time she started therapy, well into her thirties, her only relation had been a secret affair with a married mail clerk. Any time Lynn was poised to change anything in her life, she would be overwhelmed with guilt and anxiety, an example of Rosenfeld's "internal gang" experience. This internal gang offered protection of a Mafia type—you leave at your peril (Williams, 1997). The cost of membership is that any positive or loving relation where need for, and hunger to depend on, another must be destroyed. Allegiance to the leader, which I propose might be the phantasised retaliating dead sibling or rejecting parents, maintains the status quo and keeps things safe in an omnipotent world of superiority where one needs nothing and no one other than the gang.

Lynn's binges and the prodigious amount of time spent planning and shopping for them numbed her painful feelings, stuffed them down, and evacuated her mind. It consumed much of her mental and physical energy and left her feeling that she could have everything in her secret bingeing world. Her eating disorder started shortly after her sister's death. She worked hard to rid herself of sorrow rather than to digest it.

In our sessions, she reported what was on her mind in a sing-song, childlike way that at times could be irritating—usually something about whether she had stopped at the nut shop for delicious cashews, or should she go to the bagel shop on the way home, and oh, the smells wafting from Zabar's that lured her inside while en route to our session. There was a teasing, provocative quality to her telling me how she often literally filled herself up at these close-by shops right before arriving or immediately after our sessions. She left no room for hunger for our connection. Not getting a good feed from her therapy was concretised in this way; satisfactions were to be had, but not from me. I was left hungry for something more substantial, while she let me know she could feed herself. Her preoccupations and actions foreclosed emotional contact—no entry into her private world.

Lynn, like most of my patients who had suffered the loss of a sibling, derived little solace from her parents. Devastated by their loss, they were too preoccupied to attend to Lynn's pain, thus exponentially multiplying her losses. Her mother sank into a deep depression; her father withdrew. After she died, Lynn's sister's name was never mentioned again and all evidence of her life was removed from view. Years later, a relative told Lynn that her parents visited her sister's grave several times a year. Lynn was neither told about this nor included; she never let on that she knew about the visits. The exclusion bruised her heart and confirmed her feeling of being left out, and left alone—not a wanted member of the family.

The first time I referred to her sister by name, she recoiled in shock as if I had struck her. All she could say was: *"You said her name, YOU SAID HER NAME."* She could not articulate what that meant to her, but I commented that she seemed afraid that the earth would open and swallow us both. I had trespassed on forbidden ground—her sister's grave. However, by literally naming her sister, I, in essence, had taken her to the cemetery and we could acknowledge her sister's life and death together.

In her divided world, Lynn engaged intellectually at work, but otherwise dwelt in the sensuous zone of smells, tastes, sounds, and bodily sensation. The shutting down of her mind was so extensive that she could not see mental pictures, could not visualise, and, thus, did not dream; neither could she call up visual memories. She often responded to interpretations by singing a snippet from a song, lyrics from her adolescence in the 1960s before her sister's accidental death. Sometimes, her singing cut me off or drowned me out, another no-entry manoeuvre, but her occasional willingness to offer associations to these songs at times became grist to our mill, substituting for dreams or more straightforward associations. It was challenging for her to directly think her thoughts, to use symbols to shape and organise her experiences. These lyrics were symbols of sorts, but she did not experience them as belonging to her, and, thus, she could tell me about them.

Then, suddenly, she was gone. Her therapy had been going well. She had been promoted at work, had stopped bingeing and was losing weight. Instead of hiding her body, she began to dress stylishly and to experiment with make-up for the first time. So why did she leave?

I found out eighteen months later, when Lynn returned to treatment. She told me that she left because she was convinced that there could not be two attractive women in the same room; one of us would die. She was trying to preserve us both, once again at her expense. In a complex layering of motives, she was cancelling out her progress, returning to a deeply punishing place within her that would not allow her to go forward in her life, to fulfil ordinary dreams. Lynn was also enacting an envious part of her personality that resented my having helped her—making her feel dependent and "less than". In the transference, I was a sister/mother who had what she lacked, and one who might kill her for competing if she did not get me first. It took courage to come back, to slowly allow re-entry, to re-engage in coming to learn more about herself and about the experiences she had not been able to face for over a quarter of a century. It was finally time to turn down the volume of the cruel, accusing voices of her mind's internal gang.

Sadly, not long after Lynn returned, I ended my practice in New York to move to Washington. I dreaded telling her I was leaving and felt pained knowing what this would mean to her, as well as to my other patients. I also worried that she would internalise me as another member of her internal gang who punished her for daring to change, to move out into the world and for depending on me. Her first response was to say, "Washington—that's a dead place—they roll up the sidewalks at five o'clock. Yeah, you'll see—why would you ever move there?" The real question, of course, was how could I leave her? I would be dead to her and she wished me to know something about dead places, where nothing lively comes out at night. Her wishing me dead for leaving her was also part of the picture.

As we prepared to terminate, she allowed herself to tell me how sad she was that I was going and how much she regretted having left and lost that precious time we could have had together. As difficult as the ending was for both of us, our being able to say goodbye, to recognise the various meanings of our ending allowed a bit of ordinary mourning into our relation.

As a postscript, I want to note that a sibling connection was very present in my countertransference to Lynn. Lynn was close in age to me and shared the same birthday as one of my siblings. I also played a maternal role with another younger sister in my family, with whom I am very close.

I think that, over the years, Lynn managed to take in something about my feelings of connection to her, perhaps even the mix of sibling and maternal aspects of it, which I hope opened the possibility of her imagining not a retaliating or envious sister/mother, but a figure who would wish her well and want her to enjoy her life.

Several years later, she wrote to me, enclosing a photograph of her recently adopted young child. She never married.

Daniel

Sibling loss, by its life-changing, long-lasting nature, seeps into the psyche and takes up residence even when the death occurred before the birth of the surviving sibling. When the parents themselves have also suffered early losses of siblings and the death of their own first baby, the second new baby comes into the world and into a nursery crowded with ghosts—perhaps more like a haunted house than a cradle of life. This is Daniel's history—a replacement baby born into a family where tremendous losses and deprived circumstances, material and emotional, were the order of the day.

Lynn and Daniel share an important history, though their stories and presentations were different. Both were born into families traumatised by sibling losses from the previous generation. Lynn's mother's two siblings were killed during the Holocaust. She had escaped by moving to the USA with her parents before the war and was the only child in her family alive at the end of it. Both of Daniel's parents also suffered sibling loss. Two of his mother's siblings died several years apart during her childhood, one from a serious illness and the second, an infant, in mysterious circumstances that suggested neglect. Daniel's father's adolescent brother died of a congenital health problem when the father was eight years old.

Parents so besieged by their own losses and their aftermath might have been leaky, rather than sturdy, containers for their children. The heavy load of grief carried by these two families would have strained their capacities to be emotionally available, to take in and transform the primitive anxieties and fear of death that every infant experiences in those early days of life, perhaps to a point beyond what they could reasonably bear. Moreover, the parents' own painful experiences were likely stirred up and projected into their children.

This transgenerational trauma, which magnifies the losses of the current generation, has significant implications for the rise of the particular extreme protections displayed by Lynn and Daniel, and for their link with eating disorders.

Both Lynn and Daniel presented with no-entry defences, but while Lynn was primarily, though not exclusively, tied to an internal gang, Daniel most often lived under the dominion of an abnormal superego.

Along with the internal gang and no-entry defences, the abnormal superego arises from the earliest dissociations stemming from ongoing failures of containment (Bion, 1962; O'Shaughnessy, 1999; Williams, 1997). Failures of containment can find expression through a variety of defences and illnesses encountered every day in our consulting rooms. What is specific about this triad of defences is that not only are the baby's projections not received or properly interpreted and returned, but the mother/parents actually create a more destructive problem by condemning the baby for not matching an anticipated ideal. In addition, the parent(s)' own anxieties are projected into the baby (Williams, 1997). The no-entry defences we saw with Lynn and will see again with Daniel grow out of a need to keep out overpowering feelings and the toxic projections of others.

Fast forward to well into his fifties, when Daniel consulted me with two pressing issues on his mind—his dying mother and his panic that he would never have his own family. A short relationship had just ended badly—cruelly—as had most of his previous relationships, crushing his dreams of "having a baby". He suffered from severe ongoing panic attacks at the thought of his nearly ninety-year-old parents dying and at being left without a child of his own. In our first session, he questioned aloud whether he should be in therapy or simply hire a matchmaker. A veteran of many years of previous therapy in which nothing had changed, he doubted whether anything would come of our work together. His threat that he would leave unless I met his demands to help him marry and have a baby right away felt like intense pressure and denigrating at the same time—I was a hired hand and failure was the expectation. From the very first, I had a sense of the bind he was in and the harshness with which he dealt with himself and others. Almost immediately, there was a clear and oscillating rhythm of who was devalued and who was superior. This rise and fall from omnipotence to a contemptible position—an indicator of an abnormal superego—could happen in a nanosecond, and became a repeated pattern in our work.

In that first session, Daniel, without prompting, told me about his history, though he did not consciously connect what he revealed and his presenting concerns. He told me that he was born a year or so after his parents' first baby died. He said that his father had told him the story of how the couple had only married because his mother was pregnant; to not marry in those years would have been shameful. The baby was born significantly deformed and died within days. His mother neither saw nor held the baby, though his father did. His father told his wife that their daughter was beautiful. Despite their contentious and unfulfilling marriage, he worried that she would not want to conceive again if she saw the deformed baby girl. At age five, Daniel nearly died of a sudden illness—the same illness and at the same age as his mother's little brother. Shortly before or after Daniel's illness, his mother suffered a miscarriage—another lost baby.

The story, ostensibly Daniel's father's, puzzled me. It did not ring true. I was not really concerned about its veracity; rather, I wondered whose distortions they were, Daniel's or his father's, and what phantasies were embedded in the story. What was abundantly clear was that Daniel's mother was viewed with contempt, though neither father nor son could separate from her. In this family, Daniel and his father were the couple, allied against the mother.

In eating disorder patients, the coupling between father and son is unusual. Interestingly, like the other two men in my sample of sixteen sibling survivors, Daniel had a strong feminine identification. Although he did not have a diagnosed eating disorder, Daniel kept impossibly strict rules about what foods he allowed himself and an obsession with weight and fitness. A man of average height and slight build, he was repulsed by body fat, and anything less than a very toned body. Daniel was married once—in his late forties—but stopped being intimate with his wife after a few months, and divorced her after a few years because, in his words, she gained weight and did not keep her promise to be fit, to stay in shape. They never attempted to have a baby.

Early in our work, I was struck by Daniel's ritual parting words— *Be safe*. When this pattern persisted, I asked him about it. He explained, "It's a dangerous world out there—anything can happen." A profoundly lonely man, Daniel expected assault from every quarter. What he was less aware of, but what I had glimpsed, was his concern about his unconscious attacks on me during our separations. His rage at women who left him was transferred to me when I left him at the end of each session.

I also felt lonely during our time together. Daniel filled every space with detached, practised stories of what was going on in his life, along with his interpretations of their meaning, most of which seemed like stale, empty echoes from his previous therapy that stuck on the surface of his mind but had not been metabolised. There was little room for me, or my thoughts—no point of entry into his world. When I offered an occasional interpretation, usually about what was going on between us, I felt that I was being intrusive, a feeling supported by his pulling back and away from me.

A second word/idea that entered every session was his reference to my or our work as "digging". Each time he used this word I inwardly cringed; it left a terrible taste in my mouth and a feeling of wanting to shudder, as if to shake it off. One day, I took it up with him, telling him I was curious about what felt like digging to him and what came to his mind about that word. It did not take long for him to answer. He told me that digging reminds him of trudging through junk, useless stuff. He then told me his mother was a junk collector, their house always piled with this or that everywhere, not even a space to walk. Nothing was thrown away or cleaned out and nothing of worth could be found in the cramped space. I said that he seemed to feel that his own mind, his mother's body, and our work were filled with junk, nothing worthwhile, that he was worried that we would not be making babies in his therapy, we would not create any new ideas or understanding, our intercourse would be sterile. He displayed little hope and wondered if all this rummaging through things could hurt him, clutter up his life rather than help. I also understood that my interpretations—even mild comments—felt like digs to him. I further sensed some mind–body confusions between a space for creating—a containing, nourishing womb—and a repository for waste suitable only for digging out, evacuating material akin to Bion's beta elements (1962).

Daniel, a well-educated, well-groomed professional man, looked very different from the person I experienced in the room. Although he often drew back from my interpretations, he seemed to want to be as physically close to me as possible. Rather than sitting in one of two patient chairs, he positioned himself at the head of my analytic couch, but on the very edge of it, never really sitting back or settling in. He sobbed inconsolably in nearly every session, always about feeling ugly, unlovable, or not having a baby. No ordinary tearfulness or soft sobs; he sounded like a wailing baby. Tears streamed down his face as he wiped his runny nose with the back of his hand. It was distressing and distasteful to watch and I felt distracted by my urge to hand him a tissue. Some days, I wondered if he was on the verge of a breakdown. It surprised me that I felt less moved by his tears than concerned about whether he could pull himself together.

While in the throes of these unpleasant feelings, I began to wonder not only about his being turned away by women in the present, but also about how his parents had responded to him, his mother in particular. During those moments when I was not initially a welcoming receiver of his extreme states of distress, he was forced to hold on to these himself, and probably felt that I was impervious to the depths of his despair and psyche-threatening anxieties. Sitting with, and thinking about, my responses brought me emotionally closer to his states of mind, which he could only show me rather than tell me about. The "abnormal superego" type feelings that were being elicited in me alerted me not only to the presence of his self-hate, but also to what kinds of figures reside in his internal world.

Daniel expressed longings for love and a baby, but my own experience of him made me appreciate his equally powerful ambivalence about a relation and how he might push people away. When I suggested that he might be of two minds about having a relation, he became enraged, bolted upright, hands clenched in fists, momentarily scaring me. I took in very quickly that I had trespassed into territory that he could not bear to think about, that I had perhaps inadvertently touched the very ashamed part of him that felt damaged and deadly. Thus, I was reminded that only small amounts of allowable food controlled by him could be taken in at a time.

In the following session he told me directly that he wished *he could give birth*, and, in a slip of the tongue, said that *he is a woman*. Daniel wanted to be both sexes, to create himself and a baby without joining together with another person, forming a couple that could create new and flourishing life. In the transference, I was a nasty digger, a junk-filled woman, and a danger he had to be on guard against.

Throughout his growing up, Daniel's family moved almost annually from one foreign country to another, never staying long anywhere, adding to his sense of having no place in the world. Some months into our work, he Googled the address of a favourite home abroad that had been a place of considerable status when he and his family had lived there when he was nine or ten. He learned that the home had become a residence/school for orphans and had been shelled in that country's intense armed conflict. All the children were killed. As he told me this, he broke down in tears, sobbing his *mea culpas* for not having saved the children. In fact, the shelling occurred long after he lived there; there was no possibility of his either having been there or of saving the children. Despite this glaring reality, he was convinced he was responsible for their deaths. This omnipotent phantasy, attached to a real event, was, I believe, linked to an unconscious, displaced phantasy of having killed off his mother's other babies—his siblings—or, when concerns about his own destructiveness surfaced, having failed to save them.

Similarly, he panicked at the prospect of his entire family line ending with his death. He yearned to provide his parents with something alive, to expel the ghosts of dead siblings from nurseries past and empty ones present. In the treatment, it was difficult to keep hope alive for something life affirming and life changing to take place. One of my biggest challenges with Daniel was to help him loosen his ties to his abnormal superego so he might experience a more ordinary superego that could help him mourn, to turn his ghosts into ancestors (Loewald, 1960) and, thus, be able to engage more deeply with the living.

Conclusion

In this chapter, I have tried to convey the indigestible quality of sibling loss and its impact on the inner world and external reality of the surviving child or young person. Using clinical vignettes, I have made links between sibling loss and the nature of the protections put in place in the face of overwhelming psychic pain. A majority of my patients whose sister or brother died developed a full-blown eating disorder. A striking finding was their use of no-entry defences as well as primitive versions of crippling guilt and a pull towards destructiveness in the form of an abnormal superego (O'Shaughnessy, 1999) or an internal gang (Rosenfeld, 1971), which made it impossible for them to mourn their sibling losses and to learn from their experiences. Nevertheless, although both Lynn and Daniel were pulled toward destruction, the pathological organisations_they developed to cope with sibling loss and all its attendant issues and phantasies might have more to do with their struggle to answer the question of whether they have a right to exist, to live, or to come alive, than with a pull towards death.

References

Bion, W. R. (1959). Attacks on linking. *International Journal of Psychoanalysis,* *40*: 308–315.

Bion, W. R. (1962). *Learning from Experience.* London: Tavistock.

Dalal, F. (1998). *Taking the Group Seriously.* London: Jessica Kingsley.

Emde, R. N. (1988). Development terminable and interminable. *International Journal of Psychoanalysis, 69*: 23–42.

Freud, S. (1917e). Mourning and melancholia. *S.E., 14*: 243–258. London: Hogarth.

Freud, S. (1924c). The economic problem of masochism. *S.E., 19*: 159–172. London: Hogarth.

Loewald, H. (1960). On the therapeutic action of psycho-analysis. *International Journal of Psychoanalysis, 41*: 16–33.

Mitchell, J. (2000). *Madmen and Medusas. Reclaiming Hysteria and the Effects of Sibling Relationships on the Human Condition*. London: Penguin.

Mitchell, J. (2003). *Siblings*. Cambridge: Polity Press.

O'Shaughnessy, E. (1999). Relating to the superego. *International Journal of Psychoanalysis, 80*: 861–870.

Rosenfeld, H. A. (1971). A clinical approach to the psychoanalytical theory of the life and death instincts: an investigation into the aggressive aspects of narcissism. *International Journal of Psychoanalysis, 52*: 169–178.

Steiner, J. (1982). Perverse relationships between parts of the self: a clinical illustration. *International Journal of Psychoanalysis, 63*: 241–251.

Steiner, J. (1987). The interplay between pathological organizations and the paranoid–schizoid and depressive positions. *International Journal of Psychoanalysis, 68:* 69–80.

Williams, G. (1997). Reflections on some dynamics of eating disorders: "no-entry" defences and foreign bodies. *International Journal of Psychoanalysis, 78*: 927–941.

PART IV

TRANSFERENCE AND COUNTERTRANSFERENCE RELATED TO SIBLINGHOOD

CHAPTER THIRTEEN

The actual twin and the imaginary subject

Francesco Bisagni

Introduction

The content of this chapter is the account of an analytic treatment, carried on in the area of Milan, Italy, where I live and work. It is the case of an adult male patient, a twin aged forty, whom I will call Emil, who was the son of a psychotic mother. His mother was herself a twin. The patient showed confusional states and severe impairments in his capacity for abstract thinking and symbolisation processes, together with depersonalisation phenomena, which resulted in deep difficulties in his relational and professional life. The psychopathological structure and functioning were related to the dual component of introjection/identification with the persecutory ideation of the mother on one side, and the confusional/parasitic and, at times, erotised relation with the twin brother. These elements affected the transference and the countertransference in the course of the ten-year analytic treatment conducted with four weekly sessions. The analytic work could actually lead to sufficient structuring of a sense of separateness and subjectivity, with significant improvement in the analysand's life.

The main theoretical background of this paper is the post-Kleinian tradition, particularly Bion's seminal paper "The imaginary twin"

(1950) and the Bionian model in general, Joseph's (1959, 1961, 1975) and Joseph and Tabor's (1961) studies on twins, as well as the more recent book by Lewin, *The Twin in the Transference* (2004).

Having limited space at my disposal, I am afraid I cannot go into the details of theory. I just recall that Bion, in his paper on the imaginary twin, connects the fantasy about a twin, either completely imaginary or, to some extent, taken from reality, to the defence against the awareness and working through of splitting mechanisms. The purpose of this form of defence is to deal with the fear that the uncontrollable object would eventually threaten with separation and a possibly unbearable experience of separateness. The conflict with the imaginary twin is also linked with the existence of elements related to the sense of sight (and hearing) used with the aim of exploring and controlling the environment. (Bion, 1950).

In a different frame of concepts, Bion (1967) considers the notion of two-ness, which refers to the natural presence of pair elements: two eyes, two hands, two ears, and so forth. This is linked by Bion to the mating of preconception (of the breast, for instance) with a realisation (sucking) for the creation of a conception (two-ness). Tustin (1981) states that two-ness represents an important issue related to stages of early (and precocious) separation between the baby and the breast, together with the "knowledge" of the nipple not belonging to the mouth.

If elements of "twinning" are common in the transference even in singletons, the presence of an "actual twin" makes things peculiar both in the person's development as a child and adolescent and in the transference.

The "twin transference" involves intense narcissistic functioning and fantasies of merging with/adhering to the object, deeply supported by powerful adhesive and projective identifications, and has deep impact on the creation of a separate internal tri-dimensional space. The twin transference has to be carefully worked through in analysis. The countertransference is equally intense and essential to be worked through with great attention and skill. A sense of separateness might develop gradually, in terms of what has been described as a move from "the identical twin transference" to the "non-identical twin transference" (Lewin, 2004, pp. 87–88), where, in my opinion, the management of idealisation is crucial. Aspects of idealisation in the transference have to be tolerated, allowing a gradual sense of separateness to unfold.

Clinical material

The clinical material is presented in an "anti-clockwise" way. I start from what emerged when we were approaching the termination of analysis and will go backwards in time.

One week before the termination of the analysis, a patient recounts a dream:

> "I am in a bed with my twin, and I am asleep. In the dream I wake up and instead of my brother I see my wife. At that precise moment I realise I have missed an analytic session. I ask my wife, 'Why haven't you woken me up?' I wake up."

The patient tells the dream with a remarkable amount of anxiety. On listening to him, I realise I share a similar feeling, clearly interspersed with a slight feeling of anger towards him. "Again with your twin?" is my hidden thought. I know he has been furious with me for months about the planned termination of our analytic work, more and more when he progressively came to realise that I would not change my mind in order to comply with his wishes and would not continue the treatment forever. (Over the years, when wanting to address his fantasy of an endless—and therefore useless—analysis, I had used the metaphor of a "twin coffin".) The analysis really was about to be concluded, and this was the final week after ten years of therapy. Once again, on listening to this dream, I find myself working to try to distinguish whose feeling the anger is. If I feel slightly angry, to whom does it belong?

He associates by recalling what he has learnt over the years with me. He seems to realise that separating from his twin is a never-ending process. I know he is right, but I think he always needs to conceive something "never ending" in his mind. He then recalls that being able to get married was an enormous step forward in his life, and his son is most precious and deeply loved. I have the impression he is desperately trying to latch on to his gratitude for me, calling up good memories against the anxiety of separation.

Emil says he felt very upset in the dream for having missed a session. "As usual", he adds, "I try to make somebody else guilty for something I am responsible for. It's me who indulges with my brother."

I tell him that "indulging" —sleeping with his twin—speaks of his never-ending fantasy of staying with me forever. I say that he realises that there is a history, *his* history, which he has worked through over ten years in analysis, and *our* history, too, and now he feels grateful and angry at the same time. I add that I am considered guilty for not preventing him from falling asleep and indulging with this brother/ analyst, and for leaving him alone in doing this job.

Three months earlier, these are extracts from my notes taken after a session: I realise the patient is struggling with his fantasy that I will not really put an end to his analysis. Not simply denying that we came to a shared decision about termination almost one year ago, but seeming to remain within the fantasy that just before the end, or possibly sooner, I will change my mind and decide to continue. This prevents him from working through separation and the feelings related to that. While listening to him, I find myself fantasising that I will become poor after his termination, as if my very survival depended on the money I receive from him, as if I could never find any other patient to replace him. I realise it is a really delusional idea. I talk to him about his feeling abandoned and betrayed and left in an absolute state of poverty and starvation. I link it to his history, but also to his present rage towards me. I say he feels as if he had never been nourished by me, as if he could not keep anything inside.

I also fantasise that he could have a breakdown after terminating the treatment.

This vignette—as well as the dream mentioned above—describes the intensity of projective identification, and the delusional quality of this patient's ideation. Various defence mechanisms are operating here, beyond projective identification: the omnipotent fantasy of my "changing my mind about termination" is reinforced by a certain degree of denial of what was going to happen and of the feelings involved. The fantasy of poverty and starvation had been powerful over the years in this patient. This was linked with the fantasy of being unwanted/unrecognised by the mother as an "unexpected" twin, but also with strong envious feelings towards the twin brother, both of which were intensely reactivated and worked through in the transference.

The following session took place one year before the conclusion of the analytic work. It was the first session of the week.

Emil is on time and comes in quite quickly. I notice he has a grim expression on his face. He rushes to the couch. He is down on the couch before I am seated on my chair.

After a few moments of silence, Emil says he has been tired since this morning, his mind has not been working well, he is quite sleepy and numb. While saying this, he immediately creates a gluey atmosphere, the rhythm of his speech is slow and "sticky", and I feel slightly irritated. (This used to be a recurrent and much heavier situation in the first years of the analysis.)

I say that, as has happened many other times, this tiredness can possibly tell us a lot of things, and it seems that in some way he cannot wait to tell . . .

Emil starts to speak of an argument he had with his wife during the weekend. Apparently his wife—as she recurrently does—started to complain again about the money . . . accusing him of spending all his money on their child's school and for his analysis, and leaving nothing for her, she cannot buy anything for herself . . . and she has to work a lot, and their home is poor and she can't invite people to visit . . . During this fight, Emil fell into a state of great rage and anxiety, feeling trapped and imprisoned, and could only reply that he does not want his wife's help in terms of money, and that he will work more . . . (he keeps talking about this quarrel for a few minutes with great emotional involvement).

I say this is what his tiredness seemed to hide and express . . . we know that he had had this protest from his wife many times, as if she were a complaining, excluded, and jealous child, and we know he feels entrapped because he feels he cannot even think of living without her, but I think he also feels the same way (as his wife feels about him) about myself. He knows there is a break next week, he is going to miss his four sessions, and the past three-day weekend presaged this . . . I guess he also feels excluded by me, and jealous, and also enraged because he feels he cannot do without me but that I can do without him . . . and he spends so much to have me, but I leave him; he cannot "buy" me.

Emil remains silent and seemingly quieter for a couple of minutes . . . his hand on his forehead, he adjusts his position on the couch as if wanting to get more comfortable . . .

I ask what is coming to his mind. He says he remembers he had a short dream on Sunday night. [Silence]

I ask if that makes him uncomfortable.

Emil says he had forgotten the dream. In the dream, he was with his twin brother in their common workplace. The brother had to leave for a few days for some work in another town and he was preparing the truck before leaving. He asked Emil to help him and told him what Emil would have to do during his absence. The brother looked as if he could trust Emil. So the dream ends when they say goodbye.

He recounts the dream with no particular emotion or "colour", as if he were speaking of something trivial and not important, as if he did not even think of a possible "meaning". Emil remains silent after telling the dream. I do not feel this silence as openly "aggressive-oppositional", rather as if he were unable autonomously to give any meaning to it.

"You seem not to be able to say anything about this dream; you are possibly waiting for me to do the job. Does anything come to your mind?"

"Nothing special."

[Silence]

"What about the non-special? I wonder if you are uncertain of my considering you and your dream important and meaningful for me, or you might believe that I am already thinking of my next week's business."

Emil repeats the dream almost the same way as before, saying twice that his brother says goodbye at the end, and that his brother expects him to do something during his absence.

I say I do not know if he can consider this "special", but I think it has never been that easy for him to be able to say goodbye, either to his brother or to anybody, including myself. In the dream, he can experience and tolerate a temporary separation; he knows his brother will be back, there is a sense of trust, and he can take responsibility for what has to be done while his brother is absent. I think this brother stands for me also. Emil can let me go next week, he can think I can trust him, he can keep working in his mind on our common work and wait for me to get back. I say we can "dare" say this is "quite" special for him . . . can we not?

Emil says he continues to feel angry with his wife. (But he looks more relaxed.)

I say I understand that he does still feel angry with his wife and with myself, but maybe the dream suggests that rage or jealousy are not the only feelings he has . . . partly, he seems also to be able to wait, and to think I can trust him, and to trust that I will be back. In some way, he has two "options" within himself, so he is more free. I say this is quite different from the times he could only feel abandoned and left behind, with-merely the possibility of getting into over-excited fantasies ... now he feels jealous, a bit angry, but also able to wait and trust.

Emil remains silent on the couch, apparently more relaxed. When I say time is up, he gets up quite slowly; when I open the door he looks at me quite intensely and is off, but without hurrying.

The session (which is reported in its entirety) gives a clue about how feelings of abandonment raised by separation are worked through in the transference. It is significant that the wife so easily becomes a representative of the twin transference, and of the maternal transference, too. What is remarkable in this session—among many possible elements—is the dream where the twin brother (as a representative of the analyst) can tolerate separation and depicts a sense of mutual trust and an experience of memory. This might represent how pathological twinning (rooted in a weak sense of identity and massive projective identification) gives space to the experience of otherness. In contrast to the confusional situation of the transference (as well as the actual) twin, separateness can be conceived and, along with it, an "ethical" differentiation can take place—the patient has two options.

The dream was regarded as a turning point. The idea of a possible conclusion of the analysis had occasionally been considered in the previous months. This dream and its further elaboration led to the shared decision to conclude the treatment one year later.

Three years earlier (six years into treatment), Emil experienced a bereavement.

"Last night my mother passed away. She had a heart attack. I am devastated." [Emil cries with great intensity, and I feel genuinely sympathetic. Also, I feel a bit worried that he might have a breakdown.] "... my brother seems lost and cannot provide any help; he asked me to deal with everything, and I am doing it ... I have never felt such pain ... I never realised how much I loved her."

This was the first significant loss in his life. Emil could manage it, which was repeatedly underlined in the following months. He managed it properly, without a significant depressive breakdown, and mourning was, on the whole, adequately worked through, including some hypomanic fantasy of triumphing over the object, a certain amount of rage, some anal fantasies of expelling a "faecalised" mother (who was also a representative of a faecal twin), and, in the end, some painful recognition of a mother who was weak and substantially psychotic. However, some aspects of the "twin transference" were reinforced during the mourning process. Emil expected to be "understood without words", and became enraged if he felt I was "disagreeing". The atmosphere in the session was often gluey; at times, I felt a sort of dizziness; at other times, I felt like sleeping on my chair behind the couch. If I had fallen asleep, I was sure Emil would not have even realised it, or, if he did, he would not have reacted. He might have thought we were "sleeping together", one inside the other.

Five years earlier (first year of analysis), Emil had this experience:

"Yesterday I felt I was melting into the television. I could not recognise whether I was inside or outside the TV, and felt my body getting liquid. That made me very anxious. And I feel so tired and weak now. I have no energy, I could not wake up and work." [In the countertransference I feel extremely sleepy; I have to draw on all my energy and will to stay awake and be able to think.]

This is an example of how the patient frequently felt in the first years of his analysis. It is meaningful to note the particular shape taken by the problem of "confusion" of identity and of losing boundaries between subject and object. That was experienced as a truly psychotic state, in terms of depersonalisation, where the self was felt to be pouring into/dissolving into the object. The experience of feeling sleepy and exhausted was partly a defence against anxiety and, at the same time, it was another way of experiencing depersonalisation.

Countertransference responses were commonly powerful, as usually occurs when intense projective identification is operating, and required continuous working through.

"I indulged in my fantasies again and again. I always imagine becoming a famous architect and being called by the President, who is fascinated by my work . . ."

This is an example of the only way Emil could initially conceive himself as separate from his twin brother: he had to be in a state of (seemingly unavoidable) grandiosity, twinned with, and idealised by, an idealised twin parent (that was myself in the transference), and substantially representing himself as an imaginary self. This was also linked with the fantasy that the actual twin brother would die if he became emancipated (and, on the other hand, Emil imagined that he lovingly allowed the twin brother to live by making himself psychically dead). The fantasy that being oneself meant killing the other twin was very powerful. In the transference, this meant that I had to keep idealisation alive to avoid getting in touch with the idea that any differentiation between us implied that one of us would die.

Conclusions: backwards in time: how it all began and possible future developments

Emil recalls his mother saying he had been a "quiet" and "never crying", "never asking" baby. His twin brother always had to be breast-fed first, or he would scream and protest if kept waiting too long. Emil, in contrast, was considered to be able to wait, showing no sign of discomfort. Essentially, a "suicidal" baby was mistaken for "quiet", although we cannot exclude the possibility that baby Emil was also trying to spare a very weak mother by "switching off" his drives, or, on the other hand, he might have had to protect himself from being intruded upon through the mother's beta elements being massively evacuated into him.

The mother (a twin herself) was, in fact, substantially psychotic, very involved in religion, superstitious, and functioning in terms of magical thinking. She suggested—when asked how to help Emil with his psychological difficulties—that maybe an exorcist could help. A complexity of multi-generational, undigested beta elements could be hypothesised to be at work in the whole family group. Although living in the area of Milan, this family was anthropologically and culturally very primitive.

From the ages of thirteen and sixteen, the twins frequently had sexual intercourse with each other, oral sex and anal penetration, each of them being active and passive interchangeably. That was experienced as very aggressive by each of them, and seemingly reinforced subtle depersonalisation phenomena in the two of them. This was the reason why the sexual games were suddenly interrupted at the age of sixteen. The twin brother got married when he was twenty-eight and had two children, while Emil was able to get married after a few years of analytic work. Emil apparently had no sexual difficulties with his wife and they had a child one year after the marriage, a boy that Emil loved intensely. Emil did not have any other homosexual experiences (in terms of explicit sexual intercourse), although he was aware of looking quite attractive to men. Particularly, his gaze was quite "hooking". His homosexual "fantasies" (or "transferences") always had a fusional quality, serving as a defence against full awareness of separateness and as a territory in which a deadly sense of never-ending immobility (often hidden behind the belief that "we can only do something if we are two, but only do it as a hobby, not as real projects") could be enacted: the twin coffin, as I mentioned before.

Emil had always been considered weaker and more passive than his twin. His identity within the family group was to have no identity. Both brothers worked in the family firm. Emil was the "ill" and the "passive" one. Although naturally skilled in his job, and in some way sharper and more creative than his brother, possessing a sort of artistic predisposition, he could not work properly, he slept many hours during the day as he always felt tired and weak (actually, in a state of depersonalisation enhanced by intense masturbatory fantasies), he was considered by the family as a kind of servant, and given money in the guise of "pocket money". He experienced all his more creative activities in terms of "hobbies" and always needed a "special friend" to carry them out. He usually took ages to finish a job; everything was interminable. When I knew him at the age of forty, he had no ID card (but he had a driving licence because this was part of being regarded as a servant in the family—he could fetch and carry for them), he did not exist on the Fiscal State Registry, never had an official job, had no insurance, and no retirement funds. Plus, he never had a sexual/affective relation, either hetero or homosexual (apart from the sexual intercourse with his twin brother when they were adolescents). At that time (aged forty) he had been a student of architecture for twenty years, waiting to write his final dissertation. He could not finish it, and it took five years of analysis for him to obtain his degree and become an architect. His brother did not have any university degree. Emil could do better than his brother, in many respects. He was very creative in his job. Thanks to the analytic work, he managed to have his own family, his own money and properties—in many ways, his own life. He did not dare to look for a job outside of the family firm— he could not completely separate from his twin—but he could at least assume a position of responsibility in the firm and be respected by the employees and by the rest of his family. He fantasised that his son could do better than him, and take a step forward on the path of emancipation. Against his wife's and all the family's wishes and opinions, he wanted his child to attend a very prestigious international school in our area, and start to learn English. Having sufficiently worked though envy and hostility (and the *mors tua, vita mea* position) in his long analysis, he felt he could do something generous for his son. Again, a bit of idealisation (together with a slightly hypomanic position, but a lively supporting imagination) acted as potential fuel for the development of a separate self, now projected into the child. He used to say, "Maybe my child will not live in my small town. He will study at Oxford!"

References

Bion, W. R. (1950). The imaginary twin. In: *Second Thoughts. Selected Papers on Psychoanalysis*. London: Karnac, 1993.

Bion, W. R. (1967). *Second Thoughts. Selected Papers on Psychoanalysis*. London: Karnac, 1993.

Joseph, E. D. (1959). An unusual fantasy in a twin with an inquiry into the nature of fantasy. *Psychoanalytic Quarterly, 28*: 189–206.

Joseph, E. D. (1961). The psychology of twins. *Journal of the American Psychoanalytic Association, 9*: 158–166.

Joseph, E. D. (1975). Psychoanalysis—science and research: twin studies as a paradigm. *Journal of the American Psychoanalytic Association, 23*: 3–31.

Joseph, E. D., & Tabor, J. H. (1961). The simultaneous analysis of a pair of identical twins and the twinning reaction. *Psychoanalytic Study of the Child, 16*: 275–299.

Lewin, V. (2004). *The Twin in the Transference*. London: Whurr.

Tustin, F. (1981). Psychological birth and psychological catastrophe. In: J. Grotstein (Ed.), *Do I Dare Disturb the Universe* (pp. 182–196). London: Karnac.

CHAPTER FOURTEEN

The lost twin: on various types of reaction to having a twin sibling

Agnieszka Topolewska

My goal in this chapter is to explore some of the types of reaction to having a twin sibling described in analytical and popular literature. Against this background, I investigate how my patient experiences twinship, what impact it had on her development and on the nature of her defence mechanisms, and how it manifested itself in our therapeutic relation.

The event that inspired me to write this chapter was the experience of watching a sequence of short videos of various infant twins, recorded by their parents. In the majority of the videos, the twins were preoccupied with each other, whether in an act of symbiosis or an act of rivalry. It seemed as if they were enmeshed with each other, in their own hermetic world, in which external stimuli, such as a parent's voice or touch, came as a surprise. The literature on this topic also focuses predominantly on enmeshment (the phenomenon of "twinning") and sameness.

Watching these videos, I had a thought about my patient—it had been months since she last mentioned her twin brother, to whom she had not spoken for a year. I was surprised by the intensity of the relation between twins, and I wondered why twinship is a marginalised topic in therapy. I came to think that I had been ignoring the presence of my patient's twin brother. I remembered my patient's words: she told me that the twin pregnancy was at first diagnosed as a single pregnancy, and the other child was said to be a uterine tumour. She was convinced that it was her brother who had been misdiagnosed as a "tumour". It seemed to me, recalling Bion's paper, "The imaginary twin", that just as a singleton can phantasise about having a twin, a twin might phantasise about being a singleton.

Before I set out to explore psychological phenomena in twins, I would like to touch on some of the universal aspects related to my main topic. These are applicable to any analytical practice, with both twins and any other patients.

Klein (1963) suggested that the phantasy of having a twin is a common response to an "unsatisfied wish for an understanding without words" (p. 300) and to a "ubiquitous yearning for an unattainable perfect internal state" (p. 300). This

> phantasy represents those un-understood and split-off parts, which the individual is longing to regain, in the hope of achieving wholeness and complete understanding; they are sometimes felt to be ideal parts. At other times the twin represents an entirely reliable, in fact, idealized internal object. (p. 302)

What we imagine is our second self, an ideal companion, who "understands me perfectly, almost perfectly, because he is me, almost me" (Wright, 1997, p. 33).

According to Bion (1984[1967]),

> the imaginary twin goes back to his very earliest relationships and is an expression of his inability to tolerate an object that was not entirely under his control. The function of the imaginary twin was thus to deny a reality different from himself. (p. 19)

Lewin (1992, p. 11) writes that the imaginary twin can be considered a psychic retreat, using Steiner's notion, preventing development towards a depressive position (Lewin, 2002, p. 11).

In the case of real twins, the above-mentioned processes and phenomena find their embodiment in the actual presence of the other twin, alike or almost identical, and also in terms of biology and genetics. As Lewin (2002) puts it, twins face strong conflicts between remaining enmeshed with each other and separating from each other;

they also have difficulties in constituting an identity separate from the other twin. Each twin faces a conflict between the twinship, with its lack of true containment provided by the other immature baby, and the relation with the mother, a mature container, but one which interferes with the twinship (p. 4). Where the twin is the primary object, the projective and introjective identifications between the two set up powerful interpenetrating forces, creating a confusion of identities. There is a lack of individual ego boundaries and integrity, the "skin" being around the pair rather than the individual (Lewin, 1994, p. 501).

With twins, rivalry is extraordinarily strong. Where the twins are enmeshed with each other, and the mother is in some way excluded from their relation, not mediating in their intense rivalry, the only possible resolution is via one twin triumphing over and vanquishing the other (Lewin, 2002, p. 12). In extreme circumstances, it can lead to a hermetic, mutually damaging situation. Lewin (2002) quotes Wallace (1994) to describe the example of Jennifer and June Gibbons, twins who isolated themselves from other people and lived in their own world, strengthening their auto-destructive behaviour until one of them died of exhaustion. After Jennifer's death, June, the survivor, said, "At long last I am all June, not a part of Jennifer. Somebody had to break the vicious circle. We were war weary. It had been a long battle. We were both a burden to each other" (Wallace, 1996, p. 273).

"Where a maternal object is recognized", as Lewin (2002) puts it, "there is rivalry for the dominant position and possession of mother. The sibling rivalry is increased because of the special nature of the twin relation" (p. 12).

The atmosphere of twinning (or enmeshment between twins), in the phases of both confused identities and of rivalry, was well illustrated by Makuszyński in the novel "The Two Who Stole The Moon" (1928). The main protagonists, twin brothers, have established a mutual relation which excludes other people, who, in turn, view the brothers as unintelligible, intolerable, or even frightening:

> "They are so much alike that even their mother isn't able to tell one from the other; so we've tied a red ribbon to one boy's ankle, and a white ribbon to the other's. Then the one who got the white ribbon became angry and tried to take away his brother's ribbon, which he thought was more attractive, but the other one didn't want to let it go. It resulted in such screams and scuffles that we had no choice but to

remove the ribbons altogether to stop the arguments. . . ." When they started to use human language, the people of the town found it hard to tolerate the noise. . . . They shouted without any reason; it gave them some kind of strange pleasure, which only they understood. And as they always did exactly the same things, Jacek wasn't going to keep silent when Placek decided to shout, so they both yelled.

"Why are you screaming?" one of them asked out of the blue.

"Because you are!" was the answer.

"I see!" said the first one, and they kept yelling. (Makuszyński, 2010[1968], 21–35, translated for this edition)

Defensive twinning, in both actual twins and in those who have an "imaginary twin", serves as an instrument for denying or evading separateness, to maintain an apparently calm state of mind, an illusion of total control, an existence free from conflicts, separation anxieties, differences, and loss.

Since the beginning of therapy with Ms J (now in its fifth year), we have been struggling with her difficulties in separating from the object and her weak tolerance of any signs of independence. When Ms J decided to seek treatment (she was forty at that time), she suffered from bulimic disorders and had no experience of long-term relationships with men. She did not have her own place to live, and her career, in spite of a good education, was progressing only very slowly. She lived with her parents, who helped her raise her six-year-old son, a child born as a result of an affair of several months' standing. She had not seen the child's father since their son was born. Thoughts about moving out, having a relation with a man, and pursuing a more independent and satisfying career provoked intense anxiety and resistance in Ms J, even though she felt trapped by the way she had functioned until that time.

Keeping to my main topic, I shall focus on Ms J's relation with her twin brother, leaving aside the subject of progress in our treatment and other areas of our work. In the first three or four years of therapy, the patient used to talk about her relation with her twin brother occasionally, although it did not emerge as one of the main issues at this time. I think I had the opportunity to gather quite a significant amount of information about their relation. I took this information into account, of course, and considered it in formulating my interpretations, but it seems now that I lacked the perspective which would allow me to think that a person born a twin is always "in the shadow of the other twin", to use Lewin's (2002) phrase, and that this shadow also falls on transference relationships.

As I already mentioned, Ms J used to stress that the twin pregnancy was misdiagnosed as a single pregnancy, and that the other child was mistaken for a uterine tumour. Ms J was born first, so she claims that it was her brother who was mistaken for a "tumour". Due to a genetic deformation of her legs, Ms J had to undergo numerous medical procedures and a significant amount of surgery as a child. This resulted in long periods of separation from her mother and brother. Her brother was born with a dent in the temporal area of his skull. The patient imagined that, due to lack of space in her mother's womb, her legs were driven into her brother's head. She thought that there was not enough space for both of them because of her mother's petite body size. I understood this in terms of a containment deficiency; the patient felt that there was not enough space for her in her mother's mind. Piontelli (2002) suggested that because in prenatal and postnatal life twins have to compete for food and oxygen, and cope with additional stimulation coming from their sibling, they quite often have to compete for individual, limited attention from their mother (p. 72). Ms J reported that she and her twin were clearly differentiated in childhood: she was reasonable and amenable, while her brother became an impulsive trouble-maker. She told me that when her brother misbehaved at school, the teachers appealed to her reason. Her brother, in turn, used his aggressiveness to protect Ms J from other children. I came to understand that these twins developed an interdependence based on delegating specific functions, and, therefore, my patient's impulsive and active function was placed in her brother. In hindsight, I think that this line of interpretation, correct as it might have been, did not touch on the true essence of Ms J's internal relation with her twin.

Now I present material from our fourth and fifth year of treatment. At that time, the patient, then aged forty-four, had bought her own flat and moved out from her parents' house, together with her son.

Moving house was an unusually painful process for the woman, a process which I could label "chronic" (she waited a year after purchasing the apartment before finally moving in). Ms J compared this process to a painful tearing of the skin that connected her to her parents. It is interesting to note that at the onset of this phase, Ms J had a sudden, intense conflict over money issues with her twin brother, which resulted in quite a dramatic split between them. After this, she stopped mentioning him, as if he did not exist. At first, I did not pay much attention to this development. It seems that my patient's subsequent words are well suited to describing my own attitude at that time: "I never thought that the fact that I have a twin could have any consequences for me." It could be said that we both shared the same belief that Ms J lived in a world consisting solely of herself and her parents, covered with one common skin, as if they were in one single belly, which was torn apart by Ms J's leaving home. The patient herself viewed this as the effect of my *cruel therapeutic procedures*. One might think that, while the twin brother was temporarily expelled from Ms J's consciousness, her defensive twinning was very much alive in her relationships with her parents and with me. My comments on transference, though, were focusing mainly on the patient's relation with her maternal object or with the parental couple, without attaching much importance to twin transference. In time, I came to understand that, for Ms J, moving out amounted to freeing space for the other, marginalised twin. As Lewin (1994) puts it, "The baby at the breast excludes the other both from mother and from itself and, while this might lead to feelings of triumph, it will also engender a fear of attack by the other excluded, envious baby" (p. 499). Ms J's grievances, directed towards me as the perpetrator of her moving out, were more than just a projection into me of her wishes for development and separation; in her mind, I was a furious, devious, retaliating twin, who intended to appropriate Ms J's connection with her parents by expelling her from her parents' home.

It is important to note that, at that time, an unidentified tumour was discovered in the abdomen of the patient's father. A complicated diagnostic procedure began, which required Ms J's father to undergo numerous medical tests, some of which required him to travel. Ms J became involved in these procedures, at the same time monopolising the care around her father. She reacted angrily to my interpretation that she was not allowing her brother to take care of their father.

At the next session, she reported that she had had a dream.

> She had dreamt that she was in her parent's flat, which was situated on a high floor of an apartment block; she was looking out of the window at the surrounding neighbourhood. She noticed a new, low, two-storey

building, which had not been there before. She considered the building and wondered what was inside. In the meantime, her brother had gone missing and her parents were looking for him. Ms J left the flat with them to look for her brother. Together they approached the new, two-storey building; it turned out to be a Borstal. Her brother was with some other children in the courtyard, surrounded by barbed wire. He asked Ms J to help him get out, but he was emphatic that he would need a bulletproof jacket to escape. They helped him get through the fence.

In her first, spontaneous association, Ms J commented, "I don't think he would need a bullet-proof jacket to protect himself from my anger"; her next words were, "I can't remember ever being jealous of him."

Ms J remembered that during her childhood there actually had been a Borstal near their parents' house. Every time her brother misbehaved, their parents threatened to put him there. The patient, as a little girl, believed in those threats and was extremely anxious that her brother really could be sent to the Borstal. In her further associations, rich with childhood memories and extended over a number of sessions, she told me about her restless "globetrotter" brother, whom she never could keep up with due to her disability. She was told that when they were infants, and her brother was at the crawling stage, she, with her legs in plaster for several weeks at a time, would crawl after him, pulling herself forward with her arms. She also mentioned that, for a few years in later childhood, they would spend their summer holidays in the countryside at her grandmother's house. Her brother used to run around all day with the other children, but her grandmother forbade her to do the same. In adolescence, Ms J's brother used to party a lot and date various girls, while she mostly spent her time at home, waiting for him to come back. "I felt like a faithful wife who waited for him, while he kept going out and coming home. He had a lot of girlfriends, but he always came back to see me," she consoled herself.

It seems that Ms J's brother, contrary to her wishes, was not interested in developing a symbiotic relation and twinning. My patient was painfully confronted with his separateness and exposed to experiencing the significant differences between them: not only differences of gender, but also differences in degree of physical mobility. During her sessions, Ms J often recalled how she had seen me running up the stairs to my consulting room; she imagined that I owned a sports car, and she was very attentive to any sign of impulsiveness on my part. It seems that she saw me as her trouble-making brother, and she felt that my attributes made me someone more potent, mobile, and active than her, exposing her to feelings of separation. She coped with her feeling of neglect by claiming that it was her brother who was the bad twin; she thought that he was a nuisance and her parents would be better off without him. She got rid of him by convincing herself for long periods of time that there was no one else except herself and her parents. She clung to them, feeling that she shared a common skin with them. It seems that Ms J's dream indicated a movement towards acceptance of her brother's existence, his separateness, and his relation with their parents.

It was at the time of this surfacing of her memories of her twin brother that Ms J began to complain more intensively about her somatic troubles. She had started mentioning this a couple of months earlier, after the Polish plane crash near Smolensk. At that session, she was mainly troubled with the death of the President and his wife. She said, "They were such a wonderful couple, such a loving couple", but, at the same time, she complained about paresis in her right hand, and she was convinced she was seriously ill. She suspected she might have cancer in various places in her body: her head, breast, or stomach. In time, the pains and anxiety were focused specifically on her lower abdomen; she underwent numerous diagnostic tests in an attempt to locate the tumour. Until now, my interpretations had focused mainly on the patient's fear of losing her parents (the plane crash coincided with Ms J's moving house), and on her worries about her father's health (her identification with her sick father). Now I was surprised to realise that I had missed the fact that it was not just that the presidential couple had died in the crash near Smolensk: the president was himself also a twin brother. I was surprised to realise that I had been observing only a single child in relation with the parental couple. I took a risk and said that Ms J seemed to be very absorbed in searching for a tumour in her abdomen, and that it might have something to do with her brother. She answered, "I was ashamed to tell you, because it's so strange. Because on one hand I'm afraid there's something there, but. on the other, when I tried to feel something in there [she pointed to her stomach], a thought came to me—it's my brother; and I felt relieved he was there. But why relief? A tumour is something bad, something dangerous."

Samuel Beckett, the alleged "Patient A" from "The imaginary twin" (Bion, 1967), obsessively mentioned twinship in his literary art. Ms J's phantasy about the brother–tumour reminds me of Beckett's "Fizzle 4" (1976), where the narrator (a voice of undetermined gender) tells us how he/she remained inside while his/her twin was born:

"I gave up before birth, it is not possible otherwise, but birth there had to be, it was he, I was inside, that's how I see it, it was he who wailed, he who saw the light, I didn't wail, I didn't see the light, it's impossible I should have a voice, impossible I should have thoughts, and I speak and think, I do the impossible, it is not possible otherwise, it was he who had a life, I didn't have a life." (Beckett, 1976, pp. 31–33)

My patient attained oneness with her brother in this phantasy; her brother became a part of her, her own tumour, under her control. But Ms J also became her own mother, having a tumour-twin in her uterus, and her own father, who probably had a peritoneal tumour. I must add that Ms J suspected her son had cancer as well. In this way, she disavowed her brother's separate existence, her moving house, and her son's growing up. It all melted into one cancerous pulp.

One could say I managed to recognise a defensive mechanism which resulted in Ms J's enmeshment with other people, encapsulation in a shared identity. This recognition allowed my patient to move on from identifying with her brother inside herself, and to move towards mourning over the realisation that her brother was separate from her. The twin brother was now in a position to be found once again, in the patient's dream and in our sessions, in my mind and in Ms J's mind. After some time, Ms J reconciled with her brother, and they are now in regular contact. Ms J's preoccupation with her parents' life receded, and her stomach pains subsided.

Summary

For some time, my mind had seemed like a "twin" reflection of my patient's mind. I was not in a position to have my own separate perspective, which is why I could not recognise Ms J's twin-like enmeshment with her internal objects. When, in spite of these difficulties, I was able to recognise various aspects of twin relationships in the transference and in Ms J's other relations, I was able to be more effective in helping her in her move towards separateness and internal integrity.

References

Beckett, S. (1976). *Fizzles*. New York: Grove Press.

Bion, W. R. (1967). *Second Thoughts: Selected Papers on Psychoanalysis.* London: Karnac, 1984

Klein, M. (1963). On the sense of loneliness. In: *Envy and Gratitude and Other Works* (pp. 300–313). London: Hogarth Press, 1980.

Lewin, V. (1994). Working with a twin: implications for the transference. *British Journal of Psychotherapy, 10*: 499–510.

Lewin, V. (2002). The twin in the transference. In: B. Bishop, A. Foster, J. Klein, & V. O'Connell (Eds.), *Ideas in Practice. Practice of Psychotherapy Series: Book 2* (pp. 3–24). London: Karnac.

Makuszyński, K. (1928). *O Dwóch Takich Co Ukradli Księżyc* [The Two Who Stole The Moon]. Kraków: Wydawnictwo Zielona Sowa, 2010.

Piontelli, A. (2002). *Twins: From Foetus to Child*. London: Routledge.

Wallace, M. (1996). *Silent Twins*. London: Vintage.

Wright, L. (1997). *Twins: And What They Tell Us about Who We Are*. New York: John Wiley.

CHAPTER FIFTEEN

Experiences with siblings in early childhood: specific forms of transference and countertransference in therapeutic processes

Sabine Trenk-Hinterberger

Psychoanalytical thinking on siblings

My thoughts on the role of siblings in the later psychic life of patients developed when I was confronted with a lack of psychoanalytic interest and research in this field. I wondered why there were no further discussions on sibling influence in the scientific context, despite there being a change from Freudian views on the importance of the father to later aspects of the significance of the mother for psychic growth. Today, we find a predominance of research on the early mother–child relation, because oedipal concepts seem to be less important than during Freud's time. Nevertheless, transference concepts appear to focus only on the mother and father; siblings are hardly ever mentioned. Before I come to the discussion of these processes, I refer to the literature I could find in German; the neglect of sibling issues is obvious.

In 1995, there was a paper published by Wellendorf in which he described the lack of psychoanalytic discussion on conscious and unconscious conflicts in sibling relations. He mentioned the violent "sibling war" from the very beginning of the psychoanalytic movement, which possibly led to an inhibition of frank communication on this topic in written arguments and reflections. In this context, it is reported that Freud himself, one of eight siblings, had an apparently traumatic experience with a brother in his biographical development, something that appears to be completely neglected in his writings. We do not know much about the circumstances of this event, but it is a fact that Freud's little brother died at six months of age (Freud, E., Freud, L., & Grubrich-Simitis, 1989). Freud, then approximately two years old, seems to have had no chance to mourn this death due to his limited verbal capacities at that time. This death could have led Freud to withdraw silently. In all his writings, there is no direct hint that he was ever, even as an adult, concerned with the death of his brother; it is as if an unconscious feeling of guilt should remain repressed. Maciejewski (2006) sees in Freud's obsessed preoccupation with Moses a reference to the persistent traumatic effects of his brother's early death. We all know how often death wishes towards younger siblings occur in childhood, so that an actual death can have traumatic consequences for the surviving child. In Freud's theoretical work, the Oedipus complex was of central significance; a focus which did not allow the examination of sibling relationships and independent problems between sisters and brothers, as the overall attention was concentrated on the father–mother–child constellation.

Wellendorf's paper seems to have remained without any resonance. In the USA, Volkan and Ast (1997) described unconscious phantasies of siblings becoming key elements in an adult's psychic life, but there was no obvious influence on psychoanalytic thinking on siblings. The discussion on the psychoanalytic significance of siblings received a new impulse in 2007 with the publication of two papers, one by Heenen-Wolff and the other by Adam-Lauterbach. Both authors find a lack of readiness by psychoanalytic writers to address the problems of siblings and both refer to different reasons as to why this should be. Heenen-Wolff discusses the question of how fraternity can develop from sibling relationships and sees a new and progressive horizontality in social relationships. Adam-Lauterbach discusses sibling transference–countertransference development in therapeutic processes. The object relationships of adults are based on their early experiences with family members, which is why we should examine their early childhoods and, especially, the role that a sibling played for a child.

The influence of siblings in infantile socialisation

A child grows up in an environment in which both the mother and father, known as the primary objects, are of the greatest importance. Whereas grandparents often see their grandchildren irregularly, siblings live in everyday contact with each other and share many common experiences and constructive games, as well as quarrels. This is why there can be no doubt that a sibling influences the socialisation of a child. What we do not know, however, is how psychoanalysis can offer a concept that addresses the ongoing processes active in these early years. The mother–child relation (who would not refer to it as a symbiosis!) seems to be a construct of only two individuals. There appears to be no father, no siblings, no other: it is as if third objects do not exist. This focus on the early exclusive mother–child relation can be understood as an effort to develop a clear concept in clinical references. The first child in a family is born into a situation in which mother and child can be together in a relatively undisturbed way; the role of the father, of course, begins to develop at this time. Each further child has to learn that its relation to its mother cannot be exclusive, that other children demand a great deal and that it will be restricted in its desire for its mother. In accordance with this experience, each child who acquires a sibling loses its "throne" and has to realise that it is expelled from paradise with its mother. In both constellations, to discover siblings after birth or to experience the birth of siblings after a time with the mother alone, the young child has to cope with intensely negative feelings concerning its unwanted rivals, who inadmissibly demand its mother's attention. These feelings are in no way positive; the frustrated child probably experiences anger, hatred, rage, jealousy, and envy. These are feelings that nobody wants to hear or see, feelings with which the child is left alone (even the father does not seem to be able to contain such desperate states in his child). The slogan "death to siblings" appears to be a taboo, one with serious consequences, possibly even including the prohibition of thinking such thoughts.

I now present my basic hypothesis as to why the problems of siblings have not experienced a wider public discussion: early negative feelings have been repressed; children are not allowed to act them out or to talk about them while growing up. Death wishes have to be denied, any aggression towards little brothers or sisters is followed by punishment, and the older child feels guilty and attempts to forget such shameful experiences. These experiences with siblings are activated not only in early life, but also in later defence mechanisms that cannot be worked through in adult psychoanalytic therapies because of collusion between patient and therapist. There is an unconscious agreement between both not to reveal the deep psychic devastation wrought by sibling hatred.

The implicit theory of transference–countertransference in psychoanalytic thinking

When thinking about transference processes, we see that the mother and father appear to be of primary importance for our patients. They let us know during therapy that they view us as being like their parents in the past, and we try to work through with them their perceptions and their memories. The psychoanalyst expects a distortion of perception within his patient, which he attempts to understand through his knowledge, his implicit theory, and his subjective sight: that is, he already anticipates explanations while transference is still developing. His implicit theory leads him to an understanding of his patient as being in a father or mother transference process and to interpret his associations and communications in this context.

Considering psychoanalytic thinking today, there is a broad consensus that the mother is considered to be the most important object in early human life. At the time that Freud was writing, however, the father seems to have been of greater importance; the role of the male subject at that time was of wide interest and Freud discovered the Oedipus complex, which definitely influenced thinking on transference. The focus on family dynamics that were seen much more precisely at that time contributed considerably to the development of psychoanalysis. During that period, we encounter a role for women which today we find not only out of date, but completely untenable, and this is not an extreme feminist point of view. Our thinking about gender roles has completely changed over the past few decades; historical events such as two world wars involving Germany have contributed to seeing new generations with their children in a different light. The loss of fathers during the wars led to new tasks for the mothers, who had to care for their children alone. So, it is no wonder that the role of a woman and mother had to be perceived and discussed in an overall social context. Psychoanalytic theory changed to a focus on the mother-child relation, away from the father, and on early processes. As Mitchell (2003) describes, the disappearance of hysteria (as a "condition") in the twentieth century can be connected with the failure of psychoanalytic theory to give a structured and symbolic place to sibling relationships. Siblings are essential in all social relationships, she argues, including those of parents and children. A society without a father, described by Mitscherlich (1963), could not ignore the new structures; the new role for women was followed by a new sensibility regarding the processes at the beginning of life. Still, sibling relationships were not considered as important.

I think the transference concept was influenced by a change from emphasising the oedipal conflict and the role of triangulating father to a focus on the early mother, coupled with corresponding research on early emotional and mental processes: for example, mentalization (Fonagy, Gergely, Jurist, & Target, 2002), the autistic–contiguous position (Ogden, 1989), and the alpha function (Bion, 1963). In psychoanalytical work, transference development seems to follow the mother–child relation, although the gender of the psychoanalyst should be taken into account. Whereas a female psychoanalyst will be seen in a motherly aspect, a male colleague will be perceived more often as a father, at least in the beginning of the psychoanalytic process. I cannot elaborate on these thoughts at present; what I would say is that transference development follows certain patterns which should be doubted—there seems to be a consensus about the dominance of mother and father transference "tracks", although the changed social conditions suggest that the classical father–mother–child family structure cannot be the only basis for a theory of transference development. Transferences occur in all aspects of life and we can, above all, work through and correct them through psychoanalysis. That further objects are of importance for the development of relational structures, and that implies transference readiness, seems to be generally recognised, but appears to be ignored in the literature on case studies regarding sibling problems.

I wish, therefore, to pose the question of whether implicit theoretical convictions on transference, which influence the psychoanalytic process, can be verified through research. How do we know that, in an analytical process, the feelings of our patients can be led back to their early experiences with their mother? Or does the concept of transference mean, above all, feelings for the psychoanalyst originally developed in relation to the father? These two aspects, the first perhaps of an earlier origin than the latter, cannot be found in a pure form; they overlap and are probably mixed in a longer process. On the other side of these conceptions, there should be seen further important objects, besides the primaries, which I suppose influence transference in the analytic process in an effective way. As already mentioned, our focus here is on siblings, although grandparents seem to play an important role in transference processes, too.

Vertical and horizontal aspects in transference lines

Whereas a child's relation to its parents can be described as vertical (i.e., originating in a generational hierarchy), the connection to its siblings can be seen as horizontal (i.e., having equal standing). Freud viewed the relationships between siblings with regard to the relationships to their parents. He stated that as soon as further children were born in a family, the Oedipus complex extended into the family complex. Heenen-Wolff (2007) describes that, at that time, Freud did not speak about a sibling complex. She cites Laplanche, who described a triangle: not the oedipal triangle, but one defined through rivalry. In this, he saw the sibling complex, consisting of the child–parents–sibling. Although Freud saw the situation of the child and its siblings in relation to jealousy, he did not analyse his own experiences with his two brothers and five sisters. He pointed to the fact that siblings often have negative feelings for each other, but was mainly interested in hierarchical relationships. It can be safely assumed that the older child does not want any newcomers, and that the younger children are opposed to the privileges of the elder one, so that envy, jealousy, and hatred are, thus, widespread among the siblings. The vertical relationships between parents and children lead to the acceptance of gender and generational differences and the incest taboo. Sexual relationships between siblings can be seen as a heritage consequence of incestuous desires for the parents, but sibling relationships can also be understood as a counterbalance to oedipal relationships. In the horizontal relation, conflicts from the vertical relation might be expressed, or the siblings as real sexual objects cause new conflicts with each other.

According to Heenen-Wolff (2007), the psychoanalytic frame of reference represents these vertical–hierarchical relationships between parents and their children. In psychoanalytic therapies in a face-to-face position, however, therapist and patient have the same horizontal position, so that the interaction in the present is important, not the transference of the patient. Heenen-Wolff cites Ferro, who sees in the narration of the patient an exclusive reference to the emotional presence of both protagonists of the cure. In these theoretical conceptions, the transferences seem to be less significant; their relevance, nevertheless, is not clear. Does the vertical relation favour transference feelings for primary objects and the horizontal one feelings for the sibling generation? In my opinion, this view neglects the movements, currents, and trends of unconscious processes and ignores the immense variety of influences on our psychic life. The therapeutic process is definitely influenced by the setting, but the way in which we can work with transference lines is dependent on manifold factors that we get to know during our common work with the patient.

Systematic research on sibling influence on transference does not yet exist, and the role of countertransference has been neglected until now. Adam-Lauterbach (2007) has demonstrated in a case study that working through sibling relationships can lead to a changed view of psychopathology and the inner psychic world of patients. Her patient had developed a sister transference on the psychotherapist, which helped her to free herself from pathological ties to her mother. In her countertransference, the author sees a bridge function in which the deficit in the relation of her patient to the primary objects could be connected with the close pathological relation to the sister. Adam-Lauterbach sees the dynamics of the horizontal level as relatively independent, but she refers to the interdependence with the vertical (parent) level for the understanding of basic pathologies.

Viewing the many open questions in this field, and the manifold unclear influences on these processes, I turn back to the experiences of siblings and choose just a few topics: to discuss vertical and horizontal levels, I want to look at new family structures, the relationships of siblings to each other, and the special situation of twins and so-called replacement children. Transference–countertransference is the leading concept for these thoughts.

Siblings in new family structures: in relation to each other, in special constellations as twins, and as replacement children

Siblings in new family structures

In new contemporary families, we do not always find a father–mother–child structure, but a variety of new ways of living together. We find families without a father, single parents, mixed families of different origin, stepmothers, stepfathers, new siblings from new marriages, and so on. All these family members are somehow related to one another, most of them in a dyadic, some also in a triadic, manner. How transference–countertransference constellations are affected by these conditions is still to be established; there is a need for more case studies to better understand these processes. The Oedipus complex *vs.* sibling conflict, as described in the literature, does not seem to be sufficient to work with a concept wide enough to understand so many variations. Analytic work will be defined through the analyst's attitude to the vertical or horizontal viewpoint, and his perception of the complexities of his patient. Does the analyst, in his or her countertransference process, feel like the little brother of the patient, a real or a social father, a motherly friend, or even a protective sister? Perhaps there are many changes in transference lines during the therapeutic process that complicate our efforts to find regular connections in these processes.

With these thoughts, I come to the following conclusions: whether we look at relationships in either a horizontal or vertical direction, we can expect unconscious themes such as hatred, envy, incestuous impulses, and/or oedipal conflicts. We will find them in the transference–countertransference constellations with our patients, provided that there is sufficient time for them to develop. This is why it seems to me very difficult to differentiate between a vertical and horizontal viewpoint in a constructive manner.

Siblings with each other

If two children are born in a family after a short interval, their relation can be regarded as being on a horizontal level. Families with many children, however, will have a different age distribution structure and considerably differing conditions of socialisation. Siblings with many years of age difference between them have much less in common than those closer together, so a horizontal viewpoint must be seen as, at least, problematic. Whether siblings whose development is at very different stages can have feelings of equality is an open question; presumably, they can feel solidarity with each other. A horizontal viewpoint, therefore, seems to be limited when applied to the togetherness of siblings

Families in which the parents have a deficient relation to their children can interact with each other in different ways: some of them witness siblings coming together to overcome their misery by protecting and helping each other, others see children having aggressive quarrels and pursuing their siblings with extreme envy and malicious actions. This behaviour can be understood as a reaction to parental failure; some of the children try to save each other by presenting a unified front, whereas the others seem to shift their negative feelings from parents to siblings, as if parental acceptance was more important. In such constellations, we find movement from a vertical to a horizontal level, but it seems complicated to separate them, as intermeshing renders the conceptual differentiation more difficult.

Siblings might be transitional objects for each other, dependent on their mother's behaviour, so, again, it is difficult to differentiate between vertical and horizontal viewpoints. Following Freud, a seduction of a child by a sibling also appears problematic regarding a vertical or horizontal level. Freud described in the "Wolf Man" (1918b) that the seven-year-old sister of his patient, who was five years old, sexually seduced her little brother, which was presumably the basis for his later symptoms. We observe that sibling relationships cannot be understood solely through referring to horizontal connections. It would appear complicated to decide which kind of phenomenon belongs to which kind of level. In the development of transference and countertransference, it is important to realise how difficult it is to clarify the different aspects.

Twins in their relation to each other

Twins are children with a clear horizontal relation to each other, and who are in an equal position except for a few minutes of separation at birth. Other siblings, even those born within one year of each other, never find such conditions in their socialisation. Looking at this constellation can help to continue my thoughts about comparable experiences in early life and their influence in later years. Twins have a special relation to each other, never being left alone, and always having a reliable "double" whom they can trust through their whole life. On the other hand, twins have to share their primary object from the beginning of their lives; they never experience an exclusive symbiotic fusion with their mother alone. There is always a rival with identical wishes for her and high demands on her attention. In therapy, twins as single individuals are reputed to need special care; indeed, my own experiences with patients in my practice have confirmed this expectation. The early experience of being together with a similar object day and night and for a long period of time might lead in the twin to an attitude of desiring a permanent presence of the therapist. This transference can be understood on a horizontal level if the patient seeks to reconstruct the situation with his twin, if he is, in fact, looking for an ever-present object like himself. However, it could also be seen on a vertical level, as if the patient expresses wishes that cannot be fulfilled by means of a sibling, but by the mother and/or father. These could be oedipal conflicts as well as symbiotic needs for an adult object who would allow the patient to be regressive. The development of lines of transference will be better understood by carefully working through these possibilities and by considering countertransference.

Replacement children

With a so-called replacement child, a theoretical viewpoint on transference processes seems to be especially complicated. A replacement child holds the place of a previous child in the family, generally a sibling who died before the next child was born. If a family can mourn for this lost child, the later sibling has the chance of an undisturbed life. The less the family have worked through the loss, the more the next child has difficulties in developing an identity of its own. On the horizontal level, this child has to contend with a phantom sibling, a child whom he does not know but with whom his parents are often occupied. They compare the present child with the lost one and, even if this process remains unconscious, the replacement child cannot feel free in developing his personality. On the vertical level, this child discovers overprotective parents who desperately want a safe life for their child and are extremely anxious to prevent a further loss. In such a constellation, if a replacement child comes later to therapy, counter-transference would be a most important reference to the developing transference of this child. The horizontal viewpoint also seems to be very important, as phantasies about the lost sibling whom the patient never knew can contribute in forming the transference. This object, mediated through the parents, can have a clear presence for the following child, demonstrated by its talking about its sibling in a matter of fact manner. However, the previous child can remain completely in the phantasies of the replacement child when the parents remain silent and do not talk about it. Parental mourning can, thus, lead to an integration of the painful loss and help the following child to accept this fate. As Hirsch (1999) writes, the replacement child oscillates between an acceptance of parental needs through identification with their expectations and rebellion through struggling for an identity of its own, with feelings of guilt in both conditions. In working through these conflicting attitudes with the patient, the therapist can try to differentiate between the vertical and horizontal levels in examining his countertransference. Although a difficult task, this would be a way to gain a better understanding of transference processes.

Conclusion: the psychoanalyst's understanding of sibling transference

Based upon all the information that can be gathered about siblings in a therapeutic context, it is the role of the psychoanalyst that seems to be the most important in developing new concepts concerning the understanding of transference processes. First, the psychoanalyst can revise his theoretical convictions and verify his attitudes towards his thinking about the influence of additional objects, besides the primary objects, on transference. We know that our expectations contribute considerably to our perceptions, which is why we should continually reconsider our theoretical point of view. If sibling transference does not conform to the psychoanalyst's theory, a patient cannot work through his corresponding feelings; to understand the influence on his therapy we need research on these processes. A second point is the collusion between the patient and therapist that I mentioned in the first part of this chapter. If feelings about siblings are extremely threatening, there is no interest for both participants to uncover their existence—the unconscious agreement between patient and psycho-analyst prevents a further engagement in this field. Knowing the possibility of the existence of such mechanisms can change the atti-tude towards signs that hint in this direction. A third consideration about this situation is that it is up to the psychoanalyst to work on unconscious hindrances in order to create a situation in which the patient can develop. If he can understand sibling transference pro-cesses despite having different expectations, if he can see himself involved in his patient's resistance by analysing his countertransfer-ence, he can create a new basis for the common work between patient and analyst. The more he notices sibling dynamics in therapeutic processes, the more the psychoanalyst can take into consideration early sibling influences in his treatments. This knowledge, intellectual as well as emotional, will inform his interpretations and create widened, perhaps unexpected, interventions.

References

Adam-Lauterbach, D. (2007). Psychodynamische und psychopathologis-che Aspekte von Geschwisterbeziehungen. *Forum der Psychoanalyse, 23*: 203–218. [Psychodynamic and psychopathological aspects of sibling-hood. Translated for this edition].

Bion, W. R. (1963). *Elements of Psychoanalysis*. London: Heinemann.

Fonagy, P., Gergely, G., Jurist, E. L., & Target, M. (2002). *Affect Regulation, Mentalization and the Development of the Self*. New York: Other Press.

Freud, E., Freud, L,. & Grubrich-Simitis, I. (Eds.) (1989). *Freud. Sein Leben in Bildern und Texten* [Freud. His Life in Pictures and Papers]. Frankfurt: Suhrkamp Taschenbuch.

Freud, S. (1918b). *From the History of an Infantile Neurosis. S.E., 17*: 1–122. London: Hogarth.

Heenen-Wolff, S. (2007). Die Geschwisterbeziehung—Postmoderne psychoanalytische Perspektiven zur "Horizontalisierung" in der Beziehungswelt [The sibling relation—postmodern psychoanalytical perspective on 'Horizontality' in relationships]. *Psyche—Zeitschrift für Psychoanalyse und ihre Anwendungen, 61*: 541–559.

Hirsch, M. (1999). Die Wirkung schwerer Verluste auf die zweite Generation am Beispiel des Überlebendenschuldgefühls und des "Ersatzkindes" [The effect of serious losses on the second generation on example of the responsibility feelings of the survivors and the 'replacement child']. In: A.-M. Schlösser & K. Höhfeld (Eds.), Trennungen [Separations] (pp. 125–136). Gießen: Psychosozial, 1999.

Maciejewski, F. (2006). *Der Moses des Sigmund Freud. Ein unheimlicher Bruder* [The Moses of Sigmund Freud. An Uncanny Brother]. Göttingen: Vandenhoeck & Ruprecht.

Mitchell, J. (2003). *Siblings: Sex and Violence*. Cambridge: Polity Press.

Mitscherlich, A. (1963). *Auf dem Weg zur vaterlosen Gesellschaft* [On the way to a fatherless society]. Munich: R. Piper.

Ogden, T. H. (1989). *The Primitive Edge of Experience*. Lanham, MD: Jason Aronson (1992).

Volkan, V. D., & Ast, G. (1997). *Siblings in the Unconscious and Psychopathology*. Madison, CT: International Universities Press.

Wellendorf, F. (1995). Zur Psychoanalyse der Geschwisterbeziehung [Towards a psychoanalysis of siblings]. *Forum der Psychoanalyse, 11*: 295–310.

PART V

LATERAL *VS.* VERTICAL: THE INTERTWINING OF THE TWO PERSPECTIVES

Envy, jealousy, love, and generosity in sibling relations: the impact of sibling relations on future family relations

Jeanne Magagna, with observations by Andrea Amendolagine

Our early relations with our mother and father are vitally important—we often think about the roles our parents have played as nurturers, protectors, sources of companionship, and containers of anxiety. We also look at the way in which our relation with our parents has, for better or worse, left its legacy in our internal world. However, there is another important early relation which deeply affects us throughout life, and yet, this is not given the attention it deserves, in research, assessments, or in psychotherapy. I am talking about the relationships that we have with our siblings.

Our relations with our siblings are stages upon which intense emotions unfold. Jealousy, hatred, greed, love, and generosity can all be present at different times with different intensities, during different stages of the life-cycle. How we, as parents or therapists, understand the emotions present in sibling relations and appropriately support young brothers and sisters can heavily influence their ability to achieve intimate and emotionally healthy relations when they grow up and have families of their own (Coles, 2003).

Sibling relations can be internalised as a deep source of security and foster healthy emotional development and a sense of good self-esteem, but sibling relations can also determine low self-esteem and be detrimental to the development of the personality, as is shown in our book *Intimate Transformations: Babies with their Families* (Magagna et al., 2005). Sibling relations can affect not only how we parent our own children, but also how we relate to our partners, including in our sex lives and even, in some cases, in our ability to conceive. When siblings internalise good containing external and internal parents, sibling relations can generate love, promote hope, and help contain depressive pain, allowing the growth and development of family members through generations.

I assume that, just as we have an external family and many other important relations, in our internal world we have an internalised family with relations existing between the self and the internalised family members and other important people in our lives. Such internalised family members might be different from external family members, for they "are always coloured by our phantasies and projections" (Segal, 1979, p. 64). Bearing this in mind, I focus on both external and internalised sibling relations and their influence on family life. I look at the tricky question of when, how, and whether or not to intervene in a sibling relation to help the siblings develop a healthier future. I also look at what can happen when unhealthy sibling relations are internalised and later provide the impetus for re-enactment in adult life. In addition, I discuss how we can use dream analysis to observe and repair the internalised damaged sibling relations and, thus, promote the development of loving and more thoughtful intimate relations.

Anna Freud's war nurseries: two scenarios of peer relations

Between 1939 and 1945, Anna Freud (1973) kept careful diaries of the residential war nurseries where children were left without their parents. Here are some striking observations that she made.

Sam, twenty-two months

Sam had just stopped crying but still looked unhappy when Rose, also 22 months, entered the room. Rose was evidently struck by Sam's expression, she watched him critically for a moment, and then ran to him and empathically comforted and petted him. (A. Freud, 1973, p. 574)

At twenty-two months, Rose is able to be projectively identified with a caring parent and become moved by an empathic identification with twenty-two-month-old Sam. On the basis of the same needs and wishes, many young children in the nursery seemed to perfectly understand and identify with the difficulties and desires of the other children. There were many observations where the children played co-operatively, looking after one another, sharing objects.

However, what do you think happened when specific care-givers were assigned to small groups of young children? The group dynamics changed dramatically! The introduction of a substitute mother relation into the life of each child meant that the child developed more vivid and varied facial expressions and his whole personality unfolded, so that the child became more amenable to educational influences. At the same time, the children suddenly became insufferably demanding and unreasonable. Their jealousy, above all their possessiveness of the beloved grown-up, the foster-mother, became boundless. "Because the child had had an earlier permanent separation from his biological mother he was all the more clinging, with an inner conviction that the same permanent separation would repeat itself" (A. Freud, 1973, p. 590). Once there was a newly found, loved staff member, the child's beckoning for the mother figure to attend specially to himself, part of normal child–mother relations, took a variety of turns. The request to be specially thought about by a mother figure took the form of antisocial behaviour, illness, temper tantrums, and positive achievements. "Once love for a dependable person occurred there were inextricably intense feelings of jealousy, envy and frustration" (A. Freud, 1973, p. 592).

But why? It seems that the formation of a trusting attachment relation with a care-giver inextricably causes conscious frustration. The wish for *more* from the care-giver stimulates greed, jealousy of the others' special relation with "the mother figure", and envy of the care-giver, who has all the riches and keeps some for herself. Murderous resentment fuelled by feelings of extreme helplessness and impotence can also occur.

Similarly, a stable therapeutic group with a dependable group leader nourishes the group members with its warmth, accepts all parts of the group members, understanding their pain and suffering, and is destroyed neither by greedy possessive primitive love nor by destructive anger. This group entity is, essentially, functioning as "a mother" (Pines, 1978, pp. 115–128).

Just as in Anna Freud's residential nursery, once there is a stable group with the group functioning "as a mother", the group can mobilise aggressive and potentially destructive impulses, including the demand for special attention of the group for whomever has the worst problem (Nitsun, 1996). Anxieties in the group can re-create those present in the early mother–sibling relations.

Dreams brought by group members and the group's response can highlight the members' difficulty in seeing and bearing internalised sibling conflict transferred on to group members. Take the following group process, for example:

> A group member reports a dream, *I am on a kind of roller coaster, I am on a track, holding my nephew on my lap, my sister holding the other nephew on her lap in the seat behind. The countryside around looks like a burned-out forest. Suddenly the roller coaster begins going down a gorge, going faster and faster. It jumps the track and I see someone – not my sister, maybe my other sister – smash her head against a tree. I am OK and so is my nephew.* (Schlachet, 2002, p. 92)

Here we see how the group members' conscious wishes to be kind and socially acceptable lead some of them to say to the dreamer such things as, "In bringing the dream it seems you have 'warm and friendly feelings towards the group'". Split-off from the group's stream of conscious friendly dialogue is an unconscious deadly sibling rivalry. For some unexplored reason, the group's hostile feelings are being redirected to the internalised sibling/group members in the nightmare's narrative regarding the smashing of the sister's head!

The use of special time to elaborate on unconscious phantasies

It is quite normal for the firstborn to have a vast array of phantasies in relation to the parents' next baby. Many a firstborn child becomes very jealous of the new baby's intrusion between both him and his mother and him and his father (Dunn, 1984). Bettelheim scolded parents for not acknowledging and accepting their children's feelings of hate and rivalry towards "the new baby". He suggested that parental rebukes fostered repression of hostile feelings. Projections of hostility into internalised siblings turns them into frightening and persecutory nightmare figures (Rosenfeld, 1986). Bick (Magagna, 2002) suggested that with the arrival of another baby in the mother's womb, the firstborn suffers a loss of the mother accompanied by a loss of identity as "the baby in the mother's lap". Bick always felt it was useful to have the older child develop an identity with a peer group in nursery before the parents had another child.

Providing "special time" for the firstborn and enlisting the attentive support of the father can allow the firstborn to work through some sibling issues through play before the new baby is born. I now show three different play scenarios showing how twenty-two-month-old Lucia's feelings towards her new baby brother were transformed through active containment of parental figures, including a weekly visiting young child observer.

Observation one: Lucia, two years, six months

Lucia tells the mother she is having a baby and she threatens to kill her brother as soon as he is born, and adds that when the baby is born, she will wee under the table. At the moment, she is experiencing sleep difficulties, nightmares, and compulsive masturbation. Later, she embraces a baby doll, gives him to the observer and asks her to cuddle him. She then says, "The poor baby became very frightened during the night because a dragon came into the basket and frightened all the puppies."

Here we see that Lucia finds it possible to talk of her identity as a child having destructive feelings towards her brother, creating all sorts of insecurities within herself. Also, she feels herself to be someone in projective identification with a mother who will love and protect the baby (Adamo & Magagna, 2005, p. 98). Just as in Winnicott's *The Piggle* (1991), Lucia was trying to overcome some of the pain of losing her mother by projectively identifying with her and mothering the baby containing her own projected infantile feelings.

Here one sees how fury about the newborn can create somatic issues.

Observation two: Lucia, three years, seven and a half months; baby nine and a half months

Lucia is pervaded by a terrible anger, almost fury, against her baby brother. She torments him in many ways, and her mother scolds her. This prompts Lucia to leave the room, but then she quickly turns around and runs towards her brother, who is being held by mother. Lucia tugs at his shirt with her teeth and tears it . . . Sometime in the same hour Lucia says she is the very ill child and asks the observer to be a female doctor who succeeds in curing her. (Adamo & Magagna, 2005, p. 104)

Here, we see that the mother's simply scolding Lucia leaves her feeling even more the displaced, lonely child and her rage towards her baby brother increases. Unconsciously, Lucia senses that her "bad feelings" cause physical/psychological problems and internal damage.

Four months later, we see the following.

Observation three: Lucia four years; baby brother, Gianni, fourteen months

Impatiently anticipating the observer's regular hourly visit, Lucia has built a den for the two of them. She says that outside everything is covered with snow and ice and there are wolves all around. . . . She comments that she and the observer will be two polecats who will soon go into hibernation. (Adamo & Magagna, 2005, p. 105)

Lucia sucks her T-shirt and, when her brother Gianni approaches the door to the den, she refuses to let him in, saying she wants to be alone with the observer because she loves her so much. She then pretends to bring wounded puppies inside the den. They have been wandering in the nearby wood. She feeds and heals them while at the same time questioning them about their age, which each time is invariably one year, approximately the age of her brother Gianni (Adamo & Magagna, 2005, p. 105).

Afterwards, she cuddles "her baby", a doll, cuts it to pieces and pretends to eat all the pieces of her cut-up baby. "Following this, Lucia's mood changes, and she decides that she is going to let her brother in after all—but specifies that he will be a baby polecat and the observer's little brother" (Adamo & Magagna, 2005, p. 106).

Lucia takes care of the puppies in a rather haphazard way. Lucia then excitedly cuts up and eats "the baby". She has eagerly waited for the observer in order that there would be someone to accept her destructive phantasies without her having to concretely act them outside the safe space of play. In the safe space of play, Lucia's murderousness towards her baby brother Gianni diminishes. Her play enabled her to establish an internal link between her love and hate. Lucia thus enters a qualitatively different state of mind in relation to both her internal and her external brother. When Lucia is able to regain inner contact with the mother who is good and loving, Lucia is able to accept her brother Gianni. Psychologically Lucia has developed from having persecutory guilt making her feel "the sick child" to experiencing depressive anxieties and reparative activities towards her brother. She now allows her baby brother into the forbidden territory of the den. (Adamo & Magagna, 2005, p. 107)

The young child observer could not substitute for the real father, but, in her role as an observer, she did respond as he might, by providing a rescuing space, support, and understanding. The father's role in supporting the older child and the mother is crucial. This is fully substantiated in Dunn and Kendrick's book, *Siblings: Love, Envy and Understanding* (1982).

Such "special time" in the presence of a thoughtful adult is offered daily for half an hour in Tempo Lineare Nursery in Rome, where each child has a box of special toys collected by the child. The parents and teachers participate in young child observation groups to understand more about the meaning of each child's "special time symbolic play". It is only through the internalisation of good parents who offer psychological space for the firstborn to feel supported and understood that the firstborn will be able to develop the capacity for generosity and love to mitigate the destructive feelings towards the baby who has taken some of the parental nest away.

Unsupervised play of young children: when it is helpful,
when harmful, and when to intervene

As one can see from the observation of Lucia, young siblings under four years of age often will not have sufficiently internalised loving parents and the protective, limit-setting father function to contain their impulsive feelings. According to research findings, moderate conflict in the context of moderate warmth towards siblings leads to more social competence in peer relations in school (Stormshak, Bellanti, & Bierman, 1996), but what if the young children involved are finding it too difficult to develop loving and protective internalised parents who make it possible to have good relations with their siblings?

To promote thinking on this subject, I now present three observations of three young American brothers, Fred, five, Sam, three, and Bruno, one year old, who are playing without parental supervision.

Observation one: Fred, five, Sam, three, and baby Bruno, one year old

Baby Bruno is seated near his three-year-old brother, Sam. Baby Bruno starts moving his hand along three-year-old Sam's back. Sam asks baby Bruno to stop, and he tries unsuccessfully to hit baby Bruno's hand. Then baby Bruno tries to rock himself in such a way that he can lean into Sam. At this point Sam sits up, pushes baby Bruno backwards to the floor, and laughs.

Baby Bruno starts to laugh loudly and crazily as he sits up. This time, Sam pushes baby Bruno harder down on to the floor. Baby Bruno tries to sit up a third time, but Sam pushes him even more fiercely to the ground.

Baby Bruno then tries unsuccessfully to slap and punch Sam. Sam hits baby Bruno twice on the head until baby Bruno laughs and then cries desperately.

Mother runs in and shouts loudly at Sam, who becomes frightened of what mother will do to him and scurries into his bedroom.

Sam, three, who had been hit frequently by his older brother Fred, five, has become more unsettled by his baby brother Bruno, one, since Bruno has started to walk, like him. When Bruno starts walking, Sam, the middle child and nearest him in age, fears losing his identity. Sam cannot do things as ably as his big brother Fred can and now the baby, Bruno, is walking just like him! What is special about Sam? Does he have a separate identity, or is he just a squashed in-between brother?

There is a sense that baby Bruno is laughing crazily to run away emotionally from feeling scared. The mother had arranged for baby Bruno to stay with Sam, aged three, in a shared space, but the mother's plan to leave one-year-old baby Bruno with three-year-old Sam does not work.

Is this unsupervised play all right? Clearly not! We see how the mother is becoming worn out in this situation where the boys are just left grouped together without her presence. The boys' hitting is pursued each time by different actors, but it is escalating in the absence of an attentive mother. There is also a sense that perhaps the mother does not feel sufficiently supported by a thoughtful paternal function within herself or by her husband. She never mentions her husband in her conversations with the observer and it feels as though the mother is unable to keep her husband's presence in mind.

Now for Observation two. The children are sitting down watching television. They have not had any conversation or play with the mother during this half-hour. Television can become boring. So, what happens?

Observation two: Fred, five, Sam, three, Bruno, one year old

The oldest boy, Fred, looks at Sam. He then pushes Sam, who turns to him with an angry expression. Sam then pushes Fred over on to the floor in return. Sam starts to laugh. Fred laughs and pushes Sam until he falls over sideways. Sam then sits up and punches and hits Fred on his chest. Fred subsequently laughs more loudly. Fred then begins hitting hard on Sam's shoulders.

Soon the mother runs into the room and screams "Stop!" She then firmly commands them, "Come and have your snack." When Sam stands up, Fred gives him a hard shove. He falls to the ground and starts crying profusely, then runs to his mother, who had gone back into the kitchen.

Shortly, while all three are in the kitchen, baby Bruno comes up to his mother and, reaching towards her, he puts both his hands on his mother's thighs and tries to stand up. Sam, now sitting in the mother's lap, pushes baby Bruno down on to the floor. As the mother tells him off, Sam starts to laugh. Then Sam slaps at his brother Bruno's head with very fast, harsh fist punches. The mother grabs Sam's hand, telling him off. Sam looks at his mother, frowns, tilts his head back, but then starts laughing.

A week later, there is another worrying observation.

Observation three: Fred, five, Sam, three, Bruno, one year old

Fred passes in front of baby Bruno, who is seated on the sofa. Fred hits Bruno on the head several times, exclaiming, "Cry!" Immediately afterwards, Fred runs into his own bedroom. Seeing what Fred did, Sam, three years old, immediately copies him: Sam hits baby Bruno on the head and then runs into Fred's bedroom to join him. A little "gang formation" against mummy's baby Bruno is forming between the two older brothers.

In another similar incident in which his hair was pulled by both brothers, baby Bruno's body was rigid, his fist was closed tightly around his hair. He seemed to be holding on to his hair for dear life in an adhesive way. He was not crying out for mother. This was a dangerous moment, for it felt as though he had lost hope in the mother's protective function.

Now, what are we going to say about this? Will we just say, like people of times past, "Well, boys will be boys"?

Saramago (2005, p. ix) in his book, *Blindness*, wrote, "If you can see, look. If you can look, observe". I hope we can do just that. What have we seen? Hitting each other has become a way of life for the boys. They hit as a way of stimulating their brains; they hit as a way of alleviating boredom; they hit as a way of having intimate contact; they hit as a way of letting out aggression to the mother's other babies. Hitting is becoming a style of relating. Hitting is also a way in which Sam can preserve his unique position in the mother's lap and keep baby Bruno away from his mother.

In these weekly observations made during a one year period, Fred, five, in particular, begins to develop an identity as the big, strong, hard, bad boy who is always getting into trouble with mother. He has difficulty seeking sustenance from the mother. Fred experiences his two rival younger brothers as always having access to her.

This is worryingly shown in the following conversation that Fred, only five years old, had with his brother Sam, three years old.

Fred says, "But you don't cry when you are in nursery school!" Sam was absolutely clear as he plaintively responded, "Do you know why I cry? Because I want my mum! I want her to prepare my food and I want to stay at home with her!" Fred, the older boy, who is very attached to his aggressive, powerful stance, replied, "It is impossible!" Fed up, Fred walked away with a firm gait to his bedroom, where he shut the door on Sam.

We see here how Fred, the oldest of the three little boys, is most at risk of ridding himself of his dependent self, which needs a mother to love, understand, and nurture him. To protect himself from feeling helpless, jealous, and in pain, he is turning to a potent, cruel self and, thus, developing an identity as a "bad boy" with a hard cold self encrusting his vulnerable self.

It does not work for the mother to do her household tasks and simply let her one-year-old child remain alone with the three-year-old and five-year-old boys to "get on with it" and "play". Moreover, continuing to play together without sufficiently helpful internal or external paternal surveillance, limit-setting, and maternal sustenance escalates the conflictual situation between Fred, Sam, and baby Bruno. The three boys repeat what has been done to them: they get shouted at and probably hit by the mother, who, in this way, enters their sadomasochistic drama and then they hit each other again.

"Look, observe"

We are aware, of course, that mothers have a lot of housework to do and, for this reason, parents and professionals can blind themselves to the possibility of emotionally and/or physically abusive relations between young siblings.

Still, we must question parents' other motives, which blind them to cruel, perverse behaviour between the siblings. There are various reasons for this parental denial.

1. To see cruelty, one has to acknowledge one's own aggression towards aggressive children and one's own aggression to one's own internalised siblings and feel responsible for it.
2. It breaks one's heart to see and accept a loved child's hostility and aggression to one of the other children. For this reason, a parent might deny the severity of the siblings' aggression.
3. We can wonder what is happening inside the mother. Could it be that she allows the older siblings to escalate their aggression because of her own unconscious sibling conflicts, her own unconscious wishes to be rid of the younger children representing her younger siblings. Might she feel that her own mental equilibrium is threatened by three children who feel too much for her? Bruno Bettelheim thinks this is a possibility (Berke, 1989).

Now, what are we going to say about the boys' interactions?

The aggressive cycle between siblings of hitting or hurting another, feeling hurt, laughing, hitting another, laughing, and being shouted at can become addictive both psychologically and physiologically. For children experiencing some degree of emotional neglect from the parents and teachers, the attachment to perverse sadomasochistic interactions can be stronger. Why? Depending on perverse sadomasochistic interactions is preferable to the psychic pain that could come from depending on an unreliable maternal figure who might abandon one. Later, perverse sadomasochistic activities, for example, those supported by suicide websites or phantasies, such as self-harm thoughts, can be in intense competition with maintaining a link with a good object, such as a therapist or partner (De Masi, 2003).

The perverse sadomasochistic pattern can also be used as an antidepressant to project psychic pain into another human being. It might also provide an illusion of entwining closely with another, being recognised in the eyes of the other, avoiding being separate from the other, and provide a false sense of alleviating isolation and loneliness. For some young children, any human response feels better than no human contact at all.

The perverse aggressive behaviour involves the wish to inflict pain or destroy an object in anger, hostility, hate, rage, jealousy, envy. Perverse aggressive behaviour arises in reaction to a psychic wound, and the severe underlying anxiety is the fear of disintegration. It feels more potent to hurt and get sadistic pleasure than to fall apart, to disintegrate psychologically in severe distress (Gunter, 1980). Tyrannical control, a form of aggression, might also be used to project into the other feelings of vulnerability, so as to psychically survive unacceptable emotional experiences (Glasser, 1986). Sometimes this factor prompts abused children to repeat the abuse on their siblings.

"One of the primary functions of the family is to contain mental pain" (Meltzer & Harris, 1994, p. 411). That involves the parents being not too indulgent or overprotective. It also involves the parents in providing sufficient understanding, protection, and nurturing to promote sufficient love from, and love of, parents to promote the adult functions in the mature part of the personality.

What happens when these children grow up? Problems in adult relations influenced by damaged internalised sibling relations

If a husband or wife feels securely attached to emotionally containing, loving, internalised parents and siblings, or sufficiently emotionally contained and nurtured by the therapists, the husband or wife is more likely in adulthood to subscribe to good family models for caring for "the new baby". In the absence of good internalised parental figures, sufficient emotional containment and nurturing by a therapist can help. However, if hostile, perversely exciting sibling relations are inadequately modified in the course of becoming an adult, they could interfere with the development of a benign parentality. In what follows, I examine five conflictual, internalised sibling conflicts influencing the parental couple. These revived sibling conflicts occur when a woman is unable to conceive, during the time of a woman's pregnancy, when there might be female frigidity and male impotence, following the birth of the first child, and after the birth of the second child.

Inability to conceive

It appears to be the case that the ability to conceive, something most people would see as purely physical, is, in fact, affected by psychological factors. Research suggests that psychological impasses can block a woman who has no physical impediments to conceiving from becoming pregnant and maintaining the pregnancy. Impeding psychological factors can be remedied through exploring the women's unconscious hostile and loving feelings towards "the baby" with whom they will share both a physical and psychological maternal space. Once both the positive and negative feelings towards "a baby" were able to become conscious and worked through in therapy, fifty-five per cent of infertile women in a mind–body programme became pregnant (Domar, 2004).

As I mentioned before, unconscious sibling relations, as shown in dreams, are important to explore in the psychological treatment of infertility. The therapist can, for example, ask a woman to say just one sentence to her sibling at different stages of their relation. Here is one example of what one mother said to her absent sister when the therapist used the empty chair technique: "You stole my mother as a baby. At six, I knocked you down when you got on my bike. At nineteen, it was good to be with you, I like having you as a friend." Then, to the therapist, the woman recalled, "Recently I had a dream I was in the plane with my sister and she fell out."

When unconscious hostile feelings to internalised rival siblings can be unearthed and made conscious within a therapeutic relation, it is less likely that they will cause somatic impasses to pregnancy (McDougall, 1989).

Pregnancy

The internalised relations with siblings can become reactivated at the time of pregnancy and birth of the first baby. Latin American fathers commonly share a state of severe physical decline known as *chipil* when the new baby arrives. Intense envy towards the new foetus is often felt (Berke, 1989).

Jarvis (1962) reports on several men who "took flight" and began to have infantile tantrums and suffer from impotence when their wives became pregnant. Jarvis then goes into clinical details of four men regressing and having psychotic episodes during their wives' pregnancies. Jarvis suggests that we should examine a woman's post-partum depression in the light of the effect of her husband's reactions to her pregnancy and childbirth. Van Leeuwen (1966) cites examples of how a man can respond to his feelings of inaccessibility to his preg-nant wife by getting various women pregnant and insisting that they have abortions.

The *American Medical Journal* reported in 1992 that eight to eleven per cent of fathers hit the baby in the womb. One of the reasons for this is that the fathers feel left out and cannot bear the baby possess-ing the maternal space all the time. Also, a mother can be hostile to the baby in the womb for taking up residence in her body, changing her body shape, and making demands on her vitality. Alice Miller describes maternal hostility, which can also include damaging the baby through overuse of alcohol, drugs, nicotine, or nutritional neg-lect. Here is one example of a problem with pregnancy.

Three couples had fertility treatment, waiting over eighteen months to conceive, and, subsequently, the fathers had affairs. In one situation, the husband left the family home, had an affair with a pros-titute, and divorced within three months of the baby's birth. This was linked with the husband not being able to bear the wife "being with the baby". His own fragile internalised mother and his own severely hostile sibling rivalry prompted the husband's flight into sexualised excitement. Sexual excitement was resorted to in lieu of bearing the pain of sharing his wife with the baby.

Female frigidity and male impotence when the wife is pregnant

The worries held by parents-to-be regarding damage to the baby in the womb might be linked with the parents' unconscious hostility to their own internalised siblings and their own internalised parents' intercourse creating them and possibly other siblings. Hostility to these internalised parents and siblings can create damaged internalised parents and siblings. These damaged figures become frightening figures and create terror, persecution, and dread in nightmares. In addition, an internalised father's penis filled with aggressive phantasies creates an anxiety about a destructive external penis. This can lead either parent to avoid intercourse for fear that the so called "destructive penis" will harm the baby in the womb. For example, one young woman had a dream of having sex with her husband, but his penis acted as a sword that stabbed through her, emerging at the mouth.

For example, in the book *Sisters and Husbands* (Brookfield, 2002) the father-to-be, David, is anxious about penetrating his pregnant wife, Anna, for fear of damaging the baby inside. Anna, the mother-to-be, is filled with unconscious and subsequently conscious hostility to her younger sibling, Becky. Because of her unconscious hostility to her younger sister, Anna also fears that the husband's penis might "damage the baby" representing her younger sister, Becky, during intercourse. For this reason, intercourse between the couple ceases and David has a clandestine affair.

The birth of the first child

"Many men and women have commented that they wanted to welcome a newborn child but found the task too difficult because they simultaneously saw the baby as an intruder, like a younger brother or sister sharing their lives" (Berke, 1989, p. 181).

For example, during each of his wife's three pregnancies, a husband had affairs. He brought a dream to psychotherapy: "Strange men accidentally broke my glasses", and he added "I was pretty lucky my eye wasn't cut." One of his associations to the dream was to the birth of his younger brother, towards whom he felt hatred. Feelings of jealousy connected to the mother and brother were followed by his becoming bashful. As the husband continued to associate to his dream, he started to confuse words "mother" and "wife" and talked about his impotence when his wife was pregnant (Jarvis, 1962).

For the husband, the loss of the "old style" of relation, without the baby, that he had with his wife can feel like unbearable pain. The pain of the loss of some of his wife's careful attentiveness can be greeted by a re-creation of early infantile loss present when sharing the mother with siblings. Regressive re-enactments can be used to evade and evacuate pain into others. As seen in some of the men's sexual acting out above, the use of the defences of perverse sadomasochistic excitement and triumph which come through the use of sexuality and betrayal can occur. This reminds us of the earlier examples of the young boys' triumphant perverse sadomasochistic excitement to obscure the painful loss of their mother's attentive care.

For example, in the book *Sisters and Husbands*, the husband, who was happily married, started an affair. His wife had become unrecognisably "the pregnant mother" in his mind, rather than his sexually attractive, slim wife. The wife, feeling like "the pregnant mother", made it difficult for the husband to remain sexually involved with her when she was in her child-bearing role.

Both men and women may be surprised by the arrival of depression during the pregnancy and following childbirth. For both the mother and the father, becoming a parent involves identification with an internalised parental couple, which, if it is not a loving internal couple and, thus, adequate, creates further strain on the parents' personalities. A pregnancy can prompt each parent to regress to experiencing intense unconscious infantile conflicts with the creative intercourse of the internalised parents and siblings. The result is the risk of post-partum psychoses. Maternal post-partum psychosis is frequently discussed and treated, but little attention is given to fathers. Jarvis (1962) suggests that we should always examine a wife's post-partum depressions in light of the effect of the husband's reactions to her pregnancy and the childbirth. The husband might also be depressed and, therefore, unable to support his wife's maternity sufficiently.

The birth of the second child

With one baby, it is possible to put one's baby self inside the baby and identify with the baby. It is more difficult when there are two babies. Feeling "the left out baby", "being in rivalry with the baby with the other partner" can evoke depression when the internalised containing parents do not have sufficient nurturing capacity to sustain "the baby-in-the-self" sharing the space with the new baby.

The Yale researchers (Kris & Ritvo, 1983) thought that conflicts between parents and between parents and their own children were often linked with parents' earlier conflicts with their siblings of origin. Mitchell (2000), in *Madmen and Medusas*, describes how prior sibling relations affect marriage relations. For the development of parentality and the ability to share "the mother", it is essential to keep the internal mother intact as a good object. Keeping the internalised mother intact involves having reparative feelings of love for the mother and regret for the aggression towards her for carrying a rival sibling.

But how do you help a child or an adult with conflictual sibling relations? As you saw in the earlier vignettes of the three boys, simply scolding an older child for being jealous and angry with a new baby promotes more aggression to the new baby. An older child must have limits to aggression to the younger sibling, or siblings, but he also requires empathic understanding of how the child feels he is losing his identity of being at "centre stage" for the parents. Through "special time" to understand him, an older child needs to develop new psychological equipment to bear the pain of sharing the mother and father with a new sibling. Similarly, adults who are regressively acting out in a perverse sadomasochistic way to avoid mental pain require psychological understanding to develop mentalization internally and support their parentality. How can we help?

Dream analysis as a method of working through unconscious sibling conflicts

As I have described, deep-seated sibling conflicts might interfere with the development of intimacy with one's marital partner, children, and sibling representatives in the form of friends and colleagues at work. I believe that some of the more profound psychic truths about a person's sibling relations are often repressed and, therefore, most evident as one looks at the person's dream-life (Magagna, 2000).

Looking at dreams in psychotherapy can be extremely useful. The dream space can be a private theatre in which dream characters interrelate and generate a meaning that is projected on to interpersonal relations in the outside world (Meltzer, 1984). The therapist and patient can develop a more comprehensive shared understanding of the patient's current internalised sibling relations through exploring the nature of the patient's dreams and through working on split-off and projected conflictual aspects of the dream transferred to the therapeutic relation. Through the therapeutic relation, new psychological capacities can be introjected to bear pain, loss, conflict, and trauma. The current unconscious internalised relations include old implicit memory experiences with external siblings. These relations can be recovered in the therapeutic relation and brought into the present, so that the therapist and patient can lend empathic understanding to them and, thus, modify the internal world of relations with the internalised family.

During the war years, Melanie Klein used dream analysis to help ten-year-old Richard, whose internalised sibling conflicts created overwhelming shyness and school phobia. Aspects of sibling relations developing in the course of Richard's analysis were clearly shown through his dreams. Here is one of them, described in *Narrative of a Child Analysis:*

> Richard misses a bus which he intended to take. He went after all, but in a caravan with him travelled a very happy family. The father and mother were middle-aged; there were quite a lot of children, and all of them were nice. There was a new cat which chased his actual cat, but then they came to like each other. This new cat was not an ordinary cat, but it was very nice. It had teeth like pearls and it was more like a human being. (Klein, 1961, p. 430)

Klein interpreted the family in the caravan as representing how Richard had all his loved people in a happy, harmonious family inside him. This meant he had loving relations to her other patients and to his brother Paul.

Richard then indicated a second part of the dream: the sky was quite black, the trees were black, there was sand-coloured sand, but the people were also black. There were all sorts of creatures, birds, animals, scorpions, all black. All of them were quite still. It was terrifying, and Richard's face expressed horror and anxiety as he described this second part of the dream.

Klein interpreted how, in this part of the dream, Richard had attacked the parents and the siblings, turning them into black people and animals and black scorpions, all of which were motionless. These stood for his internal family figures attacked through his jealousy and anger.

Richard then said at a certain point in the dream, "Ahoy there", as he saw a patch of green on the island and the sky over the island showing a little blue. The people began to sing; the scorpions and the other creatures jumped back into the water. Everybody was overjoyed, everything turned light, and the sky became all blue.

Klein interpreted this as Richard's wish to bring to life all these attacked internal family members that had turned into threatening creatures.

In getting to know the psychic truth about Richard through his dreams, we were able to understand that this seemingly very nice, shy, school-phobic boy had an inner complexity which would not be revealed without understanding his play, drawings, and dreams, which reflected his unconscious aggressive conflicts with his rival brother, Paul.

Some recent newspaper stories tell of siblings who acted in a most loving way when their younger sibling was at risk. For example, a five-year-old English boy realised his mother was giving birth, because her waters broke. He helped the baby out and, while doing so, he noticed that the umbilical cord was around the baby's neck. He removed the cord from around the baby's neck and then called the police. Also, a ten-year-old Australian boy, caught in a flood with his mother and younger sibling, suggested that his young brother be rescued first. The ten-year-old was not rescued in time.

There are probably many examples in external reality. It is also important, though, to understand the internal reality of the sibling relations. In saying this, an example from psychotherapy comes to mind: a very charming and handsome fifteen-year-old adolescent boy, Marco, came to psychotherapy complaining of a disfigurement he wanted removed from his face and his fear of aphids flying about in his room. He was popular with teachers and school friends, but he was lonely and did not experience intimacy in his relations. He could not understand why this was the case when he consciously "liked people".

Despite his being very placatory to me and most others in his life, Marco's first year of psychotherapy was marked by an eruption of violent dreams, including some in which he wished to poison the drinking water of his peers or throw a hand grenade and thereby injure all his fellow students, with whom he was most agreeable in his external life. In the course of therapy, Marco introjected a good containing internal mother, which allowed hope, security, and the ability to improve relations to damaged internal siblings. At the end of three years of psychotherapy, the split between Marco's external agreeable and placatory attitude and internal violence to siblings and peers changed considerably. This can be seen in his more intimate external relations and this dream of his internal relations guiding his external behaviour.

In the dream, eighteen-year-old Marco is saying goodbye to a group of his best friends. They were giving presents to one another. He enjoyed his presents because he felt that people had actually thought about what they had chosen to give to him. He was so touched by their thoughtfulness that he was crying. He felt that when they were all separated, reminding themselves of their friendship would make them feel sad.

Although Marco was not yet able to own his sadness and I did not feel he should be ending his therapy, I was moved by his capacity to experience being touched, feeling love towards peers, and coming near to the pain of loss in his journey back to his home country.

Conclusion

In various publications (Magagna, 1990, 1998, 2010), I have suggested that progress in individual and family psychotherapy is marked by a transformation in the patient's dream-life representations of his relation to his internalised siblings. My theory is supported by the research of Harris (1957) who suggests that, as therapy of eight- to nine-year-old children progresses, the developing child shows pity, grief, and concern about harm done to siblings and peers through hostility. Also, the socially well-adjusted eight- to nine-year-olds have dreams in which they are preoccupied not only with their own well-being, but also with the well-being of siblings and peers. In the dreams I have observed in psychotherapy, there is a move from persecutory anxieties, linked with attacks on internal siblings who, thus, become frightening, to reparative feelings of love and generosity towards the internal siblings. Psychotherapy working with dreams holding implicit memory experiences, much in the same way as adults being empathically and understandingly present for Lucia's play, can remove some impasses to achieving intimate and emotionally healthy relations in one's current family. It is to be hoped that then there will be generating of love, promoting hope, containing of depressive pain, and maintaining thinking for the growth and development of family members in subsequent generations of family life (Meltzer & Harris, 1994). What is ultimately clear is that the quality of our sibling relations affects not just our childhood, but also our adult life, and that the right intervention, promoting introjection of good parental functions, can allow us to break out of a cycle of hostile acting out or depression and move towards a healthy, loving, nurturing family life that can bear psychic pain and promote hope and generosity for generations to come.

References

Adamo, S., & Magagna, J. (2005). Oedipal anxietes, the birth of a new baby, and the role of the observer. In: J. Magagna, N. Bakalar, H. Cooper, J. Levy, C. Norman, & C. Shank (Eds.), *Intimate Transformations* (pp. 90–111). London: Karnac.

Berke, J. (1989). It's not fair. In: *The Tyranny of Malice* (pp. 179–201). London: Simon & Schuster.

Brookfield, A. (2002). *Sisters and Husbands*. Cannock, Staffordshire: Flame.

Coles, P. (2003). *The Importance of Sibling Relations in Psychoanalysis*. London: Karnac.

De Masi, F. (2003). *The Sadomasochistic Perversion*. London: Karnac.

Domar, A. (2004). *Conquering Infertility*. London: Penguin.

Dunn, J. (1984). *Sisters and Brothers*. London: Fontana.

Dunn, J., & Kendrick, C. (1982). *Siblings: Love, Envy and Understanding*. London: Grant McIntyre.

Freud, A. (1973). *Infants without Families and Reports on the Hampstead Nurseries (1939–1945)*. New York: International Universities Press.

Glasser, M. (1986). Identification and its vicissitude as observed in the perversions. *International Journal of Psychoanalysis, 67:* 9–16.

Gunter, M. (1980). Aggression, self psychology and the concept of health. In: A. Goldberg (Ed.), *Advance in Self Psychology* (pp. 167–192). New York: International Universities Press.

Jarvis, W. (1962). Some effects of pregnancy and childbirth on men. *Journal of the American Psychoanalytic Association, 10:* 689–700.

Harris, I. D. (1957). The dream of the object endangered. *Psychiatry, 20:* 151–161.

Klein, M. (1961). *Narrative of a Child Analysis.* London: Hogarth.

Kris, M., & Ritvo, S. (1983). Parents and siblings. Their mutual influences. *Psychoanalytic Study of the Child, 38:* 311–324.

Magagna, J. (1990). On not being able to sleep. In: *Psychosomatic Disorders in Adolescence.* Bologna: CLUEB (Cooperativa Libraria Universitaria Editrice Bologna).

Magagna, J. (1998). Psychodynamic psychotherapy. In: B. Lask & R. Waugh (Eds.), *Eating Disorders in Children.* Hove: Lawrence Erlbaum.

Magagna, J. (2000). La valutazione dei tentativi di riparazione nel sogni dei Bambini [The examination of reparation in the dreams of children]. In: A. Vitolo (Ed.), *Menti Eminenti in Sogni* (pp. 133–159). Rome: Edizioni Magi.

Magagna, J. (2002). Three years of infant observation with Mrs Bick. In: A. Briggs (Ed.), *Surviving Space: Papers on Infant Observation* (pp. 75–105). London: Karnac.

Magagna, J. (2010). Sogni and incubi in bambina in eta di latenza [Dreams and nightmares in latency age children]. In: M. Lugones & F. Bisagni (Eds.), *Bambine e bambini Quale Latenza oggi?* (pp. 97–127). Rome: Borla.

Magagna, J., Bakalar, N., Cooper, H., Levy, J., Norman, C., & Shank, C. (Eds.) (2005). *Intimate Transformations: Babies with their Families.* London: Karnac.

McDougall, J. (1989). *The Theatre of the Body.* London: Free Associations.

Meltzer, D. (1984). *Dream-Life.* Strathtay, Perthshire: Clunie Press.

Meltzer, D., & Harris, M. (1994). A psychoanalytic model of the child-in-the family-in- the- community. In: A. Hahn. (Ed.) *Sincerity and Other Works: Collected Papers of Donald Meltzer* (pp. 387–455). London: Karnac.

Mitchell, J. (2000). *Madmen and Medusas: Reclaiming Hysteria and the Effect of Sibling Relations on the Human Condition.* London: Penguin Press.

Nitsun, M. (1996). *The Anti-Group.* Hove: Brunner-Routledge.

Pines, M. (1978). Group analytic psychotherapy of the borderline patient. *Group Analysis, 11:* 115–128.

Rosenfeld, M. (1986). Too old to play, Bettelheim still scolds parents. *International Harold Tribune*, 11 April.

Saramago, J. (2005). *Blindness*. London: Vintage Books.

Schlachet, P. (2002). Sharing dreams in group psychotherapy. In: C. Neri, M. Pines, & R. Freedman (Eds.), *Dreams in Group Psychotherapy* (pp. 79–97). London: Jessica Kingsley.

Segal, H. (1979). *Klein*. London: Fontana.

Stormshak, E. A., Bellanti, C. J., & Bierman, K. L. (1996). The quality of sibling relationships and the development of social competence and behavioral control in aggressive children. *Developmental Psychology*, 32(1): 79–89.

Van Leeuwen, K. V. (1966). Pregnancy envy in the male. *International Journal of Psychoanalysis*, 47: 319–324.

Winnicott, D. W. (1991). *The Piggle*. London: Penguin.

CHAPTER SEVENTEEN

The fraternal complex in the Under Five Service

Rossella Coveri and Miriam Monticelli

T he Under Five Service where we work as child psychotherapists[1] was created on the basis of the Under Five Counselling
Service of the Tavistock Clinic in London.

The Under Five model was inspired by the pioneering work of
Fraiberg in 1975 (Fraiberg, Adelson, & Shapiro, 1980) and it underwent a natural development in the light of both the therapeutic needs
of the families encountered over the years, and of the new types of
mother–child or parent–child psychotherapeutic work. The recent and
growing literature about neuroscientific research and the attachment
theory additionally supports and validates the basic hypothesis of this
model.

The model proposes a treatment for the entire family group that
has children under five presenting a developmental impasse. Families
are offered between five and ten sessions, characterised by a flexible
setting, in order to understand and eventually resolve the impasse
that led to the developmental block within the intra- and interpersonal
relationships.

The work with both the children and their parents allows interpretations to grasp not only phantasies, emotional states, and anxieties which are part of the children's internal reality, but also the

parents' transgenerational ghosts. Fraiberg explained that the parents' conflictual nuclei are passed on to children through an unconscious communication. This presentation, of course, might not be able to take such ghosts into account, as there is no time or space to work on their origin. Our work focuses on the possible transformation of the parents' and children's impasse resulting from unresolved nuclei.

In this chapter, we discuss how we work on the fraternal complex in the Under Five Service. We do this by working with the phantasies of the children and the parents' internalised transgenerational ghosts, as shown in their interaction with their children. We show how we interpret both directly to the child and the parents regarding their inner conflicts, and in this way the impediments to development seem to diminish.

Emanuel (2006) described that in many cases the spectacular nature of the therapeutic results obtained with under five children and their families comes from being able to dramatise the internal conflicts through the child's experience in the consulting room or through the words of the parents.

Watillon states,

> The child makes the interactive conflict manifest and allows the therapist to decode the message, to elaborate the emotions projected into him and to interpret the unconscious motivations of the various members of the cast of the 'play' . . . The analyst, as a theatre director, can perform a transforming function. (Watillon, 1993, p. 1041)

In this perspective, the theme of rivalry and of feelings that colour the fraternal bonding seem to be one of the most suitable "scripts" to be performed in the Under Five consulting room. In fact, as many authors recognise, the emotional states linked to the fraternal complex colour the family relationships, becoming a central issue of human existence. In addition, working with a family with young children and a "young" couple ("young" because they have only started their parental experience) provides an opportunity to observe the inter- and intrapsychic relationships being created. Many authors agree that the fraternal complex plays a role in forming these relationships and is intertwined with the Oedipus complex.

The fraternal complex, as specified by many authors, does not coincide with either the fraternal bond or with phratry. Just like the

Oedipus complex, according to Kaës, the fraternal complex is "one of the psychic organising factors of any bond" (Kaës, 2009, p. 45, translated for this edition): it has its own specificity in organising the fraternal bonds and in structuring the representations of the internal world.

In this chapter, we present two cases where the family members did not work through the fraternal complex, which led to a developmental impasse in the children and within the family relationships. In addition, we emphasise the type of assistance the Under Five counselling can provide to this kind of difficulty.

"MY" twenty-five per cent

Y's mother called the Under Five Service asking for help because Y, two and a half, did not speak yet and it was difficult to wean him from the breast. She also added that she had another boy, L, who was four and a half, and who was extremely jealous.

The parents came only with Y for the first meeting, although I told them to come with both children. The father, a railway company manager (notwithstanding his young age), had a beloved sister, while the mother, the youngest of her family, had a twin sister and three other siblings. She said that she did not have a good relation with her family, particularly with her mother, who often made her feel criticised. Her mother often told her that she raised five children by herself, while Y's mother was having difficulty with only two.

They told me that she miscarried after L was born, and then Y arrived immediately after. Unfortunately, when Y was born, the father had to be away for work. The mother said she felt terribly alone with two young children. L was extremely jealous and continuously bothered Y in various ways. She said that they could not be left alone for one minute.

At the first meeting, the mother said that they had come because Y was not yet talking. He would say only a few words, and, furthermore, it was hard to wean him from the breast. She did not know what to do any more. She even thought of placing some plasters coloured with red lipstick on her breasts and telling Y that she had "an ouch", and therefore she could not nurse him any more. I was struck by her words, and even more that she spoke as if Y was not even in the room with us.

While the parents spoke, Y, without saying a word or looking at me, took toys out of the baskets, looked at them one by one for a few seconds, and then threw them far away. He then removed all the furniture and the toy figures from the toy house.

While I was looking at him, his parents continued talking to me and I felt as if I was carried away listening to them, as if Y was not there. I had a hard time concentrating on what he was doing. I thought of this emotion as a countertransference movement in my mind. I addressed Y, who did not seem to pay attention while emptying the baskets and throwing the toys far away. He turned and looked at me quickly and then went back to the toys. I said that he never interrupted us . . . he had been playing by himself for a long time. Y turned around and looked at me a bit longer. Mother said that Y "was a good child and was not a bother" unless he was provoked by his brother, who would never have let us talk like that.

I sat on the rug next to Y and looked at him. I told him I thought he knew very well that mummy and daddy were talking about L and him. Maybe that is why he let them talk, although I noticed that he threw the toys he was looking at and also removed the furniture from the toy house and threw the toy daddy, mummy, and children away. Perhaps he wondered whether we were really talking or thinking about him or whether we were leaving him alone, far from us, like the toys and toy figures over there. Y turned and looked at me intensely. He then looked down and grabbed the train again. The father lovingly told him to listen and look at me. Y looked up at his dad.

The mother's words made me think that she felt internally angry, wounded, and harmed by her great effort in doing everything by herself. In addition, that the maternal object in her mind criticised her ferociously for her emotions, to such an extent that she tried to project her guilt on Y. To me, this was also relevant in that it stirred up my countertransference; it was as though the mother spoke as if Y was not there, as if, perhaps, he was not born from a psychic point of view.

The parents came to the next meeting only with Y again. They told me that things were better as the boy did not search for the breast any more and the mother felt relieved. The father immediately spoke about L and the difficult relation between the children. They never played together because L stopped any initiative Y might have made. The mother said that it happened even though she was careful not to arouse L's jealousy.

During the second meeting, the mother said that Y started saying "mine" when he grabbed a toy and L got angry. She tried to tell Y not to say "mine" but, rather, "ours", belonging to Y and L. In the meantime, Y was at the toy house. He took the infant, placed it briefly on the bed, and then threw it. Mother said that L was jealous. He said that Y was naughty when he said "mine" and she said, "It's true, Y is naughty . . ." She looked at me as though she had to say it in order not to provoke L's jealousy. In the meantime, Y was removing the toy furniture from the house and throwing it far away. I said that perhaps L was very afraid that he would be kicked out of his mummy's and daddy's heart because Y had arrived. Yet, Y was afraid, too. I approached him saying, "Daddy's and mummy's heart is like a home. You know that you have a place in it and L has one, too. Yet, you are scared that if L is around, then there is no space for you any more . . . and you'll be thrown far away, just like these toys!" Y stopped and looked at me.

The mother told me that she, too, had had fears as a child. She had watched a film where a girl fell down the stairs and it kept coming back to her mind, Down the stairs . . . down the stairs. She resumed speaking about L's jealousy. I said that she remembered something from when she was a little girl. She was afraid of this film where the girl fell down the stairs. Perhaps, when she was a girl, she was very afraid of not finding "her" place in her mum's heart. There were five children in the family and she also had a twin sister. The mother started to cry. The father said that she had to share everything since her birth. I pointed out that it was not from birth, but from conception; she did not even have her own space in her mother's womb. The mother said, "Yes, it is true . . ." I said that the little girl inside herself perhaps was very afraid of "falling down" from her mother's heart. She now knew that it was not like that, yet, when she was little, she might have been afraid that her mum, having so many children, might not have had a space entirely for her.

After the first session, Y said the word "mine". I thought that the work had helped the mother and father to create a space in their mind for the child. Perhaps, the work I did within myself and with them about my feeling that Y was not there with us helped the parents to look at their child and think about him. Y seemed to feel that he had "his" place and that seemed to have initiated symbol formation in his mind: for example, a word to express what he experienced.

Later, we dealt with what made it hard for the mother to help her children to feel that they had their own, undivided space in her mind.

The girl in the mother's mind seemed to not have firmly introjected the experience of having her own unique and undivided space in the mind of the maternal object. This, perhaps, led her to feel closer to the emotions of her older child, through projective identification. She also felt guilty because she had had another baby and had an even harder time protecting the space of little Y in her mind and in the external reality. Voicing this internal little girl and her emotions seemed to help the mother profoundly. Her mind created an image, the memory of the film and the words that tormented her, as in a dream, offering a symbolic representation that allowed her to have an empathic understanding of the children's experience.

This meeting seemed to mark a turning point. Six more meetings followed that included L, and just two with his parents.

L was an intelligent boy, a chatterbox, carefully competing with Y. I understood very well what his parents meant when they said that he provoked his younger brother continuously. However, he stopped and listened to my comments when I was trying to grasp the profound meaning of what he was doing. For instance, when I said that perhaps L did not really want Y's toy, but, rather, he was afraid that Y took all daddy's and mummy's love and he had nothing left. While I was looking at him, he dropped the toy he was interested in to go to grab Y's, and then ran away with angry and triumphant eyes, climbing into the armchair followed by his little brother, who instead fell down.

Mrs Bick's words came to my mind: "I can say that I found out that each member of the family loses his or her identity when a new baby is born" (Vallino, 2009, pp. 121–122, translated for this edition). The first child *is* the first one, but suddenly he becomes the older child when a second child comes along. The birth of a sibling is a great blow for the first child, who suddenly sees mummy with another baby and, therefore, wonders, "Who am I?" The mother thought it was jealousy, but, in fact, it is a matter of survival—to be or not to be. It is a strong and primitive thing, a matter of animal survival. It is not jealousy provoked by the other baby. When we feel jealous, we are not scared; we do not act in order to survive. The older child has completely lost his identity. Can you see the difference? Being jealous means, "I am myself and he is himself and he has more than me." In this case, instead, the reaction is, "Who am I? I feel lost, I will cease to exist if mummy does not come, I will collapse . . . and fall . . ." Jealousy is a misnomer that does not entail terror. Instead, one behaves as one does in order to survive (Vallino, 2009, pp. 121–122, translated for this edition).

I thought it was these kind of emotions that impelled L to stop Y's playing or to invade the space he was trying to conquer. Even his continuous and well-developed talking seemed to be used to fill up the space.

L also experienced his mother's miscarriage and, therefore, the death of a sibling in his mother's womb. I wondered about his feelings related to this event: perhaps he feared that his homicidal desires were omnipotent and he was afraid of retaliation from his dead sibling?

L seemed engaged in a fight for survival, as if accepting Y's presence meant that he would become absent from his mother's mind.

The most recent studies emphasise that the influence of the older sibling is essential for the development of the personality of the younger one. The younger child's self-esteem, the experience of feeling loved and wanted, or attacked and abandoned, is based not only on the relation with the mother and how she divides her emotional space between her children, but also her relation with the older sibling (Cooper & Magagna, 2005). "It is clear that the baby expects to meet 'the gleam in mother's eye' (Kohut, 1971), but also the baby is very attentive to the nature of the gleam in the older sibling's eye" (Cooper & Magagna, 2005, p. 17).

The gleam in the eyes of Y's mother was dimmed by a depressive cloud, while the one in L's eyes often shone with fear and hatred. Perhaps all of this had made it difficult for Y to feel that he had a space all to himself, as if he felt he had not had full permission from his parents and brother to be born, thus evoking the catastrophic change that the birth of a sibling stirs up (Mitchell, 2000).

As the work continued, Y's speech increasingly developed, both during our sessions and at home. I was touched when, at the end of the fourth meeting, while leaving, he said, "Bye Sciella!"

Summer vacations took place between the sixth and seventh meetings and the mother moved to the beach for two months, to the house of the paternal grandparents, who helped her very much, and father spent a month with them, too.

When they came back in September, Y's speech was very much enriched. He started attending nursery school and was doing well, and two months later his parents had a meeting with the teachers. They were surprised to find out that he was able to play and talk, just like all the other children. The mother found a job for three hours a day and felt greatly relieved in finding time for herself and her profession.

I think that what helped this family to unblock the situation and resume their journey was voicing their primitive anguish and the violent emotions of the two children in the presence of the entire family; this provided a space for thought and mentalization for all those issues that previously had been unspoken, but that were so vividly manifested by Y's symptom.

By understanding his anguish, his parents had largely managed to stop L's hostility and, perhaps, to mitigate his hatred.

Giving space to the mother's feelings, entitling her to say that raising two young children without their father's help was an unexpectedly exhausting job, the right that her internal object did not seem to give her, seemed to help her understand empathically the emotions of her children, in a Russian dolls' effect.

Being able to get in touch with herself, the twin sister who feared she would not have a unique and unshared space in her own mother's mind, seemed to catch the maternal transgenerational ghost roaming around Y's and L's room (Fraiberg, 1980). The interpretation of the ghost perhaps leads to the understanding of an unconscious, unresolved conflictual core and, therefore, the beginning of transformation.

The support and enhancement of the paternal function of the father, who was able to understand without judging his wife's and children's emotions, seemed to bring him back home emotionally to his family. Mother had probably felt alone during his absence. She did not feel he had supported her maternal function or that he helped her at a time of great emotional effort.

L did not seem to have experienced "a secure passage from mother's lap to father's lap" (Adamo & Magagna, 2005, p. 96); rather, it seemed he felt he was falling and was terrified. After the first meeting, the father showed himself to be aware that his absence led to a feeling of loss in his family. He also took responsibility for his role. Thus, the work probably allowed the relation between his children and him to develop. Perhaps this helped little Y to find his space in his family.

During the last meeting, the father said that he thought our meetings had helped Y to take his twenty-five per cent space in his family, the space he was entitled to. He told me at length of his work as a young manager, adding that it was very demanding. It was snowing that morning, and he feared the effects of the snow on the railway traffic. He said that last year he had had an excellent boss during the time that it snowed and had learnt a lot from him. This year, he was in charge. I said that perhaps he felt helped by our work; he now thought that he and his wife could take care of any forthcoming "snowfalls" while their children were growing up.

The ghosts of the siblings

During our work in the Under Five Service, we often observe that sibling issues and the emotional states they entail concern not only real siblings. In fact, very often we encounter only children who face fears and, sometimes, anxieties linked to phantasies of the birth of siblings or the lack of them. From Freud's point of view, they are children who often deem themselves to be permanently supported on the unshakeable love of their parents, but they fear being thrown out all of a sudden from the Olympus of their imaginary omnipotence (Freud, 1919e).

Klein, as early as in 1924, observed these phenomena in her work with Erna, a six-year-old girl who suffered from phantasies linked to the birth of siblings.

She wrote that, on the basis of Erna's and other children's phantasies, the only child suffers from anguish fed by the thought of a brother or a sister who might come at any time. The only child, Klein said, suffers from the guilt feelings resulting from his unconscious aggressive drives against these children, who, in his imagination, live in the mother's body and with whom it is not possible to have a good affective relation on a real level (Klein, 1950).

Many authors who currently deal with sibling issues draw on and develop the Kleinian idea of the only child. Kaës maintains that the fraternal complex does not coincide with the real fraternal bond and that, as the Oedipus complex and notwithstanding the existence of real siblings, "it is an essential experience of the human psyche for any subject, whether it is an only child or a sibling" (Kaës, 2009, p. 44, translated for this edition).

Laura, a four-year-old girl I met at the Under Five Service, is an only child. From a real point of view, she has fully dedicated parents who do not want to have other children. Yet, these conditions were not enough to spare Laura from conflicts and catastrophic anxieties about siblings.

Laura is a wilful and tyrannical girl who suffered from a serious form of constipation. Her parents were exasperated to such an extent that they took her to A & E to have her bowels cleaned out.

The first meeting was almost entirely occupied by Laura's difficulties. Towards the end, I asked something about the pregnancy. They said that they had wanted a child so much and everything went well, although, the mother added, the first ultrasound showed two hearts. By the second ultrasound (during the early months of pregnancy), the second heart was not evident. I looked puzzled, and the parents added that sometimes it happens that one foetus is absorbed by the other. The mother continued speaking, saying that the pregnancy went well, but then the beast was born! They both laughed, but I think that the joke allowed the parents to bring their phantasmal experiences into the session. Laura was born as a little beast in her parents' minds, one who fought for survival and suppressed her sibling.

When I met Laura during the following meeting, I wondered how the little girl received the phantasised representation of her parents and how such phantasmal experiences shaped the behaviour and the symptoms of the girl.

Laura was kneeling in front of the toy house. She placed the grandfather in the bath, saying that grandpa Rino went to take a bath. Grandma Paola was in the kitchen cooking, while mother and Laura were placed in the twin beds in the children's bedroom. Next, there was a cradle where she put a baby she called "the baby brother". Daddy was on the sofa watching television with another character that Laura said was a friend. Then daddy and his friend went to sleep, too, and were both placed in the big bed. I remarked, speaking to both the parents and the girl, that Laura showed us that it was necessary for the girl always to have her mother available. Mother and daughter were always supposed to be together, even at night. Thus, she moved all the beds into the same room, keeping them one next to the other, forming a long line, and placed daddy and mummy in the big bed, Laura next, then her baby brother, and then daddy's friend, all together, sticking to one another.

Laura seemed to suffer from something that had to do with unborn or not yet born children, based on anxieties about exclusion from the oedipal and fraternal triangle. In this session, Laura seemed to use a consistent defence through control, which omnipotently cancelled the difference among generations and the sexual quality of the relation between the father and mother. In addition, it negated the difference between the born and the unborn children, between the living and the dead children.

"All together, sticking to one another" was, in addition, the way Laura dramatised the conflictual core pervading the relation between her and her parents, which was the idea that the issue of the siblings belonged to everyone and not only to her. Her parents, in fact, seemed never to have given space in their minds to the experience of the loss of the other foetus, a loss that was always connoted by dangerous expulsive phantasies for Laura. This seemed, from a psychological point of view, to have immobilised the family around the issue of the desired, hated, and feared siblings for the girl and for her mother and father.

Interpreting the girl's play in the presence of her parents meant, therefore, working on something that belonged to them, too, and their transgenerational ghosts.

While Laura arranged her characters as described above, I commented that it seemed as if it was always necessary to be all together, sticking to one another; who knows what would happen otherwise? Laura fetched the baby brother and a small hammer. I noticed that she quickly hammered him a bit. I made a comment about it, "Oh . . . this baby brother . . . what anger!" The parents quickly replied that Laura did not want to hit him and that I was wrong. Laura fetched two giraffes of the same height. She tried to understand what gender they were. She then fetched a small giraffe and placed it next to the tummy of the daddy giraffe and said that it was nursing from him. She then fetched two big giraffes and made them kiss. I said that Laura was very confused and confused us, too, but she was also saying that she knows that mummy and daddy want to be together and that when that happens they could have babies. Laura went back to the toy house, from where she fetched baby Laura and baby brother. Baby Laura repeatedly hit the baby brother with a small hammer. I told her that she was showing us that there was a girl who was very angry with other children who could be born when mummy and daddy were together. Laura looked at the baby brother and said that he had a broken foot. She wanted her mummy to treat him. The mother proposed other games, confused her, and then asked her, "You really want a baby brother, don't you?" The father threw her a ball, thus inviting her to play.

I thought that it was difficult for these parents to observe their daughter from the outside.

I then addressed Laura directly and told her there was a girl who felt she had been bad because she hit the baby. Laura looked at me, struck, and nodded her head. I told her that she was very afraid of feeling bad towards children who could be born. She also feared that she had hurt a baby and wanted to cure him.

The session continued with the father suggesting playing with wooden blocks with her. Laura played for a little while, and then she played another game by herself, in which she had to pass a piece of a certain shape through a hole of the same shape, so that the piece fell inside the container. Through her mother's and my associations to Laura's play, we started speaking about poop and her fear that when her poop fell in the potty, it left her. Then mother said that poop ended up in a sea of poop when we threw it in the toilet. Laura suddenly stood up, grabbed a red ball with prickles and threw it violently against her mother's tummy. She ran to hide behind an armchair and she fearfully spied on her mother, checking whether her mother would throw the ball back at her.

Laura's phantasies about her siblings in her mother's tummy were particularly anguishing because, unlike with other children, there was an actual unborn baby. In addition, with respect to the "loss" of this baby, she and her parents had phantasies about her getting rid of him. Laura was anguished by the idea of her destructiveness, which was not mitigated by the real experience she has with her parents. Rather, it was exactly at that level that the phantasies about the power of the girl were unconsciously conveyed. On the other hand, the phantasy of her destructive power, shared with the parents, gave Laura an imaginary omnipotence through which she controlled the phenomenon linked to the sexuality of the parents, consisting of the birth of siblings. The intensity of the anxieties did not allow the girl to tolerate the emotional states linked to sexuality and the birth of siblings. Her dread, fear, and hatred were turned into a desire to have siblings, to be met in a way that seemed to be almost delusional, under her iron control.

The session showed how the interpretation of the anxieties allowed Laura clearly and openly to portray the unresolved issues. Her parents, although confused and resistant, showed that they had observed what was happening.

A few sessions later, we touched on the fundamental issue. While Laura changed the nappy on a doll, the mother told me that the other day the girl had a temper tantrum because she wanted a sibling, just like her friend, whose mother was pregnant. I asked them whether they were thinking about it. She said they were not, because they risked having twins. I said that when Laura was in her mother's tummy, there was also a "baby brother" who then died. The mother said that it was a girl and she would have been identical to Laura. She said, laughingly, "Can you imagine two Lauras?"

Laura arranged all the toy house furniture around the doll she had been taking care of. I told Laura that this is the way she wanted to feel when she was with her mummy and daddy and even with Miriam, at the centre of the stage. Yet, I believed that Laura had another child currently in her mind, the dead little sister in her mother's tummy. "Perhaps", I said, addressing Laura, "you feel at times as if you are to blame for the death of your little sister." Laura grabbed the ball with the thorns and placed it next to the doll. She then fetched another ball and threw it gently at first. As I was talking about Laura's aggression, which was stuck in the phantasies of destructive attack on the siblings in mummy's tummy, Laura threw the ball harder and harder. I interpreted it as an expression of her decreasing anxieties.

The concurrent work with the girl and her parents allowed me to grasp the phantasies, the emotional states, and the anxieties that were part of the girl's internal reality, as well as the transgenerational ghosts of the parents. We do not have space here to understand the nature of the transgenerational ghosts; that is, why the mother and father experienced their daughter as they did. Perhaps the unprocessed anxiety about the death of her twin sister while still in the womb led them defensively to give meaning to the surviving foetus, thus pushing away their fear of losing her, too. Therefore, did the "little beast" represent someone who would not risk dying in the fight for survival? Did they have anxieties about their child-bearing abilities?

Notwithstanding these hypotheses, which are unchecked, I believe that Laura's case shows that many "only" children are unique only from an external point of view. The minds of children and parents seem to be crowded with the ghosts of miscarried, wanted, and unborn siblings.

During the final meeting, the parents told me many good things about Laura. She did not suffer from constipation any more and defecated regularly. "In addition," the mother said, "Laura seems to be different, she is serene." Before saying goodbye, I arranged a follow-up meeting with them a few months later. I said, addressing Laura, "Well, Laura, we'll meet one more time near Christmas." The mother looked at me and then said, "You know what gift Laura has asked Santa Claus for? She wants a kitten."

Conclusions

In this chapter, we have shown that with a limited number of sessions it is possible to work on issues concerning the fraternal complex and its interaction with the Oedipus complex. We have shown that issues linked to the dynamics of the fraternal complex can knot the yarn of the family warp, thus often resulting in difficulties and symptomatic behaviours. Intervening early, as soon as the symptoms of the child come to his or her parents' attention, often prevents these difficulties from crystallising and pervading the growth and development of children and of their families.

In the cases we have presented, we have shown how, working with the entire family, it is possible to grasp unconscious aspects that, like transgenerational ghosts, are passed on to the children. The interpretative work seems to trigger a transformation, allowing development and psychic change.

Note

1. Our work takes place in two units, the Under Five Service of the City of Sesto Fiorentino, located in "Il Melograno" Family Centre, and "Il raggio Verde" Parents Space of the Health Authorities of the North-western area of Florence, in co-operation with the City Library of Scandicci.

References

Adamo, S., & Magagna, J. (2005). Oedipal anxietes, the birth of a new baby, and the role of the observer. In: J. Magagna, N. Bakalar, H. Cooper, J. Levy, C. Norman, & C. Shank (Eds.), *Intimate Transformations* (pp. 90–111). London: Karnac.

Cooper, H., & Magagna, J. (2005). The origins of self-esteem in infancy. In: J. Magagna, N. Bakalar, H. Cooper, J. Levy, C. Norman, & C. Shank (Eds.), *Intimate Transformations* (pp. 13–41). London: Karnac.

Emanuel, L. (2006). A slow unfolding at double speed: reflections on ways of working with parents and their young children within Tavistock Clinic's Under Five Service. *Journal of Child Psychotherapy, 32*(1): 66–84.

Fraiberg, S., Adelson, E., & Shapiro, V. (1980). *Ghosts in the Nursery. A Psychoanalytic Approach to the Problems of Impaired Infant–Mother Relationships.* London: Tavistock.

Freud, S. (1919e). 'A child is being beaten': a contribution to the study of the origin of sexual perversions. *S.E., 17*: 175–204. London: Hogarth.

Kaës, R. (2009). *Il complesso fraterno* [The Sibling Complex]. Rome: Borla.

Klein, M. (1950). *The Psychoanalysis of Children.* London: Hogarth.

Kohut, H. (1971). *The Analysis of the Self: A Systematic Approach to the Psychoanalytic Treatment of Narcissistic Personality Disorders.* New York: International Universities Press.

Mitchell, J. (2000). *Mad Men and Medusas.* New York: Basic Books.

Vallino, D. (2009). *Fare psicoanalisi con genitore e bambini* [Doing Psychoanalysis with Children and Parents]. Rome: Borla.

Watillon, A. (1993). The dynamics of psychoanalytic therapies of the early parent–child relation. *International Journal of Psychoanalysis, 74*: 1037–1048.

CHAPTER EIGHTEEN

Ghosts in sibling rivalry

Daniela Cantone and Carmela Guerriera

O ur contribution to the question of sibling rivalry is based on the assessment of two children who seemed not to have anything in common and whom we think can be defined as "victims" of a sibling complex, in the specific meaning attributed to it by Kaës (2008) and Kancyper (2004). The sibling complex appears as an organised cluster of hostile wishes and affects what a child feels for its siblings. Kancyper says that the sibling complex cannot be reduced to a derivative of the Oedipus complex, or to a simple displacement of the parental figures to the siblings, but has great structural importance. Each subject has a specific oedipal structure, a mix of positive and negative Oedipus complex, and, at the same time, suffers the destructive and/or developmental effects of the sibling complex (2004). Kaës states that the sibling complex derives its specificity from its organisation and function. Essentially, its structure is organised jointly by the rivalry and curiosity, attraction and rejection that a subject feels for this other similar person that plays the role of sibling in his internal world (2008). These authors suggest that this complex has a structuring and organising function, analogous to that of the Oedipus complex, but different from it, whose dysfunctions or deviations can give rise to psychic suffering at various levels and in different configurations. Surely, the tangle of pre-oedipal, oedipal, and sibling issues is difficult to unravel because young patients have different levels of functioning and development: from defensively dwelling in a primitive dimension dominated by primary processes, to reaching out to a more mature dimension that ends up being so precarious that it seems impossible for secondary processes to set in and stabilise the foundations of individuation and a healthy development. Another aspect we wish to briefly highlight are the parental ghosts that support and feed our patients' phantasies in a dramatic game of mirroring and alienation.

Luisa, six, patient of Daniela Cantone

Luisa is six and has stopped speaking at age three, although, as her parents say, she had never been a great talker. She communicates only with her parents and her sister and only for expressing her needs. She is the firstborn of a young couple, both physicians and socially well located. The mother comes from another European country but moved to Italy while attending university. The father has his own practice and says it is successful. In both parents, a narcissistic aspect is noticeable: in the father, when he talks of his professional performance with an apparently friendly but haughty attitude, and when he denies the existence of any suffering in his life; in the mother, in her generally distant attitude which becomes specifically negative and critical towards her daughter. She describes Luisa as lacking passion, resistant, tending to boredom, with superficial and passing interests. When she talks of her daughter's problems, she does not seem distressed but, rather, resentful. They come to see me because they are exasperated by the teachers' requests, as they cannot make Luisa talk and, therefore, are unable to check her learning performance (she is in the first year). The father is convinced that the problem will resolve itself in time because it is only an expression of the girl's stubborn and determined character. The mother, instead, says that she is worried that there could be an underlying disorder that she cannot explain, as she considers her family "totally normal and free of conflicts".

Luisa first showed her symptom at age three, when she had to change kindergarten because the previous one had been shut down, her sister Sara was born, and, at the age of forty days, had fallen ill with a face tumour. In addition, her maternal grandfather had died of a heart attack. All these events happening in a short period of time made me think of the expression "to be speechless". I think of the mother's mental state: she had just given birth (and she said pregnancy had not been easy), she saw her daughter's disease and her distorted face, and her beloved father died. About the disease, she says, "In a few days a small swelling on her face became enormous, as if she had grown another head." I think of Luisa, whom they describe as jealous and distressed about the birth of her sister, prey to feelings of rivalry towards the mother–sister couple, which is transformed by the illness and by unconscious ghosts into a monstrous and terrifying sight. And I think of the father, who had added to his wife's story, "Sara's breastfeeding was terrible; while she sucked her lips were bleeding due to ulcers and mother and baby were covered in blood. At times, my wife would phone me, crying, and I had to rush home and found them lying in bed in a terrible condition."

The image of a double-headed Sara is the persecutory image of a sister attacked in phantasy as the content of the mother's body due to experiences of envy and jealousy. She is a double that looks like Luisa but is different from her, a double that is distorted and, therefore, uncanny. According to Kaës (2008), the uncanny is the third element of the figure of the sibling double. It is embodied in particular in the imago of a monster sibling. In her phantasy, Luisa attacked her "sister-in-the-arms-of-beautiful-mummy" and now is haunted by a "double-headed-monster-sister". I also think of the impact that the vision of the deformity, ulcers, and blood of their second-born child must have had on these beautiful parents. I try to imagine the scene the father described through Luisa's eyes: a concretisation of what Meltzer and Harris Williams (1988) defined as an aesthetic conflict, in terms of emotional impact, between the beautiful looks of this charming mother full of milk and love and the dark interior of her enigmatic mind, in this specific case probably very depressed. A mother who offers her nipple and soothes the pangs of hunger, as Luisa had tried herself, but provides harmful food that Luisa had been able to expel, whereas it made Sara's mouth explode and bleed. It is a mix of (the mother's?) depression and (the child's?) destructive phantasies that seem to confuse, as in a kaleidoscope, Luisa, her sister, and their mother in the roles of persecutor and persecuted (I added question marks because depression seems possible also in the little girls, one because of the birth of her sister, the other because of the attacks on her body and life, just as destructive phantasies could also be ascribed to the mother).

The story of Sara's disease, with its medical implications, takes up a large part of our interview. The father even shows me two pictures of Sara on his mobile phone. In one picture, I see Luisa, too, but I feel they want me to see Sara at all costs, as if in their minds there was no separate place for each one of their daughters. I must do my best to keep my and their attention on Luisa's mutism. The final detail of this case, which might help our reflection, concerns the mother's statement that she wants her daughters to learn her language. However, instead of teaching them herself, she hired a lady who teaches the girls at home, a double denial of her origin of being a daughter, on the one hand, and being a mother, as an authentic speaking object, on the other. In *Explorations in Autism* (1975), Meltzer writes that for the development of language, it is necessary that dream thoughts are formed which are somehow suitable for communication and do not simply require to be evacuated. There must be an apparatus that turns dream thoughts into language. This apparatus consists in internalised speaking objects from which (in a process of narcissistic or projective identification) one learns the deep musical grammar that can represent the mind's states. In order for communication to take place, the internal world must find in the external world an object that has enough psychic reality and differentiation from the self to lead to the vocalisation of this internal process. I think that Sara's birth, her deforming illness, the death of the grandfather, and, before these events, the primary relation with a mother apparently impermeable to emotion and unable to confirm any expression of vitality, deprived Luisa of a basic experience for acquiring and maintaining the ability for an authentic verbal communication—that of being able to make projective identifications with a mother capable of reverie and contact. Luisa's drives, failing the transformational function of her mother's mind, could unfold only in an archaic and persecutory form and have, therefore, been paralysed and frozen, leading to the inability/refusal to communicate.

The superposing of the two sisters in the parents' minds, which I had already seen in our first interview, also pervades my first meeting with Luisa, confusing me. I am upset not only by her looks, which contrast with her mother's beauty, but also because, for a moment, I even think this is Sara here, although I had seen her pictures. I expected a girl as beautiful as her parents and, instead, Luisa is pale and tousled, wrapped up in a long anorak, with hat and scarf; she wears huge glasses with blue frames that make her eyes look larger. During her brief introduction outside the door, she looks indifferent, her face showing no emotion, while her mother cannot hide her vexation at being forced to leave her daughter alone with me (although I had told her in advance).

In the consulting room, I feel I must actively make Luisa participate. She remains still while I take her coat off, she sits very close to the table so that she can hardly move, and remains quiet and still. Telling her I understand her difficulty, I volunteer to open the box and show her its contents. She nods; she is tense and, holding her hands together, she makes regular small movements. She slowly relaxes, takes some clay, makes a disc, then a smaller one on top of the first, then bends the thing to make a half-moon shape. With the small knife, she cuts the rim, then pastes it on again. I think of the function of separating and putting together, but also of a scalpel that cuts off excess parts. After having made a second half-moon, she leaves it all and starts drawing (Figure 1). With the help of the lid of the clay pot, she draws a regular circle, then adds some lines, eyes and nose and hair. Her use of red makes me think of the image of the bleeding breast-feeding and the surgery that Sara underwent to remove the tumour, so the images of the two girls overlap in my mind all the time. When she has finished, she adds her name and smiles when I read it. She would like to take the drawing home with her, but complies immediately with my wanting to keep it. At the door, mother says hallo to her, but she does not reply: they are both very cold. I remain with a feeling of uncertainty and confusion, as if something traumatic took away the beauty from this child and gave her at times a vacant look. I think of what Meltzer and Harris Williams (1988) write about aggression, jealousy, and envy, which, by attacking the object through projective identification, distort its beauty and force the subject to identify with an ugly object.

In the second session, after playing aimlessly with clay and building blocks (as if she just wanted to waste her time) she makes the second drawing (Figure 2). This, too, is a face in vivid colours, where the huge red–black mouth makes me think of her mouth, locked up in opposition, as her father says, but also of her sister's mouth with its

Figure 1. Luisa's first drawing of a face, featuring a large red mouth (centre).

Figure 2. Luisa's second drawing, with a thin red–black mouth bisecting the
width of the face.

ulcers and bleeding. Today, too, she would like to take her drawing home, but she immediately gives in. During this session, I was discouraged because her mother told me that Luisa had fallen ill the day after the previous session and this was her first day out.

Confirming my hypothesis of the mother's resistance to consultation, Luisa does not want to enter the room for her last consultation session; she clings to her mother's coat, while she tells her to enter in a few curt words. "Come on," she says, "this is the last time. I told you. Get in!" but Luisa appears more and more afraid, which greatly irritates the mother. So she repeats, "Please, don't do that. I told you it's the last time! Come on, stop it!" The shilly-shally goes on for a while, until I decide to say something to try to contain their anxiety. Luisa, then clinging to her mother, says in a very low voice, although I can hear it, too, "But wait for me here." The mother says, "Certainly, I'll stay", but her expression is stiff and not soothing at all. Luisa keeps her coat on for the whole session. She has brought some toys along, thus rejecting the content of my box. One of her toys is a little skier that moves with a spring inside it. With it, she targets first a doll, then me. Every time she manages to hit me, she reacts in sadistic triumph with a satisfied grunt.

The restitution meeting with the parents confirms their strong resistance to psychotherapy. The mother had tried to anticipate the meeting (with the excuse she had been called to school as Luisa had wet herself because she did not want to ask to be allowed to go to the toilet). She says how terrible it has been to have to wait three weeks for consultation and even more that I might say something worrying about Luisa. With this communication, she seems to deprive me of any chance to talk without risking hurting her fragile and challenged narcissism. I have to be very tactful to contain their anxieties and put forward my idea that the child and the parents, too, need help. The mother, although listening with great attention, says she disagrees and cannot accept the idea that her daughter needs this kind of help, while the father, apparently amused, says that about a week ago (right after the previous consultation session), his wife invented a placebo in the form of drops that she has been giving to Luisa three times a day, telling her that this medicine will make her talk again. This family, with its unspeakable load of anxiety, a primitive level of defences, indifferentiation, and perverse solutions, managed to render me speechless, too. I suggest that they get in touch with a colleague of mine to see if they can get help as a parental couple and they decide to accept the teachers' proposal that Luisa is seen by the school's psychological team.

Giovanni, seven, patient of Carmela Guerriera

Giovanni, seven, is the only son of a couple of forty-year-olds. They both work, but she has a good intellectual job, while his employment is intermittent. When I meet them, he has just lost a job, but finds another a couple of weeks later and, this time, a better one. They have been referred by a child neuropsychiatrist who suggested psychotherapy for their son. They conceived the boy with the help of in-vitro fertilisation (IVF). They do not specify if it was homologous or heterologous. I do not know why, but, during the whole consultation, I keep thinking that they wilfully avoided telling me this detail. Maybe they take for granted that I know that heterologous IVF is illegal in Italy, and they never mentioned a trip abroad. In any case, probably it is just due to a general reticence about the question of assisted fertilisation. I find it hard to go back to this issue also because they mention IVF in passing and have come to talk about their son. The mother is a swollen river and speaks very loudly. She is tall and burly, while he is tall and obese. She leans towards me while speaking as if she wanted to make sure that I listen and pay full attention. She has a notebook in front of her (and she has it also in the second interview), in which she has made notes of events and sentences uttered by her son that she thinks are significant and useful for me. I remember only that in most of the sentences she read there is a reference to monsters and danger.

Mr and Mrs T are a united couple and mutually confirm impressions and memories of events that concern the boy. In their first interview, they describe his symptoms: he is afraid of dying suffocated by some object that he could swallow without realising it, so he is alarmed if he cannot find things, even if they are too big to be swallowed. He is so afraid of dying that he often asks his father if one can die in one way or another, when one dies, and if children, too, can die. A few months ago, he did swallow a small part of a toy and was taken to the hospital. The doctors took X-rays and told the parents and child that the little thing would be expelled in his faeces. The phobia of suffocating, with food for example, was already present before this episode, although in a lesser form. The child is convinced that he has swallowed anything he cannot find, imagining having put it in his mouth, which, in fact, he has not done. In most cases, his parents were present and saw him suddenly begin to be upset, believing he had swallowed something, even if he had not touched anything. When he had actually swallowed the little thing, he had thrown it up in the air towards his mouth, as he later confessed, thus showing his compulsion to gobble down things, feeling possessed of a dangerous drive. When I ask the parents what could have been the triggering cause, they look at each other and the father mentions one day when they had told the boy of "an egg with a little sister". Mother goes on minimising and says that she had told him they had put aside another egg for a little sister, but it had "dried up". The boy listened to the story and asked for explanations, but none seemed to satisfy him. The mother says, "I don't know, maybe we made a mistake, but we were just talking like that", and makes a gesture that was intended to convey that for her it was not so important.

This seems typical of the phantasies these parents have of their son and this unborn sister. For them, and for Giovanni, too, there seems to be a phantasy that they conceived two children at the same time, but "the little girl" was somehow "sucked up", annihilated, rather than never conceived other than in the mother's wish. I know very little of their families, just that their parents are all alive and present in their lives. Giovanni's uncles and aunts are mentioned, but nothing is said about their relationships. The parents tend to define the relationships they have with relatives and friends on the basis of their tolerance for their son and his behaviours and the fact that he is often nervous and upset, fights with the other children, and reacts dramatically every time he is excluded from games, so much so that his parents have to take him home, or rescue him. The father oscillates between a reassuring and rationalising attitude, when the child is worried that he has swallowed something, and a strict and brusque attitude, intolerant of the boy's liveliness, tantrums, and nonsensical statements. His wife disapproves of these oscillations because she says they are confusing for the boy and certainly painful: for example, when the boy sees that daddy does not enjoy playing with him or patronises him. In reality, she, too, finds it hard to bear her son's negative aspects and the fact that he is always "glued to her". She reacts firmly when he throws tantrums, but immediately after is seized by anxiety and consternation;

she tries to extract from him the reasons for his behaviour, she tries to make him see reason, but what she gets is "I don't know", or she feels forced to fight with him. Then she asks me, "But why does he do this? Why doesn't he accept the rules of games when he is with the other children? People are patient with him, try to engage him, but he wants to impose his own games, his own phantasies of monsters, battles, always the same, so he makes them exclude him. They think he is an oddball, as if he were crazy. Why does he always draw at school, invading the classroom with his drawings and making his teachers despair? And why does he always draw monsters?" It is clear that, although she wants quite a few answers from me, she already has a general answer, the one I try to help her verbalise: her son has a problem, he is different from his peers. She is in anguish, at times scared; she feels guilty, also, because of her own occasional rejections of her son; she would like to help him, but does not know how. This is why they came to see me. Her husband asks no questions, tries to deny the presence of a real psychological disorder in his son, and blames his wife's anxious character which makes her magnify the negative aspects and exaggerate little things that can be solved with a little common sense and reassurance of the boy.

In the first consultation session, after a fleeting uncertainty, and in the second session, Giovanni plays at staging tragedies, catastrophes, ships colliding with icebergs, causing the shipwreck of the *Titanic*, which falls apart, separating a large family, whose children are on tiny makeshift rafts and risk drowning. The adults and only one child (!) are left with the captain on the part of the ship where the engine is.

It is the mother who rescues the children. The mother, after a failed attempt, remains with her son, *to keep him company*. There is a girl, a member of an evil family deprived of children that sadistically (and he laughs) destroys the ship and attacks the original family. This girl, taken over by the evil family, ". . . is the wickedest person, but really really vicious!" he says, wide-eyed and in the kind of voice typical of readers of fairy tales. The wicked ones are hungry and greedy; they hoard whatever they find even if they have no room left, and pile up all the stolen things. Then there is a "shark" in the water, the terror of good castaways who, by now, are deprived of everything: food, a bed, light. He plays forcefully, as if goaded by the need to represent his anxiety, like his mother bringing her notebook and wanting to feel or hear from me an opinion on the normality of what he says and does.

Before using the toys, Giovanni asks me of each toy if it is small or big, and asks, "This is big, it can't be swallowed, can it?"

After the first two sessions, Giovanni falls ill, so the third session takes place after two weeks. When he arrives he immediately tells me that he had *very high temperature and a sore throat.* So, I comment that he has escaped a big danger, and he nods, raising his eyebrows. I know from his parents that he is afraid of falling ill. I am struck by the familiarity and strong contact he established with me from the beginning. He seems surprised that I take him seriously and listen to him attentively. He asks me to play with him and makes me choose the characters of one of the groups taking part in a battle to conquer a house. For himself, he always keeps "the little girl". In the last two sessions of his assessment, the game is always the same, but his confusion is more explicit.

The boy has one of the typical phantasies that Kancyper saw in twins: there is only one space, one time, and one chance for each of them. The sacrifice of one of the twins derives from the stratification of symbiotic phantasies of fusion and confusion, theft of the roles and functions of the other, and gives rise to violent remorse and resentment that usually end up inhibiting any kind of competition and rivalry. We should keep in mind that the term rivalry comes from the Latin *rivalis*, which means to have the right to the same body of water (Kancyper, 2004).

Giovanni tears the furniture out of the house, saying that thieves are stealing it, and takes the children from the house and says that they are kidnapping them. In the noisy, fast, and excited action, the identity and gender of the children change rapidly, as if by theft or fraud.

He says explicitly that a gender change has taken place, or else that one character *pretends* to be of the opposite sex or *stole the clothes* and also says: *it's a fraud*, when somebody appears to be a well-intentioned relative or a friend. Once, he says that the little girl is *an impostor.* Here, he uses a masculine word, probably because he cannot imagine how to say it in the feminine, as the word is uncommon and very seldom used. Normally, he speaks very proper Italian, with a rich vocabulary, so it is more likely that he identified with the impostor and the term referred to himself. The male characters tend to be inept and powerless, castrated. For example, he explicitly devalues the father character, which seems totally powerless. In a sequence of the game when it is necessary to clean up the house devastated by various onslaughts, he takes the father and tries to make him hold the vacuum cleaner, but gives up immediately as he finds it difficult to join two pieces and says that the father cannot clean up because he is clumsy.

He conveys a claustrophobic anxiety—when the house is attacked intensely, continuously, and recklessly, there is no escape, no space left for walking over the wreckage or preventing a survivor's death, as the character immediately falls out of the window or is flattened by a falling lift that Giovanni operates in the totally empty house.

Meltzer (1992) aptly described the phenomenon of claustrum and claustrophobia and developed the concept of "intrusive projective identification" that, in this child, could explain the feeling of being trapped in the object he violated (think of his fear of suffocating) and also the feeling of fraud and imposture. However, if we observe some features of his relation to his mother, the shared phantasy of the sucked-up content of another egg, we see also other types of projective identifications, such as the passive mutual sucking up typical of *folie-à-deux* (Maiello, 2007).

The theft of his magical skills, which Giovanni attributes to the little girl of his games, at times is attributed to a boy or to adults, but they are not successful. The ghost of the little sister resists all attacks and triumphs in being the true omnipotent usurper. She is, in fact, the boss of the gang of the evil family which violently enters the house, kills or kidnaps the children, and steals everything. The little girl has *too much power*, he says, and when I ask him what power this is, he simply says, "She can do ANYTHING!" His hate for this little sister, defensively idealised like a negative ego and described as a thief and impostor, derives from her having usurped his place in his mother's wishes and having avoided any attack, as she did not even exist as an embryo, also paralysing him in guilt for having killed a life in his mother's womb.

Once again, Kancyper (2004) helps us to understand these aspects when he writes about a double and states that it acts as a foreign body in the ego, erasing all differences between the self and the other and, thus, becoming the source of confusing anxiety. It is located in the subject's psychic space as a squatter that prevents him from being the master of his home, turning the ego into a slave. Giovanni is always threatened by swallowing, incorporating the object that is other to himself, his double, the living dead usurper, of which he would like to get hold. In fact, he tends to put anything in his mouth and swallow it in order to feel one and complete in a narcissistic investment of himself, also conquering the place of the object of desire in his mother's mind.

Kaës (2008) talks of the incorporation of another into oneself as another figure of double sibling and as a negative, persecuting version of the narcissistic, mirroring double. He says that the incorporation of another in oneself, a double that is, at the same time, a foreign body, is often the outcome of an unelaborated loss or of the hate of a sibling. Giovanni's mother has to work through a double loss: not having conceived a little girl, her true object of desire, in a phantasy of sucking up, and the loss of a perfect son who should have and could have indemnified her. It is worth remembering that in the IVF technique, one usually employs three eggs, so the idea of the two eggs derives probably from her ambivalent wish-phantasy (is she the one who sucked up the second, and maybe the third, egg in her body?), which she shares with her son. This entails the risk for him of playing the role of a "sur-dying" (Kancyper, 2004), remaining trapped in an archaic alienating imposed identification. A "sur-dying", according to Kancyper, is not only a surviving human being; he is a subject that, in psychic reality, is judged and condemned for his being, not for his acting, for his birth and not for his life. Nothing can redeem him from his role and he is obliged silently to fight a compulsive war against death.

One day, the mother comes to bring Giovanni and asks me why he does not want to play with a girl she invited home expressly for him to play with and adds, "He says he even hates her! But why does he hate her? She is so sweet and nice and warm and he rejects her", and, to her son, "Why do you act like this? Is it true, doctor, that he should socialise? It is better if he plays with a girl, since he always fights with boys." The parents tell me that he does not like to play with his peers, especially if it is a competition; he prefers to play alone or with an adult relative.

He cannot enter a conflict with a rival "sibling", especially with a "sister", probably not only because of the fear of a fight between siblings where the other is imagined as animated by homicidal drives, just like himself, but because he risks losing his identity.

Outside and beyond his symbiotic relation with his mother, Giovanni feels he cannot exist. Brunori (1996) states that the process of differentiation proceeds through the need to express desire as a differentiating element and an element for building one's identity, and after that proceeds through the fear of being rejected and the wish to be chosen. Some of Giovanni's clinical manifestations, such as his tendency to hypochondria, phobias, and confusion, suggest that these are defences against the risk of breaking the symbiosis with his mother. They are indispensable to both in order to keep under control, blocked, and, somehow, met, the needs of the immature parts of personality, which require dissociation from reality, and from the more mature and integrated parts of personality (Bleger, 2012). Here, Bleger identifies "the glutinous core of personality", which leads back to a phase preceding the development of the capacity for splitting and differentiating. What we want to stress here is that this leads to confusion and the inability to see the other as separate in siblings, in particular if intense envy is present, along with persecutory anxiety. We agree with Brunori's conclusions, according to which we can say that a persecutory idea of being a sibling is related to a glutinous mode of living a relation. The family of this child could be defined as Bleger's (1966) participation group, characterised by symbiosis, where the psychotic part of personality of all members is concentrated, and by the lack of differentiation of ego and not ego, object and subject.

As one can see, the fathers of both children are fuzzy or indefinite, as in Luisa's case, or weak and inept, as in Giovanni's case.

The father, when perceivable, is invested only as a partial object, a penis in the mother's womb, "orally incorporated by mother", as Klein stresses in the case of children's sexual theories at an age when pre-genital drives are prevailing, although genital drives are "awakening" (Klein, 1933). Attacks in phantasy on the mother's body and its contents (penises and children), due to the child's belief in the omnipotence of thought, make them confuse imaginary and real aggression.

So, the child's world is filled with persecuting and vengeful monsters. In order for the child to experience a type of guilt that has the potential to repair and mitigate the reckless severity of an archaic superego and to identify with a repairing penis, it would be necessary to keep reality away so that it does not dramatically confirm the omnipotent destructivity of the young aggressor's envy, at least, not before he is able to perform a reality check, after which, if he cannot absolve himself, at least he can find mitigating circumstances and not lose faith in his capacity for love and creativity. Luisa and Giovanni must come to terms with the concretisation of their worst phantasies.

Luisa is forced to see a distorted little sister, related to a breast that bites and bleeds. Giovanni is certain of having eaten, sucked up, his potential little sister when he was in his mother's belly with her, according to his unconscious phantasy, supported in this by his parents' more or less conscious delusional story of the birth of their only child.

Concerning the developmental function of the elaboration of the sibling complex, Kancyper (2004) notes that when the subject cannot elaborate his Oedipus complex due to sibling traumas, he remains trapped in a distressing web of rivalry with his peers that can take the form of repeated failures, as unelaborated oedipal guilt is at play in him, along with sibling and narcissistic guilt, with the accompanying need for conscious or unconscious punishment. In both children, we see signs of this tendency to failure—the girl is compromising her school performance with mutism, the boy risks marginalisation and isolation through his inability to relate to his peers. What is truly worrying is the risk of a developmental failure. Both children move at an undifferentiated psychic level and suffer owing to the repeatedly failed efforts at operating a healthy splitting from which to start to tidy up their internal and external worlds and reach a good enough integration. They have to cope with an "archaic form of sibling complex", where the mother's body is the protagonist and is inhabited by all sorts of partial objects that, in the children's phantasy, unite and complete each other and, most of all, fill up all the space that had been theirs and to which they still aspire, like a paradise lost, in a new fusion. These objects also have a threatening quality, as Kaës (2008) notes, devouring mouths, parts of the mother's body, or an undifferentiated magma of organs, a body confused with their own body. Luisa and Giovanni are on the threshold of pre-oedipal and oedipal rivalry, a triangular, more evolved form of the sibling complex, but they do not seem capable of enduring this position and rapidly regress to a more archaic form.

Luisa's parents rejected the suggestion of analysis for their daughter and reacted with a flight into delusion, confirming that they are unreachable. Giovanni's parents accepted having the child analysed, but delay the beginning of their own therapeutic path and it is not yet possible to be sure about their ambivalence and, therefore, their ability to let treatment continue. Both children fight against the risk of developing psychic disorders. We have seen their fragility and their potential, the latter implied in their "showing off" the expression of their sibling complex by means of specific symptoms, a reaction of the healthy part of their personality. Our hope is that soon this vital part can resonate with force and clarity in their parents, too.

References

Bleger, J. (1966). *Psicohigiene y psicología institucional* [Psychological Hygiene and Institutional Psychology]. Argentina: Paidós, 1990.

Bleger, J. (2012). *Symbiosis and Ambiguity. A Psychoanalytical Study.* London: Routledge.

Brunori, L. (1996). *Gruppo di fratelli. Fratelli di gruppo* [Brothers Group. Group of Brothers]. Rome: Borla.

Kaës, R. (2008). *Le complexe fraternal* [Sibling Complex]. Paris: Dunod.

Kancyper, L. (2004). *El complejo fraterno. Estudio psicoanalytico* [Sibling Complex. A Psychoanalytical Study]. Buenos Aires: Lumen.

Klein, M. (1933). *The Early Development of Conscience in the Children. Psycho-Analysis Today.* New York: Covici-Friede.

Maiello, S. (2007). Claustrum. La dimensione spaziale della vita mentale nel pensiero di D. Meltzer [Claustrum. Spatial dimension of mental life in D. Meltzer's thoughts]. *Richard & Piggle, 15*(3): 284–298.

Meltzer, D. (1975). *Explorations in Autism. A Psycho-Analytical Study.* London: Roland Harris Educational Trust.

Meltzer, D. (1992). *The Claustrum: An Investigation of Claustrophobic Phenomena.* Strathtay, Perthshire: Clunie Press.

Meltzer, D., & Harris Williams, M. (1988). *The Apprension of Beauty. The Role of Aesthetic Conflict in Development, Art and Violence.* London: Roland Harris Educational Trust.

CHAPTER NINETEEN

"We are unbeatable." The relation between siblings seen as an opportunity or as a retreat: talking about the Oedipus complex—is that old-fashioned?

Evalotta Enekvist

Introduction

In the therapeutic encounter with teenagers, one usually finds a protest of some sort against the adult world, if not directed immediately against the parents, at least directed against authorities and other forms of sovereignty. Recently, in my practice, I have met three teenage girls who did not exhibit this kind of protest. Rather, the relation to their parents and authorities has been conspicuous by its absence. Instead, all three girls have been preoccupied with the relation to a sibling. Although there are differences, the common denominator is a charged and painful relation to a sibling.

The girls, aged fifteen, seventeen, and twenty when I first meet them, all seek help after some kind of emotional breakdown that influenced their ability to function in school or at work. One of the girls explicitly seeks help because of her difficult relation with a younger brother who has a serious mental disease. As for the other two girls, a complicated sibling relation comes to the fore early in the therapeutic work. What they have in common is a self-supporting attitude leading to very limited contact with their own needs and feelings. All three have been very competent and capable, so their need for help has come as a total surprise to themselves and their environment.

The relations to the parents are, as I said, surprisingly absent in our therapy sessions, in spite of the parents participating a great deal in the girls' lives. In one case, for example, the parents drive their daughter to the therapy; in another case, the girl talks for hours with her mother in the evenings. Despite this, the parents are very seldom mentioned during therapy hours. I rather get the feeling that the subject is avoided. Instead, it is in relation to the siblings that the emotional engagement becomes visible. Two of the girls are constantly worried about their siblings, taking a great responsibility upon themselves for them. One girl carries a feeling of having been abandoned by her older sister when she chose a friend of her own age.

During the therapies, it becomes clear that all the girls have difficulties handling both aggressive and depressive feelings. A threatening lack of energy is constantly present—a fear of not being able to cope with the expectations and demands of life. A difficulty in getting involved in close relationships is also obvious. All three girls take the therapy very seriously, wanting to understand what it is that has happened, but, at the same time, they keep a certain distance in our work.

These three therapies have made me reflect on the significance of the sibling relation, both as an opportunity for handling conflicts and as a means of circumventing parental conflicts, thereby also evading the oedipal order. I use these therapies as a starting point for an examination of whether there might be an interplay between the absence of the parents in the therapeutic work, on the one hand, and the salient position of the siblings, on the other. If it is there, how can we look at this interplay? My focus is an attempt to understand a phenomenon, to elucidate the common factors, not the specific ones that, of course, are also at hand. I make a theoretical odyssey with the help of some theorists who, in different ways, have deepened our understanding of the intricate interplay within the family. I illustrate the theories with short vignettes from the therapies.

"We are unbeatable", says one of the girls when she describes the sibling relation in her family. I notice this expression. I also notice another expression that one of the other girls uses when she describes her childhood: "I was obsessed by the thought of having a sibling." Both these formulations are heavily charged. In the first case, it leads my thoughts to a sibling relation that is impossible to disturb, that no one can break. In the other case, I think of an all-consuming longing, a dream of a sibling who would save or change everything. In both cases, the sibling relation is supposed to fulfil strong emotional needs.

Freud and the Oedipus complex

In Freud's writings, the sibling relation mostly deals with rivalry, envy, and alienation. To Freud, the sibling relation was always connected to the relation to the parents and, for that reason, subordinate to the Oedipus complex (Freud 1909b, 1916–1917). The Oedipus complex is, as we know, the core complex in which the child's loving and hostile relationships to the parents are organised. This is what structures the personality, under the threat of castration and loss of love. It is the Oedipus complex that sets up the dividing lines between the sexes and the generations. When a sibling enters the scene, the Oedipus complex is expanded to a family complex (Freud, 1916–1917). The sibling becomes a threat, an intruder who competes for the parents' love. At the same time, it is the "dethronement" of the child's omnipotence that is always present in the Oedipus complex that unites the siblings and gives them a sense of community (Freud, 1921c). We are all in the same boat, leading to the formation and development of a social conscience, all under the threat of a possible greater loss. The meaning of the sibling relation for the child's development is, in other words, impossible to separate from the influence of the relation to the parents.

Mitchell and "Who am I"?

Mitchell (2006), on the other hand, emphasises the sibling relation (the lateral relation) as a autonomous line of development, in itself structuring, having a significant importance for our capacity to cope with groups.

Mitchell maintains that the breaking up of the mother–child union, besides being caused by the forbidding father, is brought about mostly by a sibling taking possession of the mother's love, something that, for the child, is seen as a serious threat. This is a dramatic event, since a sibling always causes one to question one's own existence. Who am I in this new constellation; am I no longer special or unique?

The child, with its magical thinking, just like Winnicott's "The Piggle" and Freud's five-year-old boy Hans, asks him- or herself, "Am I the mother or am I the child?" There is a confusion about who one is, what position one has in the new family. Hatred and murderous impulses are roused against the sibling, but, at the same time, the child will use the sibling as a mirror, thereby seeing him/herself in the sibling, thus creating feelings of sameness—we are alike. If the child should die, what could then not happen to me? The love between siblings is, therefore, a love of sameness. Mitchell states that all children have a real or possible sibling, and that all children, therefore, are tossed to and fro in a life-and-death struggle. She also maintains, that if a child has serious difficulties in handling a sibling, later in life he or she runs the risk of not being able to take a position in groups—as both the same as, and separated from, the other.

For the girl with a seriously ill brother, there is still some obscurity regarding her role in relation to him. When she describes a great relief when the brother finally leaves school and I comment on that by saying that it sounds as if she is the parent, she gives a laugh and says, "I have always felt that he [the brother] was my child." There is, in other words, a confusion about her relation to her brother, whether it is lateral or vertical.

Britton and triangulation

In his theory about triangulation, Britton (1989) has elaborated the dynamics between the vertical and lateral relationships, something that I have found most useful in my thinking about these three girls.

Britton says, in agreement with Freud, that one central aspect of the Oedipus complex is alienation, the child being excluded from the parents' own lateral relation. Under fortunate circumstances, the child manages to take this in, leading to a capacity to put oneself in the position of the third: that is, being able to see the other, to put oneself in the other's place, and to see oneself, to reflect upon oneself. The mental freedom that the child has thus acquired is what Britton calls "the triangular space", a capacity to handle both lateral and vertical relationships. It creates a relation to the inner world, to phantasy as such—that is, as if not "real". This third position, Britton maintains, becomes a prototype for an object relation, and in a family the triangulation can then arise in other constellations where siblings are included.

Serious deficiencies in this development emanate from the early dyadic containment. Real or felt deficiencies in the early interplay between mother and child make the entry into the triangulation more difficult. Later in life, this leads not only to difficulties in relating to others, but also to difficulties with thinking, since there is very little room for integration and modulation in the inner world, which leads to a lessened ability to handle loss and grief. That is why Britton states that the Oedipus complex is developed parallel to the depressive position. If one does not work, the other does not either. It is the triangulation that makes possible the development of symbolisation.

One of the girls experienced severe anxiety during the interview. This was preceded by her talking about an older sibling, whom she thought needed my help more than she did. At the same time, she recalls from her early childhood that her parents were always saying "Let A [my patient] have her way." I suggest to her that she has guilt feelings about that. This intervention immediately rouses a strong anxiety and it is not until the end of the session that I understand that my way of putting it, for A, meant that she actually was guilty. The intervention was taken as a concrete fact, feelings of guilt being equated with being guilty. A's ability to symbolise is deficient and one can suspect difficulties with triangulation, something that is later confirmed.

A colleague once described, very vividly, the central meaning of the Oedipus complex and how a little child can experience it: "The child wants something, but then there comes some other bugger and puts himself in the way". In other words, it is not difficult to imagine that it becomes extremely important for the child to have experienced a good enough dyadic relation before it can endure this alienation and loneliness.

The relation between siblings seen as an opportunity or as a retreat

In his article "The missing link", Britton mentions an analysand with great difficulty in handling the oedipal situation who, in outer reality, turns to a less demanding relation—with a sibling. "... her everyday relation with the outside world, which was undemanding and reasonable, was based on her relation with her sibling" (Britton, 1989, p. 93).

In her inner world, this patient has serious difficulties in integrating the parental couple, but, at the same time, she is capable of maintaining an "undemanding and reasonable" relation to a sibling. One can assume that the relation to the sibling is, in this case, both a retreat (the relation to the sister is strongly connected to the inner relation to an idealised mother) and a help, a sort of opening up to another relation.

It seems to me that this resembles the ways of relating to their siblings that I have observed in my three girls. For them, too, the sibling relation presents an opening to another object relation. It is, after all, there that they can find room for feelings of worry, concern, anger, and frustration. It is in relation to the sibling that they can have a dynamic interplay. The sibling relation presents an opportunity, in an outer relation, to test your capacity to handle inner conflicts and problems connected to growing up. One might even say that it is in relation to the sibling that they can "play" with the role confusion, with the lateral and vertical relations—try out the triangulation. Am I a responsible parent or a dependent infant? The girl I was telling you about who felt relieved when her brother graduated from school, is balancing between being both a sister and a parent. She smiles at herself when she thinks about the foolishness in what she just said, that she looks on her brother as her child. The girl who felt abandoned by her elder sister when she chose a friend the same age as herself is, in the therapy, struggling with her feelings of alienation, of being left outside of the community, asking herself who she is in this constellation. Is she the child who is not allowed to participate? Both are, quite seriously, trying out their positions—being a child or a grown-up, being put aside—and this is done in relation to a sibling.

All three girls have a striking driving force towards independence and taking responsibility. They all have been very successful in school and they have been engaged in different activities both in and outside school. They are proof of the power of initiative and enterprising spirit. One of the girls has started her own business, another has travelled around the world, and still another has made a choice of school, thus exhibiting a strong urge to make her own decisions. All this, though, stands in glaring contrast to the breakdown that brings them to me. Suddenly, all impetus is gone. They are all deeply worried, but still they can express relief. One girl says, " I have been keeping up a front, I am more honest now." Another girl says, "I want to dare to talk about the problems, to admit to myself that everything isn't that easy."

Loewald and the active urge for emancipation

Loewald (Ogden, 2009) adopts an approach to the Oedipus complex that I find useful. He elaborates the thought that the Oedipus complex is not primarily a threat of castration and loss of love, but that, instead, it is about the child's "active urge for emancipation" from the parents. What he means is that the child has an inherent urge for, or drive towards, individuation, to become a separate, independent, and responsible human being, beyond the sexual and aggressive urges. I think that it is this urge we can observe in these girls, but, before they came to me, it had come to a halt. So, how can we think about what has happened? There are, of course, several reasons behind what is occurring, but I would like to point out one common denominator— the lack, in the therapeutic work, of a relation to the parents, that in other senses are paradoxically present. The mother who talks for hours with her daughter is present to the highest degree, but the relation between mother and daughter bears the marks of a relation between two girlfriends. The relation to the parents has seemingly become difficult to handle and, at the same time, of no use for the girls in their struggle with their inner lives. The emancipation and the process of growing up has, therefore, not really taken place in relation to the parents, but instead in relation to a sibling. In this case, the sibling relation has become a substitute. But, is it possible to exchange the parental relation for a sibling relation?

Both Britton and Loewald have a very clear answer to that question. Britton says that a sibling relation can never solve the Oedipus complex. The sibling relation is incapable of becoming as big a threat as the parental relation, and, therefore, it does not have the same power. The sibling relation, a relation within the same generation, is a relation that is more equal in power and authority. Britton maintains that it, therefore, does not have the same structuring influence.

Loewald also lays stress on the fact that the Oedipus complex can only be solved in the struggle between generations. He states that the task of the adolescent is to become autonomous and take over the parents' position, and from that follows an inherent striving to symbolically "kill" the parents. He calls this "Parricide: a loving murder" (Ogden, 2009, p. 119). Winnicott, too, has a clear thought of what this is all about. He says, "In the unconscious fantasy, growing up is inherently an aggressive act", and it means taking the parent's place. "It really does" (Winnicott, 1971, p. 169). He also says that if there is death in a child's phantasy, there is murder in the adolescent's. I think that what both Loewald and Winnicott want us to understand is that there are unconscious phantasies and forces at play within the adolescent, which, in due time, will be necessary to take over power and responsibility, but that the adolescent really needs help to handle this during the process of growing up. These unconscious phantasies must not be ignored. Winnicott stresses that the adolescent has to be met in his or her challenge, and met not primarily with under-standing, but instead with confrontation—a confrontation not dealing with retaliation, but with setting boundaries. I think that this has to do with the importance of the adolescent experiencing that the surrounding world, and especially the parents, are stronger, making sure that the phantasies will stay phantasies and not become reality. The participation of the parents in this struggle for the position of being a grown-up is, therefore, indispensable. Loewald puts it thus: "In the oedipal battle, 'opponents are required'" (Ogden, 2009, p. 120). The parents must lend themselves to this struggle, let them-selves be used for that purpose. Otherwise, if the parents' authority has not been established, "the child's fantasies lack 'brakes'" (Ogden, 2009, p. 120).

All three girls have great difficulties in listening to their own needs and feelings. All the time, during the therapy, there is also an impend-ing threat of powerlessness. I understand that as an expression of a fear of a frightening and menacing inner world, an inner world where feelings of guilt can at any moment take over and turn into an expe-rience of actually being guilty. Or, as with the girl with the brother who was ill, a world where rivalry turned into a real threat of hurting the brother. Competing with an ill brother was made impossible and her strength and vitality instead turned into guilt and feebleness. What was thought to be a striving towards emancipation instead becomes a deadlock and a fear of an inner world without brakes. The struggle between generations has never come into existence. When that is the case, Winnicott says, the threat is experienced as coming from one's own generation and from within oneself.

The girl with the seriously ill brother has parents who care about her and are engaged in her life but they have, after a very difficult divorce, for many years been in constant conflict with each other. The fighting, therefore, takes place between the parents, and with a brother who is ill there has been little room for a struggle between generations. Maybe one could say that the generational struggle instead came to take place in and between the siblings. "We are unbeatable," the girl says in talking about her relation to her brother. I understand that statement as a mark of the unconscious phantasies not having properly met resistance. It is not the parental authority that is unbeatable, it is the sibling relation. That means that the omnipotent phantasy has not been curbed.

To sum up, I think that this odyssey has shown that a sibling relation offers an opportunity to test, play, and find oneself in relation to others: that is to socialise, or, as Mitchell puts it, to "negotiate self and other". However, at the same time, it can never replace the relation to the parents. If sibling relations are given the function of that kind of replacing, it will imply an avoidance of the oedipal conflict and the oedipal order, and, as a consequence, a reduced ability to handle omnipotence and mourning.

At the same time, I take the view that the appearance of the sibling relation in the therapeutic work, with its frame, limitations, and asymmetry, can function as an opener to the important triangulation and the transference work needed, in that way making it possible to approach the absent parental objects and, as a result, the work with the central oedipal problems.

References

Britton, R. (1989). The missing link: parental sexuality in the Oedipus complex. In: R. Britton, M. Feldman, & E. O'Shaughnessy (Eds.), *The Oedipus Complex Today: Clinical Implications* (pp. 83–101). London: Karnac.

Freud, S. (1909b). *Analysis of a Phobia in a Five-year-old Boy. S.E., 10*: 3–149. London: Hogarth.

Freud, S. (1916–1917). *Introductory Lectures on Psycho-analysis. S.E., 16*. London: Hogarth.

Freud, S. (1921c). *Group Psychology and the Analysis of the Ego. S.E.*, *18*: 69–143. London: Hogarth.

Mitchell, J. (2006). From infant to child: the sibling trauma, the *rite de passage*, and the construction of the "other" in the social group. *Fort Da*, *12*: 35–49.

Ogden, T. H. (2009). *Rediscovering Psychoanalysis. Thinking and Dreaming, Learning and Forgetting*. London: Routledge.

Winnicott, D. W. (1971). *Playing and Reality*. Harmondsworth: Penguin.

CHAPTER TWENTY

The psychotherapists' relation with their own siblings as a factor shaping the therapeutic relation

Joanna Skowrońska

An analytic therapeutic group is a theatre of intersubjectivity, in which the subjectivity of the therapist is particularly significant, given the presence of specific group mechanisms. The therapist's social experience, including their experience with siblings and peers, has an influence on the kind of object the group is in their mind and determines their ability to form, maintain, and understand the group, as well as the complexity of the group therapeutic situation. For these reasons, in group analytic thinking, it is natural to reflect on what the person of the conductor brings into the group. In this chapter, I would like to attract your attention to, and invite you to reflect on, the significance of the therapist's own experience with their siblings on the kind of therapeutic relation they tend to create. In order to do this, I have decided to compare the family situation and, in particular, the place among siblings of two psychoanalytic "fathers": Sigmund Freud and S. H. Foulkes, the creator of group analytic therapy, also known as group analysis. I shall also compare the things on which they concentrated and the things they neglected in their theories and therapeutic methods and apply the above-mentioned perspective to the therapeutic tools they have left us.

Some introductory remarks

Authors who write about the sibling relation on psychoanalytic grounds, Colonna and Newman (1983), Sharpe and Rosenblatt (1994), Coles (2003), Mitchell (2003, 2006), agree that this issue is strikingly neglected. What is more interesting, this situation is not better in the literature concerning psychoanalytic group psychotherapy, which, by definition, should favour the study of relationships other than dyadic. For example, in *Group Analysis*, except for articles from 1998 that followed the series of workshops by the Group Analytic Society, *Sib-Links* (Brown, 1998; Brunori, 1998; Maratos, 1998; Wilke, 1998; Wooster, 1998), very little has been written on the subject of the dynamics of sibling relationships as they are visible in groups. Colonna and New-man (1983) consider that, although the sibling relation is an object of therapeutic work, psychoanalytic literature does not reflect this fact.

One can say that in psychoanalysis, two traditions of thinking about siblings and, hence, two ways of treating the representation of siblings in the therapeutic relation, can be observed.

The first way of thinking draws on what Freud wrote on the mean-ing and the dynamics of the sibling relation. According to Freud, the relations between siblings are, from their very beginning, marked by a primary hostility and by feelings of rivalry, while the attachment that appears later on is a result of formation reaction to those emo-tions. The relation with siblings is not considered a factor in the con-struction of a person's inner world, and its traces are treated in the therapeutic relation as a displacement of feelings from the relation with parents. What is of importance to group analytic therapy is Freud's conviction that the relation between siblings gives the basis for the formation of social feelings. Formation reaction, covering impulses and feelings of jealous rivalry with one's brother or sister, leads to a desire for justice and fair share. "If one cannot be favourite oneself at all events nobody else shall be the favourite" (Freud, 1921c, p. 120). When writing about groups, Freud concentrated on the meaning of the leader and thought that group psychology is created through the identification of members of the group with the ego ideal of the leader. This opinion on groups minimises the significance of the relationships between group members. In this tradition of thought, sibling rela-tionships are overshadowed by the relation with the parents and by oedipal issues.

In the second way of thinking, sibling relationships are recognised as another path of development, distinct from the relation between children and parents, having different consequences on the development of one's personality. Those two kinds of relation are given different names—vertical relations in reference to the relation with parents and lateral relations in reference to that with siblings. Freud's contemporary, Melanie Klein, wrote in her early works that the love between siblings favours the child's development and helps them distance themselves from their parents, as well as alleviating the negative emotions, the feelings of exclusion and guilt due to the development of the Oedipus complex. Moreover, incestuous relations between siblings "where the positive and libidinal factors predominate" (Coles, 2003, p. 55) could have a positive effect on the sexual development of the child. It is known that she had a very close and meaningful relation with her brother. Sharp and Rosenblatt (1994) consider that object relation with siblings has its own development line and, as in the case of the phases of individual separation in the relation between mother and child, it is never over, but is always to be worked through in a new and more integrated form. The developmental task of the sibling relation is to achieve the capacity to tolerate the existence of, and maintain relationships with, others, who are similar to ourselves while remaining distinct and separate, writes Mitchell (2006). According to her, it is necessary to cope with sibling trauma that consists in experiencing the fact that we are not the one and only (Mitchell, 2006). Mitchell thinks that the Freudian desire for equality is preceded by a desire for being different—seeing in the eyes of one's mother one's own individual reflection and existing separately from one's siblings. Coles, on the other hand, notes that the relation with siblings is not only the basis of a trauma, but also the source of meaningful experience that determines our feelings of importance, value, and influence. She writes,

> . . . a child with a sibling can begin to gain some new control in the world. Kissing, biting, hitting, holding, are activities that can now become more powerful and effective when directed towards a sibling. The child's world is no longer peopled with giants. (Coles, 2003, p. 88)

Brunori (1998) similarly calls our attention to the fact that sibling relationships are marked by natural duality—children share at first a

common space inside the family, which is, for them, a source of security and identity, all the while fighting for their individual existence.
If this natural duality is creatively worked through in the process of
development, it will become a basis for the capacity to find satisfac-
tion in both sharing and rivalry.

In this tradition of thinking about sibling relationships, one could
speak of a sibling transference which shapes the therapist's and the
patient's experience in a way that is different from that deriving from
the vertical relation. Coles, writing about sibling transference, tries to
capture the characteristics of the transference–countertranseference
experience that can inform the therapist of its occurrence. Describing
the relation of one of her patients with his slightly younger sister, she
notes that "... we miss something if we say they were just parenting
each other, even though the relation compensated for parental
absences" (Coles, 2003, p. 14). She writes about her countertransferential experience, "... he could, at times, listen to what I had to say
from a place within himself that was untrammelled by what might be
called oedipal anxieties, such as the fear of seduction or anxieties
about my state of mind ..." and sometimes "... we played together
cooperatively, like children and 'child's play' cannot be compared to
the games between parents and children. They are different and
enrich the psyche in different ways" (Coles, 2003, p. 14). Coles also
observed the presence in the transference of a very strict super ego,
which, in her opinion, is linked to the relation between siblings left to
themselves in a situation of deficient parental care.

Siblings of Freud and Foulkes: different constellations, different experiences, different concerns

A lot of attention is usually paid, concerning what Freud wrote about
his family and what others wrote on this subject (M. Freud, 1958; Gay,
1988; Jones, 1953), to the specific family configuration that resulted
from an important age difference between the parents as well as from
the fact that, for Freud's father, this was a second marriage. When
Freud was born, his stepbrothers from his father's first marriage were
already grown up and the eldest had a son, Johann, who became
Sigmund's closest childhood playmate. Freud was the eldest of eight
children: he had five sisters and a brother; his other brother died not

long after birth. It is noted that Freud was of particular importance to his parents, especially his mother. Since he was born in a caul, it was believed that this would "ensure him future happiness" (Jones, 1953, p. 5). Freud himself wrote that he was certain of being his mother's "undisputed darling" (Coles, 2003). However, those working with families (McGoldrick, Gerson, & Shellenbergger, 1999) also point out other details of his biography. Freud's mother gave birth to eight children in ten years. Three months before Sigmund's birth, his father's father died. When Freud was one and a half years old, his brother Julius was born and died six months later. The month before that saw the death of his mother's brother, with whom she had strong enough bonds to give his name—Julius—to her second son. Shortly after Julius's death, only eight months later, his sister Anna came into the world. While she was being born, Freud's nanny was accused of theft, thrown out of the house, and put in prison. Freud's stepbrother Philip was in charge of this operation, from which it can be presumed that his father was not there at the time. It is otherwise known that he was often absent. Eight more months passed and Sigmund's older brothers emigrated, together with their families, causing him to fall out of touch with his closest companion, Johann, and his whole family to lose the tight circle of close relationships with the wider family. Thus, the first three years of Freud's life were marked by a number of losses and irrevocable changes experienced by his family. One must add that the Freud family was, at the time, suffering material hardship. Freud himself writes about this period: "nothing worth remembering" (Freud, 1900a, p. 312), (Coles, 2003). It is not hard to imagine that in a family thus downtrodden by external and internal factors, the emotional life of a little boy could attract little attention.

Coles offers a fascinating analysis of Freud's writings, searching for hints as to how he understood the signification of sibling relationships. She points out places such as those where he writes about his relation with Johann, who was brought up with him like a brother. Freud writes that Johann "had a determining influence on all [his] subsequent relations with contemporaries . . . his personality was unalterably fixed as it was in [his] unconscious memory" (Freud, 1900a, p. 424). Coles also makes note of places where Freud mentions the importance of sibling relationships but does not push the thought further, or even negates it. Such is, for instance, the case of the analysis of the Wolf Man, where Freud refused to recognise the role of the patient's relation with his sister in the development of his disorder, even though the Wolf Man himself saw a link between his depression and the death of his sister, with whom he had spent most of his childhood, since they were both rather lonely and neglected by their parents. Similarly, Coles calls our attention to a situation when Freud did not go further to understand the significance of the death of a sibling in the case of the Rat Man (Coles, 2003).

Coles suggests that Freud's concentration on the vertical relation and one of it aspects—the oedipal situation—was due to his desire to gain a sense of orientation in his generationally complicated family situation. She also suggests that his one-dimensional vision of the sibling relation was linked to his position in the family. Much was written and many disagreements arose on the influence of the birth order on the development of the structure of the personality (Coles, 2003; Mitchell, 2006; Rohde et al., 2003; Sharpe & Rosenblat, 1994; Sulloway, 1998). Nevertheless, some results are concomitant and it was proved that first children are usually more concentrated on the parents'; they tend to share their values and seek their support more often than younger siblings. It was observed that the birth of siblings increases the elder child's hostility, but, in favourable conditions, it can also help the child learn to cope with aggressiveness better than in the absence of siblings. Did Freud, having a number of siblings, have such a chance? The sentence, "If one cannot be favourite oneself at all events nobody else shall be the favourite" (Freud, 1921c, p. 120), which he attributes to all children having siblings, sounds more like a declaration of a firstborn who has lost his unique position of the one and only, which is not experienced by those born later.

In his theory, Freud concentrated on the meaning of the oedipal situation and of the relation between the child and the parents. The therapeutic technique that he developed and that evolved from the relation of domination between the hypnotist and the hypnotised, in which the patient is lying down, favours in particular the reproduction and the study of the relation between the child and a parent. It helps in reactivating the feelings of dependence, trust or mistrust, submission or rebellion towards authority (Coles, 2003).

Foulkes was born forty-two years later than Freud, into a wealthy Jewish family, as the last child—the fifth—and much younger than the others. He was reported to have said once that he took interest in psychoanalysis in order to understand his siblings and his relation with them (Brown, 1998). Quite probably, his family did not expect his birth. He was strongly bound with his grandmother, an important person in the family, and appreciated by wider family circles (Brown, 1998; E. Foulkes, 1990). His siblings, three brothers and a sister, were older than him by, respectively, seven, nine, ten, and eleven years (Brown, 1998). His father worked in a family firm. Foulkes wrote little and spoke little about himself. However, I have found a description of the experience of a similar family configuration by another group analyst, Agazarian. In an introduction to *Autobiography of a Theory* (Agazarian & Gantt, 2000), in which she describes the path she followed in formulating the principles of system centred psychotherapy, she talks about how, being the youngest among much older siblings, she would spend long lonely hours observing her family group. This childhood "analytic work" allowed her to observe how the behaviour of the members of her household changed according to the context and taught her "thinking systems".

What we know about Foulkes' family situation is that his father favoured his eldest brother, Richard. The first name he gave him was that of Wagner, his favourite composer, while the following children were given the names of Wagnerian characters. Foulkes had tried, in the course of his development, the activities at which his brothers excelled, but he eventually found both his own sporting activity and professional speciality, which differentiated him from the rest of his family. Later on, in constructing the group analytic theory, he differentiated himself from the psychoanalytic family. In his theory and his practice, he underlined the significance of a stage of development of the group in which the group rejects the authority of the therapist and gains its own authority, which represents an important turn towards individuation for the participants.

Some researchers show the importance of the identification with siblings (Coles, 2003), while Sulloway (1998) wrote that children strive, with their families' help, to occupy a separate niche, which would grant them the most of parents' attention. Younger children search for a niche that will allow them to differentiate themselves from their siblings. It could be considered that all of those findings could apply in Foulkes' case.

Foulkes was a great believer in Freudian psychoanalysis and he thought that he had merely extended its scope and its application to groups. However, one could say he behaved rather boldly with

Freudian principles. He was certain of having made a "decisive step" (Foulkes, 1990, p. 157) in both theory and in practice by treating all of the group's activity as free associations in a group context. He named this way of communicating in the group, which the therapist encourages among the patients, a free-floating group discussion. He assumed that people instinctively understand each other, so all communications of the participants of the group, verbal and non-verbal, can be considered as unconscious associations and interpretations. From this moment, free associations are no longer a two-person activity, but the activity of a group of people. Moreover, he was convinced that Freud probably would have shared his opinions (Foulkes, 1948).

Sulloway (1996) wrote about second children that they are "born to rebel", while the studies described by Rohde and colleagues (Rohde et al., 2003) have shown that the last children are often the ones to perceive themselves as rebels against family values. Foulkes, in his theory, treated the Oedipus complex in a seemingly lax manner. He was sure that from its very beginning this is a family affair and the story of Oedipus is a family story. It is not species heredity, but generational transmission that determines whether parents' unsolved problems concerning exclusivity, rivalry, love, and hate shall be reactivated with the birth of every new child. He never dealt explicitly with sibling relationships, since he thought that the whole theory of personality development had been written by Freud. However, he thought about the relation of the individual and their environment in a manner different from Freud's. He was of the opinion that in order to understand somebody, we have to see them "as a whole in a total situation" (Foulkes, 1948, p. 1). He considered that thinking about somebody's psychic life as separated from the person's environment could be a useful intellectual tool only at times. He described the human being as a nodal point in an intersubjective and interactive network, which influences us and that we influence even before we are born.

For this reason, the group analytic method lays stress upon the therapist's capacity to see the whole of the situation in which, as with figure and ground, different constitutive elements come into focus. This means that, with reference to vertical and lateral relations, we must think about the relation between siblings always as related to the one with parents. Foulkes pointed, as the source of inspiration for those aspects of his theory, at his co-operation with Kurt Goltstein, a neurologist and the author of a holistic theory of the functioning of the brain (Foulkes, 1948), as well as at the influence of sociologists from the Frankfurt School. However, one could ask if his interest in the overall situation and his capacity to see it did not, as in the case of Agazarian, come from his position in the family. In the same manner, the group analytic setting, in which the therapist is both the conductor and a participant, the group's member and its observer, could mirror the experience and the desires of the youngest sibling watching his own family group as a whole, learning from observation and yearning to be part of the things that are inaccessible at his age. In her biography, Agazarian describes how one day she got lost during a family skiing trip. What made her happy was not the fact that she finally managed to reach the hotel, but that her whole family group participated in the search for her. However modest the role we try to play in a group, it is a unique role.

It is considered that Foulkes' optimistic and enthusiastic vision of groups was linked to his relatively non-conflictual position among his siblings (Brown, 1998). Foulkes has been reproached with underestimating the hostility and destruction that the group situation generates. It is true that he showed a lot of optimism when he wrote that in a well conducted group the aggression that is innate to us all shall be used to fight the symptoms and to cope with the disorder. However, one can wonder if this optimism did not have a source in the experience of a child from a big, stable, safe family who had the chance to develop a safe attachment. Foulkes advised group conductors, in the first period of the group's development when early fears concerning survival and basic security are reactivated, to be accessible enough to create for the group members the conditions for safely forming attachments and setting a safe environment for therapeutic work. Later on, he thought, the conductor should step back and follow the group, taking care of the balance between security and challenges. This point of view could make us think of studies (e.g., Rohde et al., 2003) that show that younger children, more often than the elder ones, tend to seek the support of other family members and siblings.

My attention was captured by Foulkes' view on peer relationships. It is known that the development of peer relationships depends on the relation with siblings. However, it can also happen that relationships with peers repair what had gone wrong in the relation with siblings. Luis Ormont mentions, recalling Foulkes' stay in the USA, that

Foulkes supposedly said that in his opinion, the form of regression that takes place in a group is all together different from that in individual analysis: "we regress to our past with peers" (Brunori & Knauss, 1998). In a therapeutic group, as in a peer group, every participant has others who serve as sources of identification and mirroring. This unwritten and undeveloped thought interested me because, just like Coles, I think that in a group, as well as in individual analysis, there are moments when the participants communicate "from a place within [themselves] that was untrammelled by what might be called oedipal anxieties" (Coles, 2003, p. 14). Let us add, not by pre-oedipal ones, either. One participant expressed this when he spoke, at a time when he was ending his therapy and struggling with mixed feelings, about his childhood memory of a painful feeling that he would experience when he made little bark ships and wished both to see the ship floating freely on the waves and to keep it. At the time, being an only child, he was alone, while now, talking about his experience in the group and observing his own three children, he understands how children help each other in such moments. During this session, I felt I was taking part in a playground discussion, in which children verify together their childhood theories on the world, both internal and external. In a situation among equals, who share the same level of knowledge and ignorance, they all present a mirror to one another that has a different meaning than the one an adult represents in a child's development.

Foulkes thought that in an analytic group, horizontal analysis takes place among equals, who can enact and modify problems rooted in the past. This situation between equals, in which the conductor is also included, creates a space that is naturally similar to that between siblings and peers. In a therapeutic group, one can not only encounter one's "own siblings" on a transference level, but also, one can experience oneself fully in real contact with others and share experience with equals as with siblings and peers. Balint (1972) writes that the desire for fair share is a stage on the road to the feeling of mutual concern, which is a developmental task of peer relationships. She wonders if mutual concern is possible to reach in relationships other than the ones between peers. Following her line of thought, one could say that the relation with siblings, which finds a natural continuation in the relation with peers, constitutes a developmental achievement that is impossible to gain otherwise.

References

Agazarian, Y., & Gantt, S. P. (2000). *Autobiography of a Theory: Developing the Theory of Living Human Systems and Its Systems-Centered Practice*. London: Jessica Kingsley.

Balint, E. (1972). Fair shares and mutual concern. *International Journal of Psychoanalysis, 53*: 61–65.

Brown, D. (1998). Fair shares and mutual concern: the role of sibling relationships. *Group Analysis, 31*(3): 315–326.

Brunori, L. (1998). Siblings. *Group Analysis, 31*(3): 307–314.

Brunori, L., & Knauss, W. (1998). *Personal Encounter with S. H. Foulkes*. A movie by Group Analytic Society.

Coles, P. (2003). *The Importance of Sibling Relationships in Psychoanalysis*. London: Karnac.

Colonna, A. B., & Newman, L. M. (1983). The psychoanalytic literature on siblings. *Psychoanalytic Study of the Child, 38*: 285–309.

Foulkes, E. (1990). A brief memoir. In: S. H. Foulkes, *Selected Papers* (pp. 3–20). London: Karnac.

Foulkes, S. H. (1948). *Introduction to Group Analytic Psychotherapy*. London: Heinemann [reprinted London: Karnac, 1983].

Foulkes, S. H. (1990). *Selected Papers*. London: Karnac.

Freud, M. (1958). *Man and Father*. New York: Jason Aronson.

Freud, S. (1900a). *The Interpretation of Dreams. S.E.*, 4–5. London: Hogarth.

Freud, S. (1921c). *Group Psychology and the Analysis of the Ego. S.E., 18*: 67–143. London: Hogarth.

Gay, P. (1988). *Freud. A Life for Our Time*. London: J. M. Dent.

Jones, E. (1953). *Sigmund Freud: A Life and Work*. London: Hogarth Press.

Maratos, J. (1998). Siblings in Ancient Greek mythology. *Group Analysis, 31*(3): 341–349.

McGoldrick, M., Gerson, R., & Shellenbergger, S. (1999). *Genograms. Assesment and Interventions*. New York: W. W. Norton.

Mitchell, J. (2003). *Siblings. Sex and Violence*. Cambridge: Polity Press.

Mitchell, J. (2006). Sibling trauma, a theoretical consideration. In: P. Coles (Ed.), *Sibling Relationships* (pp. 155–175). London: Karnac.

Rohde, P. A., Atzwanger, K., Butovskaya, M., Lampert, A., Mysterud, I., Sanchez-Andres, A., & Sulloway, F. J., (2003). Perceived parental favoritism, closeness to kin, and the rebel of the family. The effects of birth order and sex. *Evolution and Human Behavior, 24*: 261–276. http://www.sulloway.org/Rohde2003.pdf

Sharpe, S. A., & Rosenblatt, A. D. (1994). Oedipal sibling triangles. *Journal of the American Psychoanalysis Association, 42*: 491–523.

Sulloway, F. J. (1996). *Born to Rebel: Birth Order, Family Dynamics and Creative Lives*, London: Little, Brown.

Wilke, G. (1998). Oedipal and sibling dynamics in organizations. *Group Analysis*, 31(3): 269–281.

Wooster, E. G. (1998). The resolution of envy through jealousy. *Group Analysis*, 31(3): 327–340.

INDEX